VIEWS FROM WITHIN

VIEWS FROM WITHIN:

The Japanese American Evacuation And Resettlement Study

Edited and With Contribution By

YUJI ICHIOKA

Resource Development and Publications

ASIAN AMERICAN STUDIES CENTER
University of California at Los Angeles

Library of Congress Cataloging-in-Publication Data

Views from within: the Japanese American evacuation and resettlement study/edited and with contribution by Yuji Ichioka.

p. cm.

ISBN 0-934052-12-3

1. Japanese Americans—Evacuation and relocation, 1942-1945.
I. Ichioka, Yuji. II. University of California, Los Angeles. Asian American Studies Center. Resource Development and Publications.
D769.8.A6V53 1989
940.53'1503956073—dc20 89-84879
CIP

PRINTED IN THE UNITED STATES OF AMERICA.

Cover Design: Russell C. Leong
Book Design and Typesetting: Mary Kao

TABLE OF CONTENTS

In Memoriam

CHARLES KIKUCHI
1916-1988

Charles Kikuchi was my best friend. During the early fall of 1988, while he was practicing his own brand of people-to-people diplomacy in the USSR, he became gravely ill and succumbed to his illness shortly after he returned to the United States.

We were kindred spirits, as we discovered when we first met as students in 1941, and so when Charlie died, a part of me died with him. As Nisei, Charlie and I had come a long way. From being outcasts in American society before and during the Second World War, we joined the American mainstream in the post-war era. We lived to see basic American attitudes transformed through the civil-rights movement, and we took a certain pride in the fact that we had been optimistic about American society changing and moving toward the ideals it espoused.

The photograph of Charlie was taken in front of my home in Maryland in August 1988 as he was about to leave for the Soviet Union to participate in the International March for Peace from Odessa to Kiev. Charlie wrote to me from the Ukraine as a member of the American contingent, saying that he was raising questions with both Americans and Russians about the status of racial minorities in the United States and the Union of Soviet Socialist Republics.

Yes, we had come a long way, but Charlie saw that we as a nation still had a long way to go in alleviating the plight of Afro-Americans and other racial minorities in finding their rightful place in American society. He was idealistic and optimistic about the future, but he was at the same time forever realistic about the road we still had to travel until America achieves genuine racial equality and social justice for all.

Warren Tsuneishi
Chief, Asian Division,
Library of Congress

PREFACE

In 1987 I organized and directed a two-day conference titled "VIEWS FROM WITHIN: The Japanese-American Wartime Internment Experience" held on September 19-20 at the University of California at Berkeley. The first day, which coincided with national and local events commemorating the bicentennial of the American Constitution, was devoted to the constitutional issues raised by the wartime internment of Japanese-Americans. The ensuing second day was devoted to a reassessment of the Japanese American Evacuation and Resettlement Study (JERS), a special wartime research project which studied the mass internment of Japanese-Americans. The California Council for the Humanities funded the first-day program; the Columbia Foundation of San Francisco funded the second-day program. The second-day participants included former JERS staff members and researchers interested in JERS.

Most of the essays in this anthology originated as papers presented on the second day of this two-day conference. Some essays are on specialized JERS topics; others are reminiscences by former JERS staff members. All of the essays reassess, directly or indirectly, one aspect or another of JERS. As editor of the anthology, I refrained from imposing my views on the contributors in keeping with the original purpose of the conference, which was to reassess JERS from as many angles as possible. Thus, for example, I did not insist upon a common, uniform language to describe the Japanese-American wartime internment experience. Some contributors use "relocation centers" and other terms originally coined by the American government, while I, following my own personal preference, employ "American-style concentration camps" and other alternative terminology.

Many people and institutions helped to make this anthology possible. First, Susan B. Silk of the Columbia Foundation generously allowed me to apply the unspent balance of the 1987 conference grant toward the publication of this anthology. The Columbia Foundation was one of the original funding sources of JERS during the wartime years. Secondly, a grant from the Institute of American Cultures of UCLA enabled me to coordinate the final research phase of the anthology. Thirdly, the staff of the Resource Development and Publications Section of the Asian American Studies Center, UCLA, made the actual publication possible. Here I would like to express my sincere gratitude to Glenn Omatsu, Associate Editor, who ably assisted me in editing the anthology;

and to Russell Leong, Senior Editor, and Mary Kao, Publications Assistant, who worked diligently at the production end to see the anthology through to publication. And, finally, I would like to thank Warren Tsuneishi, Chief, Asian Divison, Library of Congress, for writing the In Memoriam Statement dedicated to the late Charles Kikuchi, a former JERS staff member.

Yuji Ichioka

VIEWS FROM WITHIN

JERS Revisited:

Introduction

YUJI ICHIOKA

Three separate groups of social scientists conducted research on Japanese–Americans in American–style concentration camps during the Second World War. One group was in the official employ of the War Relocation Authority (WRA), the federal agency which administered the camps. Mostly anthropologists, the social scientists in this first group functioned as so–called social analysts whose job was to furnish WRA administrators with information to enable them to administer the concentration camps efficiently. Within recent years, these social scientists have come under heavy criticism.[1] Independent of the WRA, the second group of social scientists was organized into what was called the Bureau of Sociological Research headed by Alexander H. Leighton. The social scientists in this second group conducted research at Poston, Arizona, under the auspices of the Office of Indian Affairs. The purpose of the Bureau of Sociological Research was to advise the administrators at Poston and to formulate general principles of administration.[2] The third research group, which was also independent of the WRA, was the Japanese American Evacuation and Resettlement Study (JERS) under the direction of Dorothy Swaine Thomas of the University of California at Berkeley.

The essays in this anthology cover this third research group. JERS is significant for two fundamental reasons. First, JERS' post–war publications set the initial academic framework of studies of the wartime internment of Japanese–Americans. In all, JERS produced three official books. These were: Dorothy S. Thomas and Richard S. Nishimoto, *The Spoilage* (Berkeley: University of California Press, 1946) covering those Japanese–Americans who were classified as so–called disloyal persons and who were segregated eventually at the Tule Lake Concentration Camp; Dorothy S. Thomas, *The Salvage* (Berkeley: University of California Press, 1952) devoted to the so–called resettlers or those Japanese–Americans who were allowed to leave the concentration camps for work or study, principally in the midwest; and Jacobus tenBroek *et al.*, *Prejudice, War and the Constitution* (Berkeley: University of California Press, 1954) presenting the historical background of racial hostility towards Asians in the western United States, the causal factors behind the mass internment, and the constitutional issues raised by it. In addition, there was an unofficial JERS book: Morton Grodzins, *Americans Betrayed: Politics and the Japanese Evacuation* (Chicago: University of Chicago Press, 1949) which examined the role specifically played in California by state and local politicians as well as economic interest groups in the decision to intern Japanese–Americans. Secondly, JERS generated a major collection of daily journals, diaries, life histories, field reports, and documents compiled and authored by the research staff and now deposited in the Bancroft Library of the University of California.[3] JERS was launched in the spring of 1942, just as the wartime internment of Japanese–Americans was getting under way. As a research project, it did not attain all of its objectives. Prevailing conceptual frameworks, personnel changes, personality conflicts, political considerations, and difficulties inherent to the project, all influenced the development and progress of JERS. The essays in this anthology reassess its accomplishments and failures.[4]

The Role of Dorothy Swaine Thomas

The central figure in JERS was Dorothy S. Thomas (1899–1977). Up until the time she initiated JERS, Thomas had no professional interest in or personal involvement with Japanese studies, Japanese immigration, or Japanese–Americans. Born in Baltimore, Maryland, Thomas obtained her A.B. from Columbia University in 1922 and her Ph.D. from the University of London in 1924. At the beginning of her professional career, she served as a researcher with the Federal Reserve Bank and Yale University. She also taught at the Teachers College of Columbia University. In 1939–1940 she was on the research staff of the Carnegie Corporation funded study of Afro–Americans headed by Gunnar Myrdal. Her husband was W. I. Thomas, the well–known sociologist of the Chicago School. In 1940 Dorothy S. Thomas became a professor of rural sociology at the University of California, Berkeley. She stayed on at Berkeley in this capacity until June 1948 after which she moved to the University of Pennsylvania.[5]

Whatever she studied, Thomas always based her studies on empirical data. Her initial research dealt with the business cycle and children. Published in 1925, her first study, *Social Aspect of the Business Cycle* (New York: Alfred A. Knopf, 1925) examined the relationship of business cycles to birth, death, marriage, divorce, crime, pauperism, and migration utilizing statistical data. In 1928 she co–authored *The Child in America: Behavior Problems and Programs* (New York: Alfred A. Knopf, 1928), again relying heavily on statistical data. In the 1930s, her research interest shifted to social demography. During the immediate pre–war years, she published two studies, one on internal migration and another on Swedish population movements. In 1938 she published *Research Memorandum on Migration Differentials* (New York: Social Science Research Council, 1938), a treatise on approaches to the study of internal migration done for the Social Science Research Council. In this work, she viewed internal migration as a selective process, and enumerated and elaborated on what she considered the crucial differentials involved: age, sex, family status, physical and mental health, intelligence, occupation, motivation, and assimilation. In 1941 Thomas published a study of the Swedish population from 1750 to 1933 under the title *Social and Economic Aspects of Swedish Population Movements* (New York: MacMillan, 1941).

Consequently, Thomas brought an expertise in social demography to her initial conceptualization of JERS. She conceived of JERS as a study of "enforced mass migration" in which the normal selective process of voluntary migration would not be at play. After all, the so–called evacuation of all Japanese from the West Coast was not on a voluntary basis. It was, in Thomas' own words, an "unselective outmigration enforced upon the Japanese population." As such, the normal "push" and "pull" forces were not in operation. Such forces came into play only during the resettlement phase from 1943. In proposing JERS, Thomas argued that there would be a post–war utility to her study of the enforced mass migration of Japanese–Americans. World War II had caused major dislocations in the population of Europe. According to Thomas, if JERS could uncover general principles underlying the enforced mass migration of Japanese–Americans, such principles could be applied, conceivably, to foreseeable, post–war enforced mass migrations in Europe which would be necessary to rectify the population imbalances caused by the war. In applying for research funds from the Rockefeller Foundation, Thomas wrote that "the administrative and research personnel of the University of California are interested in" JERS "because of its significance [in] providing a documentary account and an analysis of an important sociological event, which they believe will be the precursor of other enforced mass migrations." JERS "is in no way connected," she claimed, "with the interests of the administration or of individual faculty members in the welfare of the Japanese group as a whole or of the students of Japanese ancestry."[6]

There were other aspects to Thomas' initial conception of JERS. As research in anthropology, JERS was to be a study in cultural conflict between "Japanese" and "American" ways and the relative acculturation to the latter by the Issei, Kibei, and Nisei generations, the three constituent elements of the Japanese population. In terms of social psychology, the study was going to examine the collective adjustment of the Japanese population to the entire process of social disorganization and reorganization which would inevitably accompany mass uprooting. Economically, it was going to focus upon the impact the uprooting would have on California agriculture. In political terms, finally, JERS was going to examine the uprooting in relation to the role of pressure groups, the formation of public opinion, the constitutional issues, and the role of various governmental agencies.[7] Other University of California faculty members were to be involved in these additional aspects of JERS: Robert H. Lowie of the Anthropology Department, Milton Chernin of the Social Welfare Department, Frank L. Kidner of the Economics Department, and Charles Aikin of the Political Science Department.

Funding and Staffing

Thomas obtained funding from three major sources totalling over $100,000, a substantial sum of money by any standard, past or present. She received $32,500 from the Rockefeller Foundation, $30,000 from the Columbia Foundation, and $29,554 from the Giannini Foundation and University of California funds. In addition, she received a supplement of $6,250 from the Rockefeller Foundation as publication subsidy. Thomas first applied for funds in March 1942 with the Rockefeller Foundation because she had a personal contact in Dr. Joseph H. Willits, Director of the Social Science Division, who was also interested in internal migration studies. In 1934 the Social Science Research Council had instituted a research project called The Study of Population Redistribution. This study was conducted under the auspices of the Industrial Research Department of the Wharton School of Finance and Commerce of the University of Pennsylvania. The Social Science Research Council Advisory Committee, which guided this study, was headed by Dr. Joseph H. Willits who was at that time a Dean at the Wharton School.[8]

In late March 1942 Milton S. Eisenhower, the first Director of the WRA, appeared in San Francisco to survey the situation on the West Coast at first hand. Taking advantage of his timely presence, Thomas paid a call on him and requested his cooperation in her proposed research project. Shortly thereafter, she received an one–year exploratory grant from the Rockefeller Foundation. In mid–May Eisenhower notified the Rockefeller Foundation of his decision to commit the WRA to full cooperation. The Rockefeller Foundation then approved funding for a full three–year period. The Columbia Foundation, a San Francisco–based foundation concerned with civil–rights issues, followed suit with a generous annual grant of $10,000 for three years.

The initial JERS staff was composed of a handful of Nisei and white college students who were recruited off the Berkeley campus. Although on the whole very young, these students had some training in the social sciences. Among the Nisei staff members, Tamotsu Shibutani had been a senior majoring in the social sciences; James Sakoda, the sole Kibei, likewise had been a senior but in social psychology; Haruo Najima had obtained a M.S. in agricultural economics; Charles Kikuchi had completed a year of graduate work in social welfare; and Tamie Tsuchiyama had passed her Ph.D. qualifying examination in anthropology. As the senior staff member among the Nisei, S. Frank Miyamoto was the only one who had no ties to Berkeley. He had passed his Ph.D. qualifying examination in sociology at the University of Chicago and was a recipient of a 1942–43 Social Science Research Council Pre–doctoral Fellowship. Among the white staff members, there were four Berkeley graduate students: Morton Grodzins in the Department of Political Science, Virginia L. Galbraith in the Department of Economics, Robert Billigmeier in the Department of History, and Robert F. Spencer in the Department of Anthropology. A fifth white staff member was Rosalie Hankey who joined JERS in 1943. She was a graduate student in anthropology, and the senior among the white staff members.

All of the JERS staff members, except Grodzins and Galbraith, became participant observers. During the initial phase of the mass uprooting, the Nisei staff was scattered in various so–called Assembly Centers: Shibutani, Najima, and Kikuchi in the Tanforan Assembly Center; Miyamoto in the Puyallup Assembly Center; Sakoda in the Tulare Assembly Center; and Tsuchiyama in the Santa Anita Assembly Center. As the transfer from assembly centers to concentration camps was about to occur, Thomas decided to make Tule Lake the principal focus of JERS with Gila River as its secondary focus. Accordingly, she had the WRA transfer Shibutani, Najima, Sakoda, and Miyamoto to Tule Lake and Kikuchi to Gila River. Simultaneously, Thomas assigned Billigmeier to Tule Lake and Spencer to Gila River. When Spencer left his position in 1943, Hankey became his replacement at Gila River. Tsuchiyama was transferred to Poston. Grodzins and Galbraith worked out of the JERS office on the Berkeley campus as liaisons to the various governmental agencies involved in carrying out the mass uprooting Besides the foregoing staff members, Thomas also employed a number of other persons, but among these people only two played a significant role: Togo Tanaka, a Nisei at Manzanar, and Richard S. Nishimoto, an Issei at Poston. As a condition of employment, all JERS staff members had to pledge not to disclose, either through publications or public lectures, any findings of the research project until the end of World War II.

Initial Problems

The Nisei participant observers automatically found themselves in a very tenuous and potentially dangerous situation. On the one hand, as participants, they were subject to all of the vicissitudes of mass uprooting; they, too, suffered the loss of their civil liberties and had to endure the physical deprivations and hardships and the concomitant emotional anxieties, fears, and tensions. On the other hand, as observers, they were expected to record and document what they were experiencing and observing as objectively as possible. Yet the collection of data was no simple task. The extraordinary circumstances in which the Nisei participant observers found themselves precluded the use of conventional methods of social research such as survey questionnaires or formal interviews. Even when they informally sought information from their fellow Japanese–Americans, they had to exercise more than ordinary caution and discretion since they were in danger of being perceived as "informers" for the WRA or FBI, as were many members of the Japanese American Citizens League (JACL) who cooperated with WRA officials. Thus they had to be on constant guard to avoid being so perceived in order to function as effective participant observers.

Thomas was sensitive to this problem. She realized that "representative sampling was out of the question, schedules and questionnaires could not be used, and even note–taking in public was a hazard, because of the experiences of the evacuees with FBI and other intelligence officers and the tendency on their part to confuse research workers with 'informers.'"[9] As the principal means of amassing data, she therefore urged her fieldworkers to write up daily field notes and maintain personal journals of what they were experiencing and observing. From her point of view, the participant observers had a "unique opportunity" of obtaining "a socio–historical record on the spot and at the time the events are occurring" [underline included].[10] She believed that they could best accomplish this by keeping personal diaries and by writing copious daily field notes, weekly summaries of such field notes, and special reports on unusual events.

Besides the difficulties of collecting data, the fieldworkers had the problem of determining what was relevant to JERS. Put in another way, they had to decide what to record and document from a welter of unpredictable events. Thomas had no theoretical framework which gave a clearcut guideline to the participant observers. She simply wanted them to write up detailed descriptive data, free from theoretical considerations, of what they were experiencing and observing. In June 1942 Tamotsu Shibutani, Haruo Najima, and Tomika Shibutani (Tamotsu's wife) produced a report entitled "The First Month at Tanforan."[11] This report presented a description of initial life at Tanforan organized under three headings: administrative organization, social organization, and social maladjustments. The administrative set–up and physical facilities at Tanforan fell under the first heading; the family, religion, recreation, social and political groups, education, and economic activities fell under the second; and intra–group conflicts, sexual problems, theft, delinquency, poverty, and individual deviance fell under the third. In forwarding the report to Thomas, Shibutani said: "We have pulled no punches," and "we feel that the paper gives a fairly accurate picture of what is going on." "After reading over the stuff we put in," he parenthetically added, "I don't think that any of it should get out to anyone."[12] Thus Shibutani asked for the report to be restricted to JERS staff members. In August 1942 Thomas recommended the outline of this Shibutani–Najima–Shibutani report to all other JERS fieldworkers as a model for their own reports.

Towards the close of 1942, there was a noticeable shift in the content of reports filed by the fieldworkers reflecting new developments in the concentration camps. In late 1942 spontaneous strikes, protest demonstrations, and violence erupted at Poston, Gila River, Tule Lake, and Manzanar. Recognizing these unexpected events as politically significant, the fieldworkers began to concentrate on them and probed into the causes underlying the conflict between the Japanese inmates and their WRA keepers. Many of the topics covered by the Shibutani–Najima–Shibutani report no longer loomed so important, so that by the time of the registration crisis in early 1943, the fieldworkers were reporting almost exclusively on events of a political nature.

A few were dissatisfied with Thomas' inability or unwillingness to give theoretical guidance to their fieldwork. They felt that the problem they were asked to investigate was not defined precisely enough. S. Frank Miyamoto was among them. Trained as he was in sociology, he believed that social theory should guide research. "One point of departure between the Director and field workers who desired to work with a specific problem," Miyamoto recalled, "was the degree of faith in the usefulness of existing social theory in guiding social research." In other words, he believed that any field research program, JERS included, should be planned on the basis of social theory which "allowed for verification with empirical data."[13] No meaningful interpretations of data could be arrived at without a theoretical framework. Miyamoto felt that Thomas' concept of enforced mass migration was too vague. Thus he faulted her for neglecting social theory.

Tamotsu Shibutani was of like mind. As he was working on the Shibutani–Najima–Shibutani report, Shibutani informed Thomas of the difficulties experienced by the Nisei fieldworkers at Tanforan. He reported that "our experience...has left us convinced of one thing: we must have some notion of what we are looking for and some preparation <u>before we begin our investigation</u>" [underline included]. Looking ahead to his transfer to Tule Lake, Shibutani asked Thomas for direction:

> I have worked out an outline that I intend to use to write up our experiences in Tanforan. I wonder if some[thing] like this could not be worked out for our study of Tule Lake <u>before we go there</u> [underline included]. After squandering around here for three weeks, I am convinced that we would have less inefficiency, less overlooking of valuable stuff, more organization, and less overlapping if we have some plan. Going into a project with an open mind would be fine if all of us had sufficient training to know what to look for, but we don't. Therefore, some outline must be worked out.[14]

Shibutani expected instructions from Thomas, but he never received them. "We waited and waited for D.S. [Thomas] to send us her instructions," he lamented to Virginia L. Galbraith, "but she kept promising and didn't come through. I guess she was so damn busy that she just couldn't get around to it."[15]

This problem of a lack of direction was never resolved to the satisfaction of those who wanted a theoretical framework within which to operate. In 1943 Grodzins, writing from the Chicago JERS office, relayed to Thomas that "T (meaning Tamotsu) is raising hell that he needs more direction—that he can't 'collect everything'—and all (referring to JERS staff members in Chicago who were engaged in studying the so-called resettlement phase of evacuation) are agreed that you should define some problems for them with more precision than you have in the past."[16] Since his undergraduate days at Berkeley, Shibutani had been interested in social theory. In the winter of 1943–1944 he began taking graduate seminars in sociology at the University of Chicago which intensified his interest. For her part, Thomas viewed Shibutani as a disruptive person. She frankly told him:

> You have shown evidence of great discontent with the study, its objectives, the jobs that you have been asked to do on it, the work that some of your colleagues are doing, and the way in which the study is being directed. I have wondered whether these attitudes were merely evidence of immaturity, and whether they would be overcome in time. I have, however, notice[d] little change in your tendency to be unwilling to do what I have asked of you. Your negativism has not only been a source of distress to me, but it has unquestionably been disruptive to the morale of your co-workers.[17]

For the benefit of the Chicago JERS staff, among whom were Miyamoto and Shibutani, Thomas drafted a memorandum in October 1943 in which she restated her conception of the fundamental goal of JERS:

> The primary purpose is not at all mysterious. A minority group was, in a period of crisis, forcibly uprooted <u>en masse</u> [underline included], and forcibly concentrated in camps. Later, part of the group was forcibly segregated, and the other part was permitted to disperse and resettle. The purpose of the study then is to collect, organize, and analyze "relevant" data on (a) the nature of the restrictions that were imposed on the group; (b) how the persons affected behaved under these restrictions and after the restrictions were removed.

According to Thomas, sociologists were, "perhaps, the worse offenders of all" among social scientists who weave "unrealistic and fanciful theories." To those JERS staff members who wanted a theoretical framework, she said that "your major difficulty, as I see it, is an unwillingness to accept the essential simplicity of our project." All she wanted, she said, was "a record of the way of life of a people in a specified situation."[18] Given Thomas' persistent refusal to incorporate social theory into JERS, those fieldworkers in favor of a precise theoretical framework had no choice but to pursue their interest on their own.[19]

The Resettlement Phase

Thomas opened the Chicago JERS office in the spring of 1943. She secured office space at the University of Chicago through the help of Dean Robert Redfield. After the registration fiasco of early 1943, the WRA began to grant "clearance" to so–called loyal Nisei, enabling them to leave the concentration camps and resettle in the midwest, mainly in and around the city of Chicago. The Chicago JERS staff, consisting of Miyamoto, Shibutani, Togo Tanaka, Charles Kikuchi, and a few others, was entrusted with the responsibility of recording and documenting this resettlement phase. From Thomas' ideal point of view, the resettlement phase of JERS was going to study the "train of individual experience" of selected individuals, tracing their experience from the pre–war period, through their wartime uprooting and incarceration, and closing with their resettlement and adjustment to a "normal" American life in the midwest. These individuals were to be representative of the resettlers in terms of sex, occupation, and generation (Issei, Kibei, and Nisei), and their families and groups to which they belonged were to be considered an integral part of their life experience.[20]

Kikuchi became a central JERS staff member in the study of the resettlement phase. Since he had been raised in an orphanage, he was not a typical Nisei.[21] He fit the classic mold of a marginal man. Without any roots in his own cultural past, he had no positive self–identity. Kikuchi was so riddled with conflict that he was incapable of identifying with any group or institution. He was alienated from his own family, the Japanese immigrant community, his Nisei peers, as well as the larger society. While incarcerated at Tanforan and Gila River, he had kept up a copious daily journal which highly impressed Thomas and which made him, in her eyes, a valuable JERS staff member. In Chicago she assigned Kikuchi the job of interviewing the resettlers and writing up their life histories.

During the resettlement phase, Kikuchi believed that the Nisei had to disperse themselves throughout white society if they ever hoped to solve their racial problem. This meant that, in principle, the Nisei had to minimize interacting with each other, or, in the extreme, sever all their intra–ethnic ties. For if the Nisei reconstituted Nisei groups in the midwest, Kikuchi was convinced such groups would not only perpetuate Nisei "clannishness," but, more importantly, would also obstruct the solution of their very own racial problem. He noted in his diary in June 1943 that he had come out to Chicago to work for JERS, but that he had "inner inhibitions" about establishing contacts with an emerging "Nisei society" in that city. "I just haven't the appetite for it yet," he wrote, "because I think that [such a society] will be harmful for the group in terms of long range adjustments."[22]

Kikuchi's background and orientation inevitably affected his relations with his fellow Japanese–Americans. To begin with, Kikuchi could not communicate with any Issei or Kibei because he was unable to speak Japanese. This restricted his interviews to Nisei resettlers. Some Nisei resettlers, however, were hostile to Kikuchi and reluctant to be interviewed by him. Such Nisei probably perceived Kikuchi as condescending or patronizing in the light of his aversion of Nisei groups. Ultimately, Kikuchi wrote up 60 complete and four partial life histories following an outline, drawn up by Thomas, which limited the histories to the "factual, 'behavioristic' aspects" of the lives of Nisei resettlers.[23] Social psychological factors were conspicuously omitted. Thomas published 15 of these life histories in *The Salvage* as Part II because, she believed, they fit the "patterns of social and demographic change" which she outlined in Part I. As representatives of "selective" outmigration, according to Thomas, the resettlers, or the so–called salvage, consisted largely of nonagricultural, college–educated, Christian–secular, young adult Nisei of both sexes who tended to be from the Pacific Northwest. The 15 published life histories in *The Salvage* served to illustrate this selective pattern which characterized the so–called resettlement phase.

JERS' Relationship to WRA

The relationship between JERS and WRA began with the appointment of Milton S. Eisenhower as the first WRA Director. According to Thomas, there were "no strings attached" when Eisenhower promised that his agency would cooperate fully with JERS. As soon as Eisenhower designated John H. Provinse, Chief, Community Management Division, as the WRA liaison to JERS, Thomas notified Provinse of JERS' research goals and forwarded a copy of her proposal to the Rockefeller Foundation. Provinse expressed a keen interest in JERS, but felt it lacked concrete, practical goals. "Is it not possible to shift the emphasis from one for the testing of scientific hypotheses which 'may have practical implications,'" he asked, "to one which definitely recognizes that objective judgements can be procured on matters of practical import?" Provinse amplified on his view by saying that "the desire to give some shift of emphasis is not a desire to impede the work." Rather it was "to bring findings into some closer relationship to administrative need."[24] By this of course he was referring to the WRA and its problems of administering the ten concentration camps into which the Japanese were to be herded. To placate Provinse, Thomas assured him that "we are quite willing to shift the emphasis, as you suggest."[25]

A fundamental issue in JERS' relationship to WRA was the degree to which JERS would share its reports and findings with WRA. This issue was first raised by Provinse. Thomas gave the following account to Richard S. Nishimoto:

> Just a few weeks after we had started work at Tule Lake, Province (*sic*) came over to my office and demanded that I give him carbon copies of everything that our staff was sending in from the projects. I explained the total impossibility of carrying on the study under those conditions and predicted that my workers would resign rather than submit to this policy. He said I wouldn't have to tell them that their reports were being submitted to WRA! I controlled my temper with difficulty and explained mildly that this was a cooperative study with no secrets from the staff members. Naturally, I sent in no documents and nothing happened for a couple of months.[26]

In September 1942 John F. Embree, Senior Archivist, Reports Division, again raised this issue with Thomas. "I would like...copies," he requested, "of any general reports you may make on your own data and also copies of reports sent in by your field men."[27] According to Thomas, Embree also ordered Solon Kimball, his WRA subordinate, to visit Thomas once a week and "examine documents and question [her] about 'unwritten' materials."[28]

As a social scientist employed by WRA, Embree was acutely aware of the dearth of reliable information about concentration camp life, especially from the perspective of the Japanese inmates. In order to compile such information, the WRA established the Community Analysis Section in February 1943. It was no accident that this section, headed by Embree himself and staffed by people trained in the social sciences, was formed in the wake of the political conflicts which had erupted at Poston and Manzanar in November and December 1942.

Its mission was to provide WRA administrators with inside information which would enable them to carry out their administrative responsibilities more effectively and therefore enable them to avert similar conflicts in the future. As a JERS staff member at Gila River, Robert F. Spencer asked Thomas for clarification on whether or not he should cooperate with Embree and his staff. Thomas ordered Spencer to refer all requests from Embree or his staff to her at Berkeley. She instructed him: "Under no circumstances should you offer your services as a social analyst."[29]

Eventually, Thomas worked out a mutually acceptable, cooperative relationship with WRA. On February 10, 1943 she signed a formal agreement with Embree in his new capacity as the Principal WRA Social Analyst. Thomas did not consent to provide Embree and his staff with copies of JERS reports. According to the agreement, Thomas agreed, first, to submit a monthly letter to the Community Analysis Section regarding the "significant findings of the [JERS] field workers." Secondly, she agreed to periodic consultations with a WRA representative "concerning [JERS] field data." And, thirdly, she agreed to allow her fieldworkers "to cooperate informally with any social analysis that may be undertaken by WRA."[30] In this way, Thomas agreed to furnish selective information to satisfy WRA demands for data bearing on its administrative problems, but managed to avoid having to hand over copies of JERS reports.

Thomas had conferred with WRA officials in December 1942 and had shared data on administrative matters with them. To WRA Regional Director E.R. Fryer, Thomas wrote about the value of such meetings:

> We believe that this method of making our material accessible to WRA works out very well, since we were able to draw out the material pertinent to specific administrative problems and to give them some idea of the nature of the data we have that bear on questions of immediate importance. We realize that, although our whole program is geared to the long–run type of analysis, many "bits" are turning up which might be useful to WRA.

"In not letting the [JERS] material out" of her hands, she felt that she was "keeping faith with [her] collaborators" in the field. Above all else, Thomas wanted to protect her fieldworkers. Since they were in danger of "being considered 'informers,'" she wanted to restrict access to their field reports as much as possible.[31] As far as the WRA was concerned, she believed that she accomplished this through her agreement with Embree. In sum, in order to insure the continuation of WRA cooperation, essential of course to JERS, Thomas agreed to furnish limited information, thereby compromising, to that degree, JERS' own independence.

This policy of denying the WRA direct access to JERS field reports appears to have been upheld throughout the wartime years. In June 1944 JERS staff members assembled in Salt Lake City for a conference to evaluate their own work. John A. Rademaker, a WRA social analyst at Amache, Colorado, asked if he could participate in this conference. Thomas declined to extend an invitation to him on the grounds that the conference was only for JERS staff members.[32] According to S. Frank Miyamoto, Thomas "established the policy of not letting outsiders in on our discussions" in order not to compromise "our relations with those who have given us information."[33] In other words, her unwillingness to permit Rademaker, or any other outsider for that matter, to participate in JERS discussions was in line with the policy of not allowing any outsider direct access to JERS material, at least for the duration of the war.

Reassessing JERS

The first three essays in this anthology cover broad aspects of JERS. In the first one, S. Frank Miyamoto evaluates Dorothy Swaine Thomas's central role as JERS director and researcher. In order to understand Thomas as JERS director, Miyamoto contends, it is first essential to grasp her "neo–positivist" scientific orientation. Because her neo–positivism heavily influenced JERS' research orientation, he presents the basic tenets of her neo–positivism. In addition, according to Miyamoto, JERS' research orientation was influenced by W. I. Thomas, her husband. Although he was retired and never officially connected with JERS, his influence nevertheless was always felt, albeit indirectly, particularly his view on the value of empirical data in general and of life histories in particular. Moreover, JERS' research orientation was also affected by the early withdrawal of Professors Robert H. Lowie, Milton Chernin, Frank L. Kidner, and Charles Aikin from JERS. All four University of California faculty members had been scheduled to participate in JERS, but were drawn away by other war–related jobs. Willy–nilly, the onus of leadership responsibility fell entirely upon Thomas' shoulders. Thomas never felt comfortable with fields lying outside her own field of specialization. Consequently, with the untimely departure of her colleagues, she directed JERS almost exclusively within her enforced mass migration framework and dispensed with the anthropological, economic, political science, and social psychological components of the original JERS research goals. In terms of Thomas as a researcher, Miyamoto rates her contributions to JERS highly, especially her social demographic profile of the salvage in contrast to the spoilage.

Among all the JERS staff members, Richard S. Nishimoto served the longest stint as a JERS research assistant. In the second essay, Lane Ryo Hirabayashi and James Hirabayashi trace and analyze Nishimoto's contributions and virtually unknown multiple roles. Nishimoto had an unusual background. A younger Issei, he had an American high school education and a college degree in engineering from Stanford University. His high educational background and fluent command of English enabled him to maneuver himself into a leadership position between the WRA administrators and the Issei population at Poston. Tamie Tsuchiyama, the sole JERS staff member at Poston, first introduced Nishimoto to Dorothy Thomas; and on Tsuchiyama's later advice, Thomas placed him on staff in 1943 as an additional participant observer at Poston. In 1945 when every JERS staff member either had quit or had been terminated, Thomas elected to retain Nishimoto on staff as her only post–war research assistant. As a result, Nishimoto not only served as a participant observer at Poston during the wartime period, but also played a role in the publication of all three official JERS publications after the war. Indeed, he had a direct hand in putting together *The Spoilage* and subsequently was involved indirectly in both the *The Salvage* and *Prejudice, War and the Constitution.*

One of the bitterest conflicts within JERS occurred between Thomas and Morton Grodzins. The Grodzins affair involved Thomas' refusal to recommend Grodzins' doctoral dissertation for publication by the University of California Press and its eventual publication by the University of Chicago Press in 1949. Grodzins was employed by JERS from July 1, 1942 to March 31, 1945 as a research assistant. His job was to collect data on the various political factors behind the mass internment of Japanese–Americans. In 1945 Grodzins obtained his doctoral degree from the Department of Political Science. His dissertation was entitled "Political Aspects of the Japanese Evacuation" which advanced the thesis that, in California, state and local politicians and economic interest groups had applied pressure on the military to remove all Japanese from the state. Although Grodzins utilized the material he had collected as a JERS research assistant to write his dissertation, he wrote it at his own initiative and on his own time.

The conflict arose shortly before the end of the Pacific War. In early August 1945, Grodzins wrote to Thomas from Tennessee where he had secured a position. He inquired about her post–war publication plans and asked if his dissertation might be included in a JERS monograph series. He reminded her of how he had faithfully honored the pledge, required of all JERS staff members, not to disclose any JERS findings for the duration of World War II, even though he had "not been in full agreement with the restrictions imposed." "I have turned down every invitation to speak, and one invitation to write an article," Grodzins recalled. With the end of the Pacific War so imminent, however, he believed that "immediate plans should be made to publish several monographs." Anxious to see his own dissertation included, he closed his letter by asking Thomas for "detailed criticism" of his dissertation, promised to "revise" it "accordingly," and requested some kind of specific publication timetable.[34]

In her reply to Grodzins, Thomas ignited the controversy. She unequivocally stated that she and Professor Charles Aikin of the Department of Political Science had the "discretion" to decide "whether or not" his dissertation would be "published as a monograph." Thomas noted that Grodzins had been properly paid for his work and that she had proprietary rights over his dissertation since it was based upon JERS data. Regarding the publishability of the dissertation, Thomas minced no words, emphatically telling Grodzins: "Your thesis is unsuitable for publication. It is excessively verbose. It includes a number of intemperate and immature judgements about the behavior and misbehavior of government officials."[35] Grodzins was shocked and angered by her remarks. "I refrain from commenting on your extraordinary letter," he replied, "only because I now fully understand your conception of my status as a research assistant who, as you so ably and eloquently pointed out, was 'paid for [my] work.'" And he sarcastically signed his reply: "Y'r h'mble and ob't s'vt."[36]

In the third essay, Peter Suzuki presents a detailed study of this conflict between Thomas and Grodzins and offers a political interpretation that centers on Grodzins' interpretation of the role played by Earl Warren as California State Attorney General in the decision to intern all Japanese. Throughout the conflict, Thomas maintained that Grodzins' study was "unscholarly" and "propagandistic," thus unworthy of publication by the University of California Press or the University of Chicago Press. She even attempted to prevent the latter from publishing Grodzins' manuscript by reasserting her proprietary rights over it and threatening possible legal action if the University of Chicago decided to publish it. Thomas left the University of California in 1948, a year before the University of Chicago Press came out with *Americans Betrayed.* Before leaving Berkeley, however, she arranged for Jacobus tenBroek to produce an alternative political study, in part, to refute the thesis advanced by Grodzins, and that study turned out to be *Prejudice, War and the Constitution.*

The next three essays cover early camp life. The first by S. Frank Miyamoto looks at the Japanese inmates at Tule Lake before the 1943 "loyalty" registration crisis. Specifically, he examines the prevailing sense of resentment, distrust, and insecurity, felt in varying degrees by all inmates at Tule Lake, and interprets the resulting differential protest responses on the part of the inmates in the light of collective behavior theory. Robert F. Spencer and S. Frank Miyamoto follow with their personal reminiscences on their experience as JERS researchers, Spencer at Gila River and Miyamoto at Tule Lake. Inasmuch as Spencer was a white fieldworker, his experience, understandably, differed from that of his Japanese–American counterparts, which is evident in his account of conducting fieldwork at Gila River. Miyamoto begins his reminiscence with an account of his personal background prior to World War II to help us understand what he brought to JERS. Both he and Spencer discuss the misgivings they had about Thomas' research orientation, Miyamoto from his sociological perspective and Spencer from his anthropological perspective. And both discuss the many difficulties they encountered as fieldworkers and conclude with their own retrospective reassessment of JERS.

Two subsequent essays deal with the JERS life histories. As the compiler of the JERS life histories, Charles Kikuchi gives us a sensitive reminiscence of his work with JERS, especially during the resettlement phase. He discusses the influence W. I. Thomas had on him, how he went about interviewing Nisei resettlers in Chicago, and how he wrote up the life histories. And he concludes with the meaning JERS had for his own life and the Nisei generation as a whole. Dana Takagi reassesses the value of the Kikuchi life histories, first by placing them within the context of W. I. Thomas' concept of life histories and second by placing them within the context of subsequent concepts of life histories, including those advanced by contemporary feminists. Takagi believes that, notwithstanding the passage of time and changing concepts, the Kikuchi life histories hold up well even today. They are, in her opinion, by far the best accounts of the resettled Nisei generation.

During the immediate post–war period, Dorothy Thomas had planned to publish another JERS book which was to be devoted to those people who remained in the concentration camps for the duration of the war. Thus far virtually nothing has been written about these people, the so–called "unresettled" Japanese–Americans who were mostly old Issei and young Nisei. This projected volume was supposed to be based on James M. Sakoda's fieldwork at Minidoka and was tentatively entitled "The Residue" in order to contrast the unresettled people with their counterparts, the spoilage and the salvage. The final two essays in this anthology consist of Sakoda's reminiscence and his special study of the unresettled Minidokans. After the war, Sakoda returned to Berkeley and took a Ph.D. in social psychology with a dissertation on Minidoka. According to Sakoda, Thomas was prepared to recommend his dissertation for publication, provided he agreed to drop the section on his theoretical framework, something which Sakoda says he was unwilling to do. Hence "The Residue" was never published. Like Miyamoto and Spencer, Sakoda notes Thomas' hostility to social theory and her unwillingness to provide a theoretical framework for JERS. In his special essay, Sakoda presents his interpretation of the unresettled Minidokans, premised on the validity of his typology and couched in his unquestioning usage of WRA terminology. He also presents an intriguing account of the closing of Minidoka in late 1945 during which the last remaining inmates had to be forcibly expelled.

Taken together, the essays in this anthology do not constitute an exhaustive or definitive reassessment of JERS. Other special topics still remain to be explored. A study of the monthly reports filed by Thomas to the WRA should shed light on how much information she actually supplied to WRA administrators, which in turn will enable us to make a reasonable judgement as to the exact extent to which she compromised JERS' independence.[37] A study of the two key female JERS staff members, Tamie Tsuchiyama and Rosalie Hankey, needs to be done. The fact that both women were successful graduate students at Berkeley in the Anthropology Department, dominated by the arch–patriarch, Alfred L. Kroeber, is evidence enough that they were extraordinary women for their time. Thomas held them in high regard when she placed them on staff, but her relationship to both ended on less than amicable terms.

After Tule Lake was transformed into a segregated camp for so–called disloyal Japanese–Americans in 1943, Thomas asked Hankey, assigned at first to Gila River, to visit Tule Lake and report on events occurring there. Hankey visited Tule Lake in 1944 and 1945. With each visit, she witnessed and reported on the politically–charged conflicts which erupted there. The breach in the relationship between Thomas and Hankey occurred soon after Hankey's last visit in 1945. Hankey has written a highly personal account of her experience as a JERS fieldworker, but her account fails to explain the precise cause of her breach with Thomas.[38] Interestingly, Thomas never consulted with Hankey in the writing of *The Spoilage*, despite the fact that a good portion of the book was based on Hankey's field reports. Peter T. Suzuki has assailed Hankey's conduct at Tule Lake, especially in terms of her alleged betrayal of Ernest Kinzo Wakayama.[39] In his essay on Dorothy Swaine Thomas, S. Frank Miyamoto defends Hankey in her difficult role as a participant observer at Tule Lake. Recently, Violet Kazue de Cristoforo, a former Tule Lake inmate, has also raised very serious charges against Hankey.[40] She accuses Hankey of betraying her, of relaying false information about her to WRA authorities, and of causing her to be expatriated to Japan against her will. In order to substantial or refute these and other charges against Hankey, future researchers will have to examine all of her Tule Lake fieldnotes which are now deposited at the Bancroft Library.[41]

Finally, in my opinion, *The Spoilage* should be looked at more closely. Lane Ryo Hirabayashi and James Hirabayashi have interpreted Richard S. Nishimoto's probable role in the publication of *The Spoilage*, but they have not given us a critique of the book itself. On the other hand, S. Frank Miyamoto defends *The Spoilage* in his essay on Dorothy Thomas. He feels that it accurately documents what happened at Tule Lake, both before and after the "loyalty" registration. In my view, three key assumptions underlying *The Spoilage* need to be questioned. The first of these is that all inmates at Tule Lake had "an initial cooperative and surprisingly unprotesting acceptance" of concentration camp life.[42] The second is that human behavior is explainable in terms of how people perceive situations in which they find themselves. And the third is that the situational changes which occurred at Tule Lake between 1942 and 1945 and the inmate perceptions of those changing situations are sufficient to explain the shifts in behavior among the inmates from initial cooperation to hostility, rebellion, resegregation, renunciation, and even expatriation.

The Spoilage starts on December 7, 1941 in a historical vacuum. Hence the first assumption that all Tule Lake inmates had an initial spirit and attitude of cooperation toward their WRA keepers. Had the authors considered the pre–

war Japanese–American experience, such an assumption would not have been warranted. The second and third assumptions conveniently and neatly permit the authors to explain the shifts in inmate behavior by situational analysis exclusively confined to the 1942–1945 period. All three assumptions rule out a historical linkage between the pre–war past and the wartime present, and therefore narrowly restrict explanations of behavior to the wartime present. Put in another way, the assumptions preclude a broader reconstruction of Tule Lake history in which the pre–war past would have a direct and important bearing on inmate behavior in the wartime present.

Conclusion

Today, with the benefit of hindsight combined with a political perspective derived from the 1960s, some may condemn JERS out of hand as an unethical research project with no redeeming value. Doubtless, such people would argue that it was carried out solely for the sake of academic professionalism. Those who reaped the benefits were Dorothy Thomas and those JERS staff members who were able to advance professionally as a result of their participation in JERS. On the other hand, Japanese–Americans, the objects of JERS research, gained nothing—JERS neither improved their condition or status, nor promoted their political interests, either during the wartime years or after. Indeed, some may go so far as to argue that JERS was fundamentally inimical to Japanese–Americans. Detached or divorced from their interests as it were, JERS was necessarily for the benefit of others.

It goes without saying that JERS was not a research project in the service of a political cause on behalf of Japanese–Americans. To say that it should have been is to engage in wishful thinking; to criticize it for not having been is to be naive. Given Dorothy Thomas' research orientation, the development and progress of JERS, and the entire circumstances surrounding the mass internment of Japanese–Americans, JERS, in all probability, could not have been other than what it ended up to be—an academic research project conducted within the framework of Thomas' enforced mass migration framework. To recognize and admit that does not mean JERS has no redeeming value. The JERS sources, especially those in the form of daily journals, diaries, life histories, and field reports, expressingly produced at Thomas' insistence upon creating and preserving an empirical record of the internment experience, retain an enduring value because they lend themselves to the writing of a social history of concentration camp life. The sources on the so-called assembly centers at Tanforan, Tulare, Puyallup, and Santa Anita are virtually untouched, while those sources on Gila River, Tule Lake, Poston, and Minidoka have yet to be mined systematically.[43] For those who question or doubt the worth of JERS sources, they would do well to heed S. Frank Miyamoto's advice. Instead of making *a priori* judgements, they should research them first and then compare them to other available sources to arrive at a meaningful conclusion. In the hands of a discerning historian, in my opinion, the JERS sources—augmented of course by other sources—can be the basis of a rich social history of concentration camp life.

Notes

1. For a blanket indictment of all social scientists employed by the War Relocation Authority, see Peter T. Suzuki, "Anthropologists in the Wartime Camps for Japanese Americans: A Documentary Study," *Dialectical Anthropology*, 6:1 (1981), 23–60. For a less hostile but nonetheless very critical view, see Orin Starn, "Engineering Internment: Anthropologists and the War Relocation Authority," *American Ethnologist*, 13:4 (1986), 700–20. For a defense of the use of social scientists by the WRA, see E[dward] H. Spicer, "History of the Community Analysis Section," Community Analysis Section, War Relocation Authority, December 30, 1945; Edward H. Spicer, "The Use of Social Scientists by the War Relocation Authority," *Applied Anthropology*, 5:2 (1946), 16–36; and Edward H. Spicer, "Anthropologists and the War Relocation Authority," in Walter Goldschmidt, ed., *The Uses of Anthropology* (Washington, D.C.: American Anthropological Association, 1979), 217–37.

2. Alexander H. Leighton, *The Governing of Men: General Principles and Recommendations Based on Experience at a Japanese Relocation Camp* (Princeton: Princeton University Press, 1945).

3. For a bibliography of the JERS Collection, see Edward N. Barnhart, *Japanese American Evacuation and Resettlement: Catalog of Material in the General Library* (Berkeley: University of California, General Library, 1958).

4. The only study to date of JERS is Peter T. Suzuki, "The University of California Japanese Evacuation and Resettlement Study: A Prolegomenon," *Dialectical Anthropology*, 10 (1986), 189–213, a one-sided, polemical essay.

5. David L. Sills, ed., *International Encyclopedia of the Social Sciences: Biographical Supplement* (New York: THE FREE PRESS, 1979), v. 18, 763–65.

6. Dorothy S. Thomas, "The Mechanism and Consequences of the Wartime Civilian Control Program for the Evacuation and Resettlement of Certain Classes of the Population" (May 1, 1942), Japanese American Evacuation and Resettlement Study (JERS), 67/14c, Supplement, Carton 1, Bancroft Library, University of California, Berkeley

7. *Ibid.*; Dorothy S. Thomas, "Progress Report" (July 3, 1942), *ibid*; and Dorothy S. Thomas, "Evacuation and Resettlement Study, University of California, Annual Report, 1942–1943" (July 1, 1943), JERS W 1.00.

8. This project produced two major studies: Carter Goodrich *et al.*, *Migration and Economic Opportunity: The Report of the Study of Population Distribution* (Philadelphia: University of Pennsylvania Press, 1936); and Rupert B. Vance, *Research Memorandum on Population Redistribution Within the United States* (New York: Social Science Research Council, Bulletin 42, 1938).

9. Thomas, "Evacuation and Resettlement Study, University of California, Annual

Report. 1942–1943" (July 1, 1943).

10. D[orothy] S. Thomas, "Memorandum to Field Collaborators" (August 27, 1942), JERS W 1.20.

11. Tamotsu Shibutani, Haruo Najima, and Tomika Shibutani, "The First Month at Tanforan: A Preliminary Report" (June 1942), JERS B 8.31.

12. Letter, Shibutani to Thomas (June 6, 1942), JERS B 12.51.

13. S. Frank Miyamoto, "Field Research in Relocation Centers," Part II, 90, JERS R 20.18A. See also letter, Miyamoto to Thomas (October 30, 1943), JERS W 1.25C.

14. Tamotsu Shibutani, "Proposed Outline for the Study of Japanese Evacuees in the Assembly Centers" (May 23, 1942), JERS W 1.20.

15. Letter, Shibutani to Galbraith (August 21, 1942), JERS B 12.51.

16. Letter, Grodzins to Thomas (October 20, 1943), JERS, Supplement, Carton 2, Staff Correspondence.

17. Letter, Thomas to Shibutani (April 6, 1944), JERS, *ibid.*

18. Dorothy S. Thomas, "Memorandum to Staff" (October 28, 1943), JERS W 1.25C.

19. After the war, Miyamoto, Shibutani, and Sakoda produced doctoral dissertations, based upon JERS data, within the framework of their own theoretical interests. Miyamoto and Shibutani dealt with aspects of collective behavior in their respective dissertations: Shotaro Frank Miyamoto, "The Career of Intergroup Tensions: A Study of the Collective Adjustments of Evacuees to Crises at the Tule Lake Relocation Center," Ph.D. dissertation, University of Chicago, 1950; and Tamotsu Shibutani, "The Circulation of Rumors as a Form of Collective Behavior," Ph.D. dissertation, University of Chicago, 1948. Sakoda placed his study of Minidoka within a social psychological framework: James M. Sakoda, "Minidoka: An Analysis of Changing Patterns of Social Interaction," Ph.D. dissertation, University of California, 1949. Besides Miyamoto, Shibutani, and Sakoda, Spencer also produced a doctoral dissertation but his was on the Japanese Buddhist churches within the context of an acculturation framework: Robert F. Spencer, "Japanese Buddhism in the United States, 1940–1946: A Study in Acculturation," Ph.D. dissertation, University of California, 1946; and Rosalie Hankey Wax focused her own dissertation on a comparative analysis of how "authoritarism" had developed among Japanese–Americans at Tule Lake and Germans in Germany: Rosalie Hankey Wax, "The Development of Authoritarism: A Comparison of the Japanese–American Relocation Centers and Germany," Ph.D. dissertation, University of Chicago, 1951.

20. Dorothy S. Thomas, "Evacuation and Resettlement Study: Resettlement Phase" (May 19, 1943), JERS W 1.20.

21. John Modell, ed., *The Kikuchi Diary: Chronicle From An American Concentration Camp* (Urbana: University of Illinois Press, 1973), 1–39; Louis Adamic, *From Many Lands*

(New York: Harper & Brothers, 1940), 185–234; and Yuji Ichioka, "'Unity in Diversity': Louis Adamic and Japanese-Americans," *Working Papers*, Asia–Pacific Institute, Duke University, 1987.

22. "Charles Kikuchi Diary" (June 11, 1943), Special Collections, University Research Library, University of California, Los Angeles.

23. Dorothy S. Thomas, "Evacuation and Resettlement Study: Resettlement Phase" (May 19, 1943).

24. Letter, John H. Provinse to Thomas (May 21, 1942), JERS, Supplement, Carton 1.

25. Letter, Thomas to Provinse (May 26, 1942), *ibid.*

26. Letter, Thomas to Richard S. Nishimoto (April 27, 1944), JERS W 1.25A.

27. Letter, John F. Embree to Thomas (September 26, 1942), JERS, Supplement, Carton 2.

28. Letter, Thomas to Nishimoto (April 27, 1944).

29. Letter, Thomas to Robert F. Spencer (February 2, 1943), JERS K 8.80B.

30. "Memorandum of Agreement" (February 11, 1943), *ibid.*

31. Letter, Thomas to E.R. Fryer (January 18, 1943), *ibid.*

32. Letter, Thomas to John A. Rademaker (May 29, 1944), JERS W 1.25C.

33. Letter, Frank S. Miyamoto to Rademaker (May 31, 1944), *ibid.*

34. Letter, Morton Grodzins to Thomas (August 9, 1945), JERS, Supplement, Carton 1.

35. Letter, Thomas to Grodzins (August 18, 1945), *ibid.*

36. Letter, Grodzins to Thomas (August 29, 1945), *ibid.*

37. As to JERS' relationship to the War Department, a few documents have been published recently. See the section titled "The War Department and the Japanese Evacuation Resettlement Study, October, 1942-October, 1943," in Roger Daniels, ed., *American Concentration Camps: A Documentary History of the Relocation and Incarceration of Japanese Americans, 1942-1945* (New York: Garland Publishing, 1989), VIII.

38. Rosalie H. Wax, *Doing Fieldwork: Warnings and Advice* (Chicago: University of Chicago Press, 1971), 59–174.

39. Suzuki, "The University of California Japanese American Evacuation and Resettlement Study: A Prolegomenon."

40. Violet Kazue de Cristoforo, "A Victim of the Japanese American Evacuation and Resettlement Study (JERS)," Salinas, unpublished manuscript, 1987.

41. See Rosalie H. Wax, "Tule Lake Fieldnotes, 1944–1945," 83/115c, Bancroft Library. Two restrictions, in effect until the year 2008, have been placed on the usage of these fieldnotes. First, researchers must obtain the permission of the Director of the Bancroft Library to use the fieldnotes, and, secondly, they must pledge not to disclose the names of individual "evacuees" identified in the fieldnotes.

42. Dorothy S. Thomas and Richard S. Nishimoto, *The Spoilage* (Berkeley: University of California Press, 1946), 45.

43. Recently, a few scholars have made extensive use of JERS sources with fruitful results. For example, see Isami Arifuku Waugh, "Hidden Crime and Deviance in the Japanese American Community, 1920–1946," Ph.D. dissertation, University of California, Berkeley, 1978; Jerrold H. Takahashi, "Changing Responses to Racial Subordination: An Exploratory Study of Japanese American Political Style," Ph.D. dissertation, University of California, Berkeley, 1980; Arthur A. Hansen, "Cultural Politics in the Gila River Relocation Center, 1942–1943," *Arizona and the West*, 27 (1985), 327–62; and Richard Drinnon, *Keeper of Concentration Camps: Dillon S. Myer and American Racism* (Berkeley and Los Angeles: University of California Press, 1987).

PART I

Dorothy Swaine Thomas as Director of JERS:

Some Personal Observations

S. FRANK MIYAMOTO

One purpose of this anthology is to provide researchers interested in the JERS archives with a basis for judging the reliability of the material. For a variety of reasons, which will be discussed below, the reliability of JERS data has come under question.[1] Because these questions revolve especially around the role of its director, Dorothy Swaine Thomas, it is important to understand her background if a fair judgment is to be made of JERS. It will become evident that I do not share others' doubts about Thomas' scholarship, but I hope it is clear that I am attempting to present her as objectively as possible, and that it is certainly not my aim to minimize the shortcomings of the project.

Thomas' Scientific Orientation: Neo–positivism

To understand Thomas' approach to JERS, it is necessary to understand her scientific orientation, best described as neo–positivist. It is a view that is not well understood by the general public or even by many social scientists, and it may be that a good deal of the misunderstanding of her role in JERS is due to not understanding her scientific orientation.

It may be somewhat misleading to call Thomas a neo–positivist, for the term implies a philosophical position. Thomas was not a theorist—she was throughout an experimentalist, a person concerned with carrying out research, and was not disposed to spend much time considering the abstract substructure of her studies. But it is the label which her longtime friend, George A. Lundberg, in his theoretical examination of fundamental perspectives underlying sociology,[2] applied to the point of view he shared with William F. Ogburn, Stuart Chapin, Samuel Stouffer, as well as Thomas. The label, therefore, permits us to use Lundberg's discussion to represent Thomas' position.

Positivism, especially in its contemporary form, is difficult to explain in simple, non–technical terms,[3] but a brief summary is needed. Since our concern is only to describe Thomas' orientation and not to assess the logic of her approach, it should suffice here to outline some basic features of positivism without giving attention to the subtler issues. The following are four basic features[4] of positivism which were clearly reflected in Thomas' work.

1) *The experiential basis of knowledge.* Positivism holds that the basis of knowledge is experience, and that the truth or falsity of any statement can be determined only by subjecting it to a systematic, empirical test. Thus, statements which cannot be empirically tested cannot constitute a basis of knowledge.

"Experience" is understood to mean an observable response of an organism in an observable environment. The ultimate concern of positivists is to insure that the reported experience of one person may also be observed or reconstructed by another, and be confirmed or disconfirmed. The point of view is clearly reflected in *behaviorism,* a neo–positivist position in psychology that Thomas adopted for her child studies. Behaviorism holds that observable *behaviors* constitute the only legitimate data, and rejects non–behavioral (subjective) phenomena. For example, if person A physically attacks person B, the attack is observable and may be taken as datum, but if an observer asserts that A attacked B because A was jealous of the latter, the alleged motive must be regarded as unverifiable. On the other hand, the behaviorist would agree that "jealousy" could be defined in behavioral terms and then could be empirically verified. In short, the effort throughout is to exclude from scientific discourse references which are not verifiable by means of observation.

2) *Nominalistic basis of knowledge.* Nominalism asserts that the only real objects to which knowledge can be referred are individual, concrete objects. According to nominalists, only individual persons act, and if a group is said to "act," it is only the configuration of individual actions that is being perceived as a group action. For example, when sociologists speak about a group, an institution, a social class, or a community as "acting" in one way or another (e.g., that the evacuees were angered by the WRA's action), nominalists would say that the references (such as "evacuees" and "WRA") are only a manner of speaking and cannot refer to actions of real entities.

Thomas was not a purist in the matter of nominalism, but she tended to avoid analyses of groups and social categories unless the members could be enumerated. Her main field of research, population studies—where population figures are generally based on enumerations of individual members—was ideally suited to the nominalist approach. Similarly, in her studies of children, her observations were invariably reports on individual actions. Even in her JERS work, I believe that Thomas tried to minimize references to group actions.

3) *The aim of quantification.* The neo–positivists among sociologists regard quantification as the best way to represent and communicate knowledge. Quantification facilitates precise communication inasmuch as it requires that the objects to be measured be clearly identified, that observational devices be reliable and valid, and that methods involving the rigorous logic of mathematics be applied in the analyses. The caveat with respect to quantification, of course, is that the measures must be valid and the analytical methods appropriate.

Thomas was from the outset a strong advocate of quantitative methods in sociology, and virtually all her research studies reflected her concern for quantitative rigor. Her best contributions in JERS, I would say, are those parts involving statistical analyses.[5] However, for the bulk of the project, she was unable to collect and use quantitative data. Thus, the question may be asked whether she was seriously hampered in JERS due to her inability to employ her preferred mode of research.

4) *The value–free orientation of science.* The term "value" refers to judgments which may be made concerning an object's desirability, approvability, or goodness. Positivists hold that objects of experience contain no value judgments, and that an experience itself provides no grounds for upholding one value over another. Value preferences arise not from experiences of the external environment, but from internally generated motives, feelings, and attitudes. So the aim of the scientist in seeking a value–free science is to minimize or eliminate the effect of his personal inclinations on the findings he reports.

Because of the complex, internal influences which affect an observer's perceptions of external objects, it is virtually impossible to establish a science or any body of knowledge that is totally value–free. This is especially a problem in the social sciences. But the neo–positivist's contention is that the behaviors under observation contain no value implications, and the scientist must strive to record each behavior without adding value to it. Or, if biasing values necessarily affect the observations, he must devise methods of data analysis which will eliminate those biases or correct for them. The point is clarified with an illustration from the history of physics. Prior to Copernicus, Galileo, and Newton, observations of the physical world were intimately linked to religious values. Copernicus and Galileo insisted on a separation of religious conceptions from scientific observations of the physical world and devised methods to achieve objectivity. Two centuries after Newton, Einstein proposed a revision of Newton's earthbound conception of the physical world with a more universal, relativist view. Thus, it must be conceded that no science, including physics, can claim to be absolutely value–free. But it should be emphasized that some methods of observation and data analysis are much more value–free than others. For example, the degree of objectivity gained by Galileo using his scientific methods of observation over the perceptions of his religious–minded predecessors was enormous; while Einstein's gain in objectivity over Galileo and Newton was relatively small.

The basis of the neo–positivist's argument for a value–free sociology lies in the contention that methods of observation and analysis exist which can minimize the effect of value–oriented preconceptions on observation. Thomas was acutely aware of the unanticipated ways in which observer biases could distort scientific observations, and in all her research took great pains to try to minimize the effects.[6]

In summary, during the first 15 years of her research career, Thomas was a firm believer and advocate of the neo–positivist principles outlined above.[7] She continued throughout her life to favor these principles as the ultimate standard of research, but by the time she was fully involved in JERS, she became less fixed in her views. Two influences probably caused her to modify her orientation. First, her husband, W. I. Thomas, the internationally renowned sociologist, approved of the behavioristic orientation, but he was a pragmatist by background and was much less of a purist about positivism. Second, the experience of the JERS research, where she found it impossible to adhere closely to neo–positivist principles, undoubtedly caused her to adopt her husband's more pragmatic approach.[8]

Thomas' Pre–war Research: Population Studies and Child Behavior

Thomas' pre–war research was primarily in two fields: population studies and child behavior. These fields seem far removed from JERS, but her earlier research, in fact, had a significant bearing on the evacuation study.

Thomas' doctoral dissertation, *The Social Aspects of the Business Cycle*, was a study of social change, an interest she inherited from her mentor, William F. Ogburn. Ogburn was especially interested in the effects of a major event such as a war or a depression, or a major invention such as the airplane or automobile, in changing society. The business cycle, the fluctuations between prosperity and depression, was such an event; and both Ogburn and Thomas were no doubt also attracted to the subject by the excellent statistical data, not only of annual business conditions but also of various related social conditions, which were available. Thomas did brilliant work in developing carefully controlled measures of each variable, and of running time–series correlations among them (this at a time when only crude table calculators were at hand).

There were parallels between Thomas' dissertation and JERS. The evacuation was a major event that seriously affected every evacuee. And since it was the military and the federal government which were to carry it out, she no doubt assumed that careful statistics would be kept on all who were moved.

Thomas' special interest was in differential migration: the questions of why some people migrate and others do not, and why migration has varying effects on different people.[9] Typically, she examined differences between migrants and non–migrants with respect to such characteristics as age, sex, family status, physical health, mental health, intelligence, occupation, and motivation; and then complicated the question by asking why people with certain combinations of these characteristics migrated.

These earlier population studies had three implications for Thomas' study of the evacuation. First, demographers may interest themselves in population structure as well as change, but Thomas clearly was more interested in change. JERS was likewise a study of change. Second, her specialty in demography was migration. The evacuation, as a forced migration, was different from an ordinary, voluntary migration. But migration, whether forced or voluntary, is a migration. It was this fact that aroused her interest in the evacuation. Third, the methodology of differential analysis developed in her migration studies proved directly applicable to her studies of the evacuees' differential behavior during "loyalty" registration and in the WRA's resettlement program.

Thomas' other major line of research, her study of child behavior, also clearly reflected her neo–positivist orientation. In the introduction to a publication that was intended to be the first in a series of child development monographs at Columbia, she declared:

> The studies presented in preliminary form in this volume represent an experimental approach to social behavior. For this reason we are calling the

> methodological scheme on which they are based *experimental sociology*. It is sociological in the sense that its aim is the study of overt behavior in varying situations in the field of social interaction. It is experimental in the sense of developing techniques for the control of the observer in order that scientific records may be obtained both of behavior and of situation, and that statistical analysis—ultimately the necessary tool for evaluating behavior–situation relationships—may eventually be applied.[10]

The emphases in this statement are on such terms as: experimental sociology, study of overt behavior, control of the observer, and statistical analysis. Thus, in these studies, Thomas tried to treat human behavior as objectively and as rigorously as a physicist would the phenomena he studies. Unfortunately, in JERS, Thomas found herself severely restricted in collecting quantifiable data. Nevertheless, there is no doubt that she tried to maintain her behaviorist standards. She repeatedly emphasized the need for careful, behavioral observations relative to significant situations in the camps, and she was obviously concerned with the problem of "the control of the observer."

The Role of W. I. Thomas

The distinguished sociologist W. I. Thomas was 78–years–old when the JERS project was initiated.[11] To my knowledge, he accompanied his wife on all field trips to the WRA centers and the Chicago field office and participated occasionally in our discussions. I have no evidence, however, of his specific involvement in the project. Yet, there is at least one good reason to consider the influence he might have exerted. For Dorothy Thomas, JERS proved to be a type of research quite different from anything she had done before. On the other hand, its heavy dependence on personal interviews, letters, life histories, and written reports involved precisely the method of research which W. I. Thomas had used with great success in his Polish immigrant study.[12]

W. I. Thomas was a theorist of a kind, but his was not the broad and general theorizing about society that was characteristic of Durkheim, Weber, Park, and others in his day. He was interested more in indicating concepts, such as attitudes, values, definition of the situation, disorganization, and crisis, which he showed not only to be basic and important features in human relations but also especially useful as research tools. His, in short, was more a theory for research.

The conceptual scheme of research underlying JERS was explicated in *The Child in America*,[13] co–authored by W. I. and Dorothy Thomas, and also in his last book, *Primitive Behavior*.[14] Dorothy Thomas shared in the final development of the point of view, but if one examines W. I. Thomas' earlier works, it is evident that he was the one who specified the main parameters of the research orientation which they came to share.[15]

The ultimate concern of sociologists, the Thomases declared, is to predict the social behavior of humans. In seeking to predict *behavior*, the variables are to be found in the *situation* and in the *definition of the situation.* The "situation" refers to objective conditions of the environment to which individuals could be observed to make adjustmental responses. In their references to the "definition of the situation"—a concept that W. I. Thomas made famous in his earlier studies—the Thomases acknowledged that subjective definitions play a critical role in determining adjustmental behavior. This way of approaching social research produced a pragmatic open–mindedness that precluded the use of any particular theory of human behavior as the underlying scheme. Rather, the approach directed the researcher's attention to problemmatic situations and to adaptational responses as the main objects of the study.[16] I believe it was this very general formula that guided the JERS fieldwork. Inasmuch as these ideas derived from W. I. Thomas' theory of research, I believe that he exerted a fundamental influence on the project.

Dorothy Thomas' Roles in JERS

Dorothy Thomas functioned in three different capacities in JERS: as mobilizer of the study, as its director, and as a researcher. These functions necessarily overlapped, but they were differentiated enough to be seen as distinct roles.

1) *As mobilizer of the study.* The question of who specifically initiated JERS may now seem a matter of little interest, but the question is important because it had a bearing on the form which the study ultimately took.

In her own account of how the project was initiated, Thomas simply states: "Early in 1942, a group of social scientists in the University of California undertook a study of the evacuation, detention, and resettlement of the Japanese minority in the United States."[17] Besides Thomas, this group included Robert H. Lowie of Anthropology, Charles Aikin of Political Science, Milton Chernin of Social Welfare, and Frank L. Kidner of Economics. She states that they all "participated in the early stages of planning," and describes the resulting plan as follows:

> The study was conceptualized on an interdisciplinary basis: (a) viewed as a sociological problem, it was to include analysis of the social demography of forced mass migration and voluntary resettlement, with special reference to the dislocation of habits and changes of attitudes produced by the experience; (b) viewed as a study in social anthropology, it would be oriented around the modifications and changes in the two cultures represented in the group, first under the impact of constant, enforced association, and later in the process of dispersal into the "outside world"; (c) viewed as a study in political science, it would emphasize policy formation and administrative procedures: the interaction of state and national political forces, the part played by local government units in determining both state and national policy, the development of organized pressures and their result; (d) viewed as a problem in social psychology, the primary focus would be on the nature of the collective adjustments made by this population group, following the crisis of evacuation, to the way of life imposed by the government during detention and on the extent and kind of institutional reorganization and individual readjustment following resettlement; (e) viewed as an economic problem, it would be concerned with the economic conditions predisposing the formulation of policies, the economic consequences of evacuees themselves, and the governmental efforts to protect the interests both of the areas and of the classes of population involved.[18]

Very soon after the study was initiated in the spring of 1942, however, all the other participants were drawn into other wartime governmental activities, and Thomas was left to carry out the study by herself.[19] They did not leave her totally unassisted, for Lowie helped to appoint three, mature anthropology graduate students as research assistants, one of whom, Rosalie Hankey, eventually played a crucial role as a field researcher; and Aikin helped appoint a graduate student in political science, Morton Grodzins, who later published a major work on evacuation policy formation. Nevertheless, the loss of her professorial collaborators no doubt left Thomas with more responsibilities than she had bargained for and also critically affected the way the project was carried out. It certainly affected the way in which Lowie and Aikin's students functioned on the study.

The early, unexpected withdrawal of her colleagues is understandable in light of the major disruption of the American manpower system that occurred in the first year of war. Thomas herself, however, could not leave the project so easily, for she had more basic commitments to it than did the others. In the first place, she probably was from the outset the prime mover behind the project. Two Nisei students in her sociology class—Tamotsu Shibutani and James Sakoda who began observations of Japanese–Americans in the Berkeley area immediately after the Pearl Harbor bombing—were instrumental in arousing her interest in such a study very early in the discussions of the evacuation. Furthermore, the initial funding for the project, which was received from the Rockefeller Foundation on unusually short notice, probably was due to Thomas' very strong research reputation within the foundation. Thus, she had a compelling obligation to carry through with the project in accordance with the original plan.

As described in the plan, Thomas' own research was to be on problems of differential migration. This objective would have given her a much more delimited study than the one she, in fact, undertook. However, once the project was mobilized as the wide–ranging, interdisciplinary study described above, it must have been impossible to retrench. For one thing, graduate assistants from anthropology and political science had already been appointed, and work had to be found for them. Also, it seems likely that Thomas needed as background for her own research the studies of evacuee lives which her colleagues were to help provide. In their absence, she apparently found it necessary to get that background herself.

In brief, the evidence suggests that when Thomas first became involved in JERS, she conceived of her role more narrowly than the one she ultimately adopted, and that the unpredictable conditions of the early wartime period thrust on her responsibilities she had not expected.[20] Some of the major difficulties which later surfaced in the project, I believe, may be explained by these unexpected responsibilities.

2) *As director of the study.* Following the withdrawal of her colleagues, Thomas was the only professorial member left in JERS, the remaining personnel being graduate students. Consequently, there was no question as to whom the staff should look for direction. But, in retrospect, it is apparent that throughout the study Thomas gave minimal direction to the field research staff, and most were troubled by the lack of more explicit instructions.

In the first year, all attention was given to studying the evacuees in the WRA relocation centers. At that time, fieldworkers were located in Tule Lake, Poston, and Gila River. At least for the initial period, Thomas apparently intended to have her field staff concentrated at one place, Tule Lake. Those scheduled to be evacuated to other centers were generally transferred to Tule Lake to accommodate the study. It was accidental that Tule Lake was chosen for the main laboratory. Located in northern California about 350 miles from Berkeley, it was the center closest to her university office, and she chose it to give her the readiest access to the field staff. However, because some staff appointees had to accompany their families to other centers such as Poston and Gila River, Thomas set up supplemental research sites to accommodate these researchers. In other words, Thomas modified her plans in order to meet unexpected requirements created by the evacuation.

Thomas' directorial activities were conducted largely by correspondence, occasional visits to the relocation centers, and once–a–year conferences of the entire staff at suitable locations outside the centers. She and her husband visited Tule Lake every three or four months in the first year, but spent no more than a few days at the center and attempted no direct contacts with the residents. She made similar trips to Poston and Gila River. Supervision of the evacuee assistants, therefore, occurred mainly via written correspondence, and there was relatively little direction given regarding the specific kinds of observations she desired. Rather, she focused on reacting to materials submitted by the field researchers and suggesting further lines of inquiry.

From the beginning, each fieldworker was asked to keep a daily journal of significant and interesting events, evacuee reactions, and attitudes and behaviors, which reflected features of camp life. The researchers were also expected to collect documents concerning policies and center events. But in my recollection, Thomas distributed only some broad outlines of topics to be investigated, and never discussed the problems under study, the research design, or methodological procedures.

The chief complaint among the research assistants, seldom expressed directly to Thomas but often hinted, concerned feelings of uncertainty as to what they were supposed to be studying. Some were concerned about the study's lack of a theoretical orientation. Others fretted over the lack of explicit instructions. By standard criteria of sociological research, Thomas clearly failed to give adequate direction to her staff.

On the other hand, Thomas was seriously handicapped in the directorial role she was called upon to play. There were major aspects of the study, especially of life in the center communities, for which she was ill–prepared by training and experience to research. It should also be added that the evacuation was inherently difficult to research, and the situation would have required an exceptional social scientist to have produced a thoroughly satisfactory study. Events occurred so rapidly that researchers had almost no time to plan their studies in the manner that research generally requires. Also, such an uprooting was unparalleled in modern American history, and researchers were mentally unprepared to determine how the study should be carried out. Finally, the evacuation aroused distrust and resentment among Japanese–Americans, so they became an especially difficult group among whom to conduct research.

The inherent difficulty of relocation center studies, I feel, is revealed by examining all the major studies which were done. When these studies are compared, I feel a strong argument can be made for Thomas' strategy of minimizing direction over her field staff and of having them focus on ongoing events and recording evacuee reaction. The strategy clearly was in line with the theory of social research which she and W. I. Thomas had developed earlier, namely, to identify some significant adjustmental *behavior* and determine the *situation* to which the behavior was a response; or vice–versa, as in the case of the center studies. Given the unpredictability of life in the centers, there was much to be said for this kind of open–ended approach to research.

The one aspect of Thomas' directorship that is almost inexplicable was her attitude toward the rights of graduate assistants on the issues of co–authorship and publication of studies. As noted above, she had relatively little direct contact with the field research and, from the standpoint of the field staff, gave minimal supervisory guidance to the data collection. Because of the critical role that fieldworkers played in the data–gathering process, they tended to develop a strong proprietary sense with regard to the data they collected.

Thomas granted co–authorship to only one research assistant, namely Richard S. Nishimoto, the only one of the assistants not working toward a graduate degree. Otherwise, the research assistants were acknowledged on the title pages of publications, below the authors' names, with such references as "with contributions by" and "with the assistance of." This level of acknowledgement was probably reasonable for most of the assistants, but there were significant instances in which a more substantial recognition seemed warranted.

One of the more flagrant cases was the treatment accorded Rosalie Hankey (later Rosalie Hankey Wax) on the question of co–authorship of *The Spoilage*. Hankey was the sole fieldworker at the segregated Tule Lake center, and with an astonishing display of research skill and energy assembled the bulk of the data that formed the basis of the book. Yet, she is simply listed as one of the four research assistants who "contributed to" the publication.

Similarly, in *The Salvage,* which is mainly a compilation of 15 Nisei life histories done by Charles Kikuchi, Kikuchi is acknowledged on the title page only with the reference: "with the assistance of, Charles Kikuchi and James Sakoda." Sakoda helped to compile a very interesting set of statistical tables which analyzed the differences between those who resettled from the WRA centers and those who did not, but he, too, was discouraged by Thomas from publishing his own material. Other research assistants encountered similar problems. Thomas freely granted permission to use JERS materials for dissertation purposes, but she never offered graduate assistants the privilege of co–authorship and resisted all requests for permission to publish separately.

The disagreement between Morton Grodzins and Thomas concerning Grodzins' right to publish his dissertation resulted in the bitterest conflict.[21] With Professor Aikin's recommendation, Grodzins was initially hired in the summer of 1942 and rapidly moved into the role of a senior assistant fulfilling major administrative duties. In this period he began, quite independently according to his account, investigations of pressure groups amd political and military influences which might have played a part in bringing about the evacuation. As a JERS employee, he collected a wide range of material bearing on this topic, and on his own time wrote a lengthy dissertation. In March 1945, he successfully defended the dissertation before a committee which was chaired by Aikin and included Thomas.

In August 1945, as Japan's surrender became imminent, Grodzins pressed Thomas for permission to publish his dissertation on grounds of its timeliness, but she declined to grant permission. She contended that because he had collected his material as a JERS employee, the material was the property of the study; and that she and other JERS committee members needed to decide on the study's publication plans before anything could be published.

Until this issue arose, Grodzins had worked closely with Thomas, and their relationship had been friendly. But as Grodzins continued to press for permission to publish, their relationship deteriorated rapidly. Grodzins was unquestionably a JERS employee during the period when the data of his dissertation were collected, but he argued that he had been the one who had insisted on the need for the pre–evacuation study and had planned its design. Thomas contended that his analysis of the persons and groups who had provoked the evacuation was biased, propagandistic, and incompetent. Surprisingly, Aikin, Grodzins' dissertation chairman, strongly agreed with Thomas, and she stated that other referees whom she had consulted also criticized the manuscript on similar grounds.

Grodzins originally had hoped to have his study published by the University of California Press as one of the JERS publications, but due to Thomas' opposition, he submitted it to the University of Chicago Press. An eminent committee of social scientists approved its publication, but when Thomas heard of Chicago's plans, she protested strongly. A struggle over the right of publication ensued, but ultimately the University of Chicago Press prevailed in its insistence on the right to publish. Grodzins' book, entitled *Americans Betrayed,*[22] appeared in 1949 to generally positive reviews. My own judgment is that it was a very important book, and that Thomas, in effect, spited herself and the prestige of JERS by disassociating Grodzins' book from the project.

I believe I understand some of the reasons why Dorothy Thomas behaved as she did on the publication issue, but I still feel she erred in adopting the policy she did.

3) *As a researcher.* In evaluating Thomas' research, we are interested only in her work on JERS and not with her research before and after the war in other areas. As I have mentioned already, unusual conditions surrounded the wartime research, and allowance should be made for the special problems she faced.

This evaluation of Thomas' research will be restricted to her statistical analyses of evacuees, and her study of the segregated evacuees at Tule Lake published in collaboration with Nishimoto as *The Spoilage.* Since the statistical analyses provided a background for all of her JERS work, they will be considered first. These analyses appear in *The Spoilage*[23] and *The Salvage,*[24] and concerned evacuee responses to two crucial WRA programs: the "loyalty" registration and the subsequent segregation of one group and resettlement of the other.

The registration occurred when, after six months of overseeing the evacuees in detention centers, WRA executives came to a crucial decision: that continued incarceration of the evacuees was mentally and morally unhealthy for them. It was decided that they should be resettled in non–restricted zones as soon as possible and allowed to reestablish themselves in the mainstream of American society. To accomplish the latter, the WRA also wanted Nisei young men to be eligible again for the Selective Service draft.

In February 1943, the WRA and the Army carried out a "loyalty" registration that was designed to accomplish these two aims. The registration required every evacuee 17-years of age and over to respond to a detailed questionnaire in which two items, Questions 27 and 28, were critically important.[25] In brief, Question 28 was a "loyalty" question, and Question 27 concerned willingness to serve in the U.S. armed forces. All persons were asked to sign a WRA application for leave clearance, which emphasized the WRA's aim of resettling all center residents. For a variety of reasons, the registration proved confusing and suspect to the Tule Lake residents, and a substantial resistance to the program developed.

Thomas' statistical analyses were primarily concerned with the evacuees' responses to Questions 27 and 28, and the implication of those responses for subsequent migration movements.[26] The large majority of evacuees responded either "Yes–Yes" or "No–No" to the two questions. Thomas focused especially on the 18,700 evacuees (16 percent of all evacuees) who answered "No–No" or refused to register and who ultimately were labeled "disloyal" and segregated at Tule Lake.

Marvin Opler has criticized Thomas for her use of the term "disloyal," claiming that those who chose to be segregated generally did so for many logical reasons other than disloyalty.[27] Thomas likewise considered the term misleading but used the reference, always within quotation marks, apparently because the term was Congressionally legislated, persistently used by the WRA, and was a real part of the stigmatized climate within which the segregants thereafter lived. The usage clearly reflected Thomas' neo–positivist belief. "Disloyal," always in quotation marks to warn of its potential, subjective bias, indicated the exact contextual climate existing at Tule Lake.

Her main interest involved the identification of every segregant from the four principal center groups in her study[28]—Tule Lake Californians, Tule Lake Northwesterners, Minidokans, and Postonians—and a determination of each segregant's background: sex, generation (Issei, Kibei, Nisei), religion (Buddhist, Christian/secular), and occupation (agriculture, non–agriculture). If each person is categorized by the five traits—for example, Tule Lake Californian, male, Issei, Buddhist, and agriculture—every evacuee could be identified as falling into one of 96 categories (4 x 2 x 3 x 2 x 2). Thomas then calculated the percentage of each category which chose segregation. For example, she showed that for all Kibei males from the Tule Lake Californian group with a Buddhist and agricultural background, 78.9 percent chose segregation; whereas for all Nisei males from the Poston group with a Christian/secular and non–agricultural background, only 1.5 percent chose segregation. The other categories fell at intermediate percentage points. The percentages were then used in a simple but ingenious scaling method.[29]

Thomas was able to demonstrate that certain background characteristics produced much higher percentages of segregants than did others. Thus, those prone to choose segregation included: Kibei more than Issei or Nisei, Buddhists more than Christians, Californians more than Northwesterners, farmers more than urban workers, and males slightly more than females. Thomas also carried out a similar analysis for a second data set, namely, the percentage of evacuees in each center who chose to resettle (out–migrate), and again found the same pattern, except of course in reverse: that out–migrants were more likely to be Nisei than Issei or Kibei, Christian than Buddhist, and so on.[30] From these analyses, Thomas concluded that segregation (the "disloyal" response) was chosen by the least assimilated, and out–migration by the most assimilated. This is a very important finding, but its significance is more clearly brought out by interpreting the results in terms of discrimination and segregation than of assimilation. That is, the data indicate that those who chose segregation at Tule Lake were those who had experienced the greatest amount of discrimination and segregation before the war.

My own observations at Tule Lake before segregation tend to bear out this interpretation. Many Californians whom I observed were from farming communities of the Sacramento valley—places like Clarksburg, Isleton, Florin, and Walnut Grove—and I observed exceptionally heavy "No–No" responses among them. Japanese–Americans in these areas generally experienced more discrimination and segregation than elsewhere on the Pacific Coast, and it is understandable why very high percentages of them chose to be segregated rather than resettled.

The high percentage of Kibei who answered "No–No" should also be interpreted as responding to a similar background of prejudices, but their situation was more complex. The Kibei's Japanese training on the whole gave them little advantage in the United States and, if anything, tended to subject them to greater limitations of job opportunities and to more discrimination and segregation than their Nisei peers. Furthermore, the Kibei often felt themselves discriminated against within the Japanese–American community. And the fact that they were, on the whole, less assimilated into American society than the Nisei also contributed to their "No–No" responses. There were many Kibei who did not match this profile, but I believe it is fair to say that those who chose segregation did so because of their resentment of past treatment.

In short, to understand the long–term consequences of majority group prejudice and discrimination against the Japanese minority before World War II, I feel there is no more succinct statement than is found in these statistical analyses. And for understanding what may have been the background of attitudes that led one out of six evacuees to respond negatively at registration, I again feel there is no better data than these analyses.

Controversy Surrounding *The Spoilage*

We turn now to an evaluation of *The Spoilage,* which was a study of about 18,000 evacuees who responded negatively on the "loyalty" question or refused to give an answer and consequently were removed to the Tule Lake Segregation Center.[31] This book was co–authored by Richard S. Nishimoto, a relatively young Issei. (Information about Nishimoto's background is provided by Lane and James Hirabayashi in their article in this volume.) Although a very perceptive observer of Japanese–American community life, he was not a trained social scientist. His contributions were no doubt substantial, but Thomas would have determined how the work should be conceptualized and ultimately shaped. In the following evaluation, therefore, I shall assume that Thomas was responsible for the main features of the work.

The book has come under very sharp criticisms from two anthropologists: Marvin Opler,[32] who was the WRA Community Analyst (researcher) at the Tule Lake Segregation Center; and Peter Suzuki,[33] who in recent years has critically examined JERS. Inasmuch as their critiques raise major issues regarding the merits of the work, this evaluation must be directed at the questions they raise. And because Suzuki's attack is particularly contentious, my remarks will no doubt seem more a response to criticisms than the straightforward evaluation I would have preferred it to be. Also, because Suzuki incorporates much of Opler's review in his own critique, the tone of my rebuttal of Opler will be stronger than if I were treating him separately.

The chief criticism of *The Spoilage* by both Opler and Suzuki is that the picture presented of the evacuees at Tule Lake is biased and distorted. Suzuki questions why it was that the original plan listed Minidoka and Poston, as well as Tule Lake, among the "major laboratories" of the study, but in the final report virtually all attention is given to the violent conflicts at Tule Lake. Suzuki charges that Thomas focused on Tule Lake due to her interest only in sensationalist and ultra–dramatized aspects of center life.[34]

Sensationalism had nothing to do with Thomas' special interest in Tule Lake. Indeed, examination of her total research career clearly indicates that her research interests were utterly prosaic and non–sensational. It was accidental that Tule Lake was chosen for the main research site. She chose Tule Lake for the main laboratory because it was closest to Berkeley and most accessible for her; and when the WRA selected Tule Lake for its segregation center, she had good reason to continue the study there. As to why Thomas failed to do the planned work on Minidoka and Poston, I do not know, although there are reasonable explanations. Space does not permit their discussion here. But I find Suzuki's suggestion that Thomas lost interest in these centers because they were unsensational extremely far–fetched.

Both Suzuki and Opler criticize *The Spoilage* for its one–dimensional interest in conflict and factional strife and lack of attention to other important aspects of Tule Lake life. I believe there were good reasons why Thomas chose the singular focus she did. First, after Tule Lake was transformed into a segregation center, she had only one fieldworker at the center and necessarily had to restrict the range of subjects to be covered. Moreover, after Lowie, Aikin, and other colleagues withdrew from JERS, she was probably wise to avoid study areas for which she was poorly prepared.

The underlying issue here is: did *The Spoilage* give an accurate or a false picture of life in Tule Lake? Did the emphasis on conflict and factionalism falsify what was generally true of segregant experiences?

To assess this question, we need to review briefly the kind of experiences the Tule Lake segregants underwent from September 1943 to the closure of the center in March 1946. Here, I must depend on *The Spoilage* for the history, but the events were so major and their documentation so complete that I shall assume no one will question their importance to the experiences of the Tule Lake residents.

I want to turn for a moment to the last chapter of *The Spoilage*, entitled "Renunciation."[35] It describes a program, carried out by the Department of Justice in the last months before Tule Lake's closure, that permitted Japanese–Americans to renounce their citizenship. The book reports that 80 percent of the Kibei and 60 percent of the Nisei, 17.5-years of age and over at Tule Lake (over 5,000 citizens), renounced their citizenship. Especially in light of what we know today, this seems an incredible outcome. Even granting the injustices of the evacuation, why should thousands of youths have taken so drastic a step?

One of the principal aims of *The Spoilage*, I believe, was to try to answer this question. The book begins with the evacuation, relates the deeply felt sense of injustice that prevailed among the evacuees, and leads up to the critical experiences of the "loyalty" registration. The study then analyzes in detail the differential reactions of evacuees to registration, and thus explains why a certain group of 18,000 or more chose segregation.[36]

The story of the Tule Lake Segregation Center began with a series of disagreements between the evacuees and the WRA administration, climaxed by an unfortunate truck accident in the farm crew that caused the death of farmer, which residents blamed on the WRA. Evacuee committees requested permission to hold a public funeral to express their feelings about the tragedy. The WRA refused permission. Incensed by what they felt was the administration's heartlessness and fueled by a series of other grievances, the residents staged a massive march on the administration building.[37] The conflict later developed into physical attacks, and ultimately the WRA called in the military and declared martial law to suppress the uprising.[38] WRA officials incarcerated those considered to be the worst troublemakers in a stockade.

The suppression led, some months later, to a tentative resolution of differences and to accommodations by the community. But it also generated an underground movement, which engaged in attacks on those it considered accommodationists (including an assassination). These developments led to further incarcerations, to demands of radical leaders for a further resegregation of the population, and, ultimately, to the demand for renunciation.[39]

The Spoilage presents every event in detail, describes both the reasonable and unreasonable efforts of the WRA to control the uncontrollable, and describes also the rational and irrational responses of the evacuees.

The criticisms raised by Opler and Suzuki of this account are so numerous and interrelated that it is difficult to know where to begin. There is a sentence in Opler's review, however, which I believe expresses in a nutshell what fundamentally troubles him about this book. He says, "Ending with renunciation rather than with Center closure, the entire final chapter of Center history is missing, including the complete transformation of Tule Lake to the most relocation–minded Center of all."[40] The sentence also expresses in a nutshell what troubles Suzuki as well, for he not only quotes precisely this statement in the closing paragraphs of his discussion,[41] but for emphasis italicizes the clause that reads, ". . . including the complete transformation of Tule Lake to the most relocation–minded Center of all." And Suzuki adds, "Even today there is a definite stigma in the Japanese–American community surrounding former Tuleans . . ." because, as he implies, *The Spoilage* depicted them as "disloyals" and "renunciants," rather than as those who simply demanded the right to return to their former communities.

I agree that *The Spoilage* is missing an important final chapter. I also concede that the book, by its concentration on conflict and the accompanying factionalism, failed to examine numerous other aspects of the center's life that would have given a more complete picture of what happened. But I do not concede that *The Spoilage* has given a false or distorted picture of Tule Lake. I feel the study focused on the central problems, and that the observations made were not heavily biased.

The argument which Opler and Suzuki emphasize, that Tule Lake was in the end transformed into "the most relocation–minded Center of all" (I am not sure what is meant by this phrase), suggests that they want us to believe the large majority of Tule Lake residents were basically no different from those who remained in other centers until the end of the war. Of course, they were basically not very different. And, certainly, those who chose the segregation center should not be stigmatized for that choice.

On the other hand, they were different enough to have made a choice that differed significantly from other evacuees on a very important issue: to be segregated or not to be segregated. Thomas showed by her statistical analyses exactly what the differences were,[42] and by these analyses she connected the history of the Tule Lake Segregation Center to the half century history of the Japanese minority in California before the war. Furthermore, by their choice, the segregants were exposed to a radically different set of experiences than were those who stayed at other centers. Thomas and Nishimoto tried to describe what those distinctive experiences were. All the centers went through the closing resettlement program, but no other center had anything like the renunciation movement that swept Tule Lake. To understand Tule Lake, therefore, it was appropriate to ask: what series of events could have led to such an extraordinary (and from my personal point of view, "tragic") outcome?

One of Opler's principal criticisms is that *The Spoilage* is seriously marred by an "overstress on one set of factional leaders (Daihyo Sha Kai) and the boundless credence afforded them which reifies their rationalizations."[43] He goes on to add that the book treats the Daihyo Sha Kai ("Representative Body") as the "favored faction" whose "position is presented approvingly," and the resulting tendency "to play sides in factional disputes" produces innumerable errors and a misrepresentation of what took place at Tule Lake.

I fail to see that the book treats the Daihyo Sha Kai as a favored faction, or that the book plays sides in factional dispute. As in any interracial conflict, the minority group was divided between *protesters*, on the one hand, and *accommodators*, on the other, and as the book clearly shows, each type of leadership had influence at different times in the center's history. But for reasons which we cannot stop to clarify, protesters generally are more prominent and exert greater influence over a minority in conflict than do accommodators. In recounting the various events in Tule Lake's history, therefore, Thomas and Nishimoto undoubtedly gave more space to the protest leaders (including those in the Daihyo Sha Kai) than to the accommodators, but I fail to see that there was favoritism. They did nothing more than describe each faction in relatively straight–forward terms.

The largest single group in camp may have been what Myrdal would have called the "passive reactionists,"[44] the middle range of people who resisted commitment to either the protest or accommodationist orientations. It is true that Thomas and Nishimoto gave relatively little space to describing this group, but because the "passive middle" tends to be non–committal, it is always difficult to describe. In any case, it is the swings of sentiment to and away from factional leaders which reflect the moods of a community in conflict, and this, I feel, Thomas and Nishimoto described in detail and with care.

Instead of a questionable, factional analysis, Opler argues that the basic study that was needed at Tule Lake, which Thomas and Nishimoto totally ignored, was the cultural revivalism that came to preoccupy center residents.[45] I am not sure what Opler had in mind, but I understand him to say that in this community, increasingly cut off from the larger world and simultaneously subjected to dominance by an external power, the residents more and more found meaning in their lives by absorption in activities drawn from an earlier, more gratifying time—from things Japanese. Thus, an exceptional preoccupation with Japanese poetry, dance, drama, music, art and crafts, sumo, *go*, and ritual and ceremonies of all kinds came to dominate the interest of residents. Opler goes on to argue, however, that as the pressure of life increased, cultural revivalism became a base for a new identity, and thus for involvement in the movement toward a renunication of American identity.[46]

I am not sure how Opler meant to interpret the role of cultural revivalism at Tule Lake, but I sense that he saw in it a culture–change (or perhaps a cultural–regression) interpretation of events that was superior to an interpretation based on an analysis of factions. In any event, I am puzzled by what he may have included under "cultural revivalism," for in the Japanese immigrant communities of the Pacific Coast before the war, there was always a great amount of interest in things Japanese. My interpretation of the "revivalism" is that in the centers the residents found the time to indulge interests for which they had lacked time before the war. Personally, I would choose a different scheme of analysis, a collective behavior theory, to explain the rise of "pro–Japanese" fervor at Tule Lake.

Suzuki, in quoting from Opler's very critical review of *The Spoilage*, refers to "the observations of the greatest authority on all aspects of Tule Lake, Marvin Opler, . . ."[47] I have found Opler's observations about Tule Lake interesting and have no reason to question his scholarship, but I consider it gratuitous for Suzuki to call him the greatest authority. As an anthropological researcher at Tule Lake, Opler had to contend with several, major disadvantages.

First, he was an employee of the War Relocation Authority whose policies, practices, and authority the evacuees often attacked, especially at Tule Lake. It would have been difficult for anyone in that position to be an unbiased observer.

Second, Opler mentions having had a staff of 16 technical assistants and hundreds of contacts. But considering the intense fear of the *inu* that existed at Tule Lake, I find it hard to believe that important information was not withheld from a WRA community analyst.

Third, to my knowledge, Opler had no pre–war background knowledge of the Japanese minority on the Pacific Coast, and even if he had diligently read the pre–war literature after becoming a WRA community analyst, I doubt that he could have gained the kind of intimate understanding of the Japanese minority that the JERS staff had. Intimate knowledge of the group before the war had an important bearing on understanding evacuee behavior.

Fourth, at the risk of making invidious comparisons, I believe that cultural anthropologists of the 1940s were not well equipped to study processes such as those which occurred at Tule Lake. The changes which occurred among the evaucees were not fundamentally cultural changes; they were rather problems related to status and identity changes, and the ensuing power struggles. For analyses of these situations, a conflict theory (a social process theory) was much more appropriate than a culture change theory, which Opler appears to have favored. For all of the foregoing reasons, I am reluctant to grant that he was "the greatest authority on Tule Lake."

Role of Rosalie Hankey Wax

There is one criticism by Opler and Suzuki that I find difficult to rebut, namely, that *The Spoilage* was based on the observations of only one field researcher, Rosalie Hankey (later, Rosalie Hankey Wax). It is true that Wax was the only fieldworker at the Tule Lake Segregation Center, and that her principal informants numbered only about 20 persons. It is obvious that one fieldworker covering a community of 18,000 residents could not have had access to a representative sample of the population. Thomas should have hired additional field staff, but there were major difficulties about doing so. She could not have found suitable non–evacuees on short notice, and given the *inu* fear, it would have been extremely difficult to hire evacuee fieldworkers who could function effectively.

Granting that the reliability of *The Spoilage* is subject to question because its data were collected mainly by one field researcher, I still believe that the account is not seriously distorted. First, Wax was an extraordinarily energetic and talented fieldworker, recognized as such by some very prominent anthropologists and sociologists who themselves were well–known for their fieldwork.[48] In fieldwork, one truly gifted worker can sometimes get material that literally dozens of researchers who lack the "magic touch" cannot. Second, the formula which the Thomases emphasized for making field observations—identify significant *situations* (events) and observe the adjustmental *behaviors*—was ideally suited for Tule Lake, where there was an almost regular occurrence of significant events. The formula might not have worked so well for observing more structured aspects of center life, but it was ideally suited for following the power struggle in the center. Once Wax understood the utility of the scheme for observations at Tule Lake—that is, once she knew what to look for—she was able to concentrate all her talent on getting a day–by–day chronology of events. By comparison, when researchers are uncertain of where to focus attention, large numbers of them may only magnify the confusion rather than get answers to research questions.

Third, contrary to Opler's claim that Wax got her information entirely from representatives of one factional group, her informants included members from a range of factions and different points of view, although, to be sure, she had the least information from the large, uncommitted middle. Furthermore, the way in which Thomas and Nishimoto used Wax's field notes tended to minimize biases which may have been inherent in her notes. Their framework presented a chronology of events at Tule Lake from the opening of the center in May 1942 to the end phase in September 1945. The basic facts about these events are not easily distorted, especially since Thomas, as a true empiricist, tried to check all pertinent information. In the analyses of the events, Thomas and Nishimoto brought to bear not only the Wax field notes but also a large body of documentation: WRA reports and directives, minutes and reports of evacuee organizations, the camp newspaper, outside newspapers, diaries and letters, and reports of outside organizations such as the Spanish Consulate. Thus, in their interpretation of each event, Thomas and Nishimoto were able to consider views drawn from varied sources and thereby to balance the bias of one data source against that of another.

Furthermore, the events which Thomas and Nishimoto reported were sequential: WRA restrictions led to a revolt, the revolt led to martial law and suppression, the suppression to the rise of an accommodative leadership and also to an underground, which led to suspicions of informers and to beatings and murder, and so on. That is, the evidence had to be consistent with the developing sequence of events, and Thomas and Nishimoto were in a position to check each source to ensure that they did, in fact, yield a consistent account.

But there are more serious charges of bias brought against Wax. In the appendix of *The Spoilage* are several pages of biographical notes describing Wax's principal informants.[49] Suzuki quotes brief excerpts from the notes, samples of which include the following:

Abe, Shozo (pseudonym). Of medium height and slender; physically unattractive. Manner forbidding in general and arrogant toward WRA officials and other Caucasians.

Sasaki, Milton (pseudonym). Short and slender; distinguished appearance; dressy and dandified.

Kira, Stanley Masanobu (pseudonym). Short and stout; effeminate appearance; small features; beard.[50]

The original descriptions are much longer, but the samples given are direct quotes. Opler and Suzuki contend that these statements are judgmental and should not have been data of the research, and they further charge that the biases demonstrate how little objectivity there was in the observations. I agree that Thomas and Nishimoto should have avoided biased references, although I frankly doubt that any anthropologist or sociologist is totally non–judgmental in observations of their human subjects. To illustrate, D. O. Hebb, the well–known behavioral psychologist who used simians extensively in his research, points out that to understand chimpanzees it is sometimes necessary to impute to them motives, emotions, attitudes, and other tendencies of behavior, all necessarily expressed in anthropomorphic terms. Indeed, he points out the danger of handling chimpanzees if one fails to use such imputations intelligently.[51]

In short, observational processes necessarily involve attributions. On the other hand, every effort needs to be made to minimize subjective judgments in analyses and in reporting. Thomas and Nishimoto can be faulted for their use of biased references, but these errors were generally minimal, especially considering that they were discussing situations of intense conflict.

The strongest charge Suzuki brings against Wax is that she was unscrupulous and unethical in her fieldwork at Tule Lake,[52] so that little credence can be placed on her work. Suzuki claims that Wax initially ingratiated herself with a man whom she called "Kira" (pseudonym), from whom she received very useful information concerning the radical, resegregationist group of which he was the leader. But she subsequently turned against Kira when she suspected him of leading a terrorist group that attacked some of her evacuee friends. The force of Suzuki's charges arises from the fact that he is able to quote directly from Wax's own detailed account, *Doing Fieldwork: Warnings and Advice*,[53] concerning her research at Tule Lake. On the other hand, I feel

Suzuki has distorted what she said by taking things out of context. For example, Suzuki states:

> She [Wax] asserted that Kira was a "selfish and dangerous man who wished only to become a big shot," and that Kira was nothing more than a gangster. It came to a point where she felt so enraged about Kira, owing to allegations of terrorism she had heard charged against him, that she pictured herself running to the section of the camp where Kira lived "like a berserk . . . and beating up Mr. Kira." She then plotted to get vengeance on Kira.
>
> Wax ultimately wreaked her vengeance on Kira in another, more effective, way. She informed on Kira to the Federal Bureau of Investigation at Tule Lake.[54]

Suzuki's allegations need to be compared against Wax's own writings, for her account gives a different picture. She describes her deep concern for "my benevolent and reasonable respondent, Mr. Itabashi" because of the recent assassination of the Co–op director and beatings of those who opposed the resegregationist movement. She continues:

> On 10 October Itabashi told me that he had spoken up at a meeting and exhorted the young men to follow the higher ideals of Japan, which, he stated, were not compatible with agitation or violence . . . He also told me that he was telling the resegregationist leaders, "The Japanese government is not so narrow–minded as you." Kira, he remarked, was a selfish and dangerous man who wished only to become a big shot. I was moved to caution Itabashi, for he was, after all, a frail little man and no match for Kira's gangsters. So I remarked that there were some very dangerous men in camp. But Itabashi laughed and said not to worry about him. "These people are cowards . . . When the Japanese talk big they don't bite." But five nights later, when Mr. Itabashi and two older men were leaving a church meeting, they were assaulted and badly beaten.[55]

Thus, what Suzuki claims Wax asserted turns out to be her quotation of what Itabashi said. And technically speaking, she did not call Kira a gangster, although she very likely thought he was. Later, she does indeed describe how when she heard from her most trusted informant, Joseph Y. Kurihara, how the resegregationist gang had beaten up Itabashi with clubs and a hammer, she fantasied going to Kira's home and "like a berserk . . . beating up Mr. Kira." But I feel Suzuki exaggerates when he says Wax plotted vengeance on Kira. What she mainly writes about is her intense concern to try to stop the beatings and violence and especially the clear threat upon Kurihara's life. Throughout Suzuki's assault on Wax, I have the feeling that he fails to understand how, in observing situations of intense conflict, a fieldworker (if he or she is a sensitive observer) can scarcely avoid developing acute feelings about those whom he is observing. Indeed, an observer would not truly understand a conflict unless he himself felt the intensity of feelings surrounding him. The objectivity is achieved by re–examining the observations made under the heat of events within the more objective circumstances of the analytic phase.

As for Suzuki's statement that Wax informed on Kira to the FBI, we need to look at her own account to understand exactly what she did. In a paragraph that begins, "During the internments I did two unprofessional deeds," she explains that the first of these deeds was to protest to the FBI that one of the men, Wakida, whom they were about to intern for presumed participation in unlawful, resegregationist activity, was innocent and, in fact, had spoken openly against the resegregationists. Wakida was not interned. The second deed concerned Kira, about whom she says:

> Again, after the first internment, I found out that Mr. Kira had not applied for denationalization. This surprised me, for Mr. Kira had been one of the most vigorous exponents of the renunciation of citizenship—for other people. Thereupon I once again talked to the Justice Department's investigators and suggested that they call in Mr. Kira and question him about his loyalties in the presence of some of the young *Hokoku* [Resegregationist] officers. Mr. Kira applied for denationalization. Subsequently, he was sent to Japan with the other expatriates, and they were all once again confined in a "center," this time by the Japanese government. Many months later, a friend sent me a clipping from a California newspaper. The clipping told how a certain expatriate, Stanley Masanobu Kira, confined in a detention area in Japan, had appealed to the American army to remove him because certain of the young men confined with him were threatening to kill him.[56]

Wax committed a serious mistake in giving information she had gained as a researcher to the FBI. In passing judgement, however, two things need to be understood about this action. First, from personal experience, I would say that participant observational research in intense conflict situations, especially in the close circumstances of a WRA center, is radically different from research in a normal community setting. For one thing, the researcher experiences the same high levels of tension which the residents feel and needs to endure them over a span of time. And when the observer comes under attack, or friends are seriously threatened or attacked, the person can scarcely avoid having fantasies about protecting self and friends and may do things that he normally would not do. Second, in the book from which Suzuki quotes, Wax wrote in detail about her feelings and actions while doing research at Tule Lake for the purpose of teaching anthropology students about the problems of fieldwork. As the subtitle indicates, her book was intended as "Warnings and Advice." For the purpose, she apparently felt it important to describe as truthfully as possible all that she felt and did as a fieldworker. I want to suggest that if, as Wax has done, every fieldworker described in detail his or her private thoughts about the people who were observed, and admitted all the misdeeds which were committed, very few studies could avoid being charged with bias. Later, in the analytical and writing phases of a study, every good researcher uses methods by which to control the biases which might have crept into the study.

There is in Suzuki's criticisms of *The Spoilage*, I feel, an ideological thrust that is clearly reflected in his discussion of Kira. He devotes almost four pages to this man and the grave injustice which he felt Wax committed against him. Suzuki points out that Kira, whose true name was Kinzo Ernest Wakayama, was, in fact, one of the handful of persons who at the time of evacuation had challenged its constitutionality. Suzuki declares:

> What student of the Japanese–American experience or of constitutional law has not heard of the Yasui, Hirabayashi, Endo, and Korematsu cases? However, one wonders how many have heard of Kinzo Ernest Wakayama (Wax's "Kira")? Yet, had "Kira" not been turned in by Wax there is a good possibility that Wakayama would be as highly respected as the other four, a thesis which will be explored in greater detail shortly.[57]

There is no question that Wakayama and his wife applied for a "Writ of *Habeas corpus*" to challenge the evacuation and that the American Civil Liberties Union of Southern California for a time supported the effort. But we are not told why the case was not pressed on to the U.S. Supreme Court as the other test cases were. There is also no explanation why Wakayama and his wife chose, finally, to be segregated at Tule Lake. According to accounts presented by Wax in *The Spoilage*, Kira (Wakayama) ". . . had been the leader of a gang at Terminal Island before evacuation and is said to have held this gang intact at

Manzanar where it took a prominent part in the 'riot' of December, 1942."[58] These accounts go on to indicate that by August 1944 Kira (Wakayama) had become one of the two main leaders of the resegregationist movement at Tule Lake, which ultimately became the movement to renounce American citizenship. Suzuki offers no information on Wakayama's background at Terminal Island, Manzanar, or Tule Lake.

What is generally troubling is that Wakayama was the leader of a group to whom much of the violence in this period was attributed. The documentation on Wakayama that Wax offered was substantial and included statements from one of her principal informants, Joseph Y. Kurihara, whose background in many respects was very similar to Wakayama's. The major difference was that Kurihara opposed Wakayama's tactics of intimidation of political opponents. Suspecting that Wakayama intended to silence him forcibly, Kurihara took steps to forestall it. The pages of material which Suzuki presents to exalt Wakayama derive almost entirely from Wakayama's own statements. He offers no independent evidence.

At the time he challenged DeWitt's evacuation orders, Wakayama may have been very much like Hirabayashi and those who contested the constitutionality of the evacuation. But by the time he emerged as the leader of the the resegregationist movement, there was very little similarity between them. The striking thing about the behavior of Hirabayashi, Korematsu, Endo, and Yasui was that they placed their faith in the American democratic system and challenged the system to demonstrate that their faith had not been misplaced. By contrast, most of those who chose segregation at Tule Lake did so because they distrusted the American system, thought seriously of expatriation or repatriation, or intended to wait out the war to decide at a later time what course of action they should choose. The background characteristics of the four litigants, in fact, were so markedly different from most of those who chose segregation that I consider it very unlikely they would have agreed with much of the thinking at Tule Lake. This is not to say that those who chose segregation were not justified in their choice. But a warranty for Suzuki's contention that Wakayama's actions were comparable to those of Hirabayashi et al. requires much better proof than he has offered. I believe an ideological bias has seriously affected Suzuki's reading of *The Spoilage*.

In summary, it is my view that *The Spoilage* is a very important study that is unappreciated, and perhaps will always remain so, because readers fail to understand it for what it is. Opler and Suzuki, and I suspect almost all readers, tend to see it as an unsympathetic account of those who the authors perceived to have been *the disloyals* and of the more sensational aspects of their behavior. However, if the book is read without ideological bias, as a straightforward account of a set of conditions which were created at Tule Lake and as a history of behaviors which followed, I believe it will be seen that the authors had no such intent.

Thomas no doubt contributed to misreadings of the book by her choice of the title. The title is a value–laden concept, which, it seems to me, stands in marked contrast to the neo–positivist, value–free reporting she generally adopted in the book. She chose the title, I believe, from the perspective of a migration specialist. The Japanese immigrants had migrated to this country to make a future for themsleves here. Those who overcame the adversity of the evacuation and continued to seek a future in this country she called "the salvage." Those who decided in favor of renunciation or repatriation became "the spoilage." Having known Thomas, I am quite sure she did not equate "spoilage" with "disloyalty"; if there was any ideological intent in her choice of title, it would have been that the American policy toward the Japanese minority caused the spoilage of some residents.

Thomas also contributed to the misreading by not placing the events at Tule Lake within the larger context of the Japanese immigrants' history in California. Her own statistical analyses offered the basis for interpreting Tule Lake in a larger historical context. My reading of her data is that those who chose segregation came, on the whole, from those sectors of the population who had experienced the greatest amount of pre–war discrimination and segregation and, therefore, had the strongest reason to distrust white society. Thomas, however, was not an historian. Indeed, because of her neo–positivist, atheoretical bent, she was not disposed to speculate beyond the immediate, examinable data.

Concluding Remarks: The Legacy of Dorothy Swaine Thomas

I have argued that to understand Dorothy Swaine Thomas' directorship of and contributions to JERS, one needs to understand the background she brought to the project: her neo–positivist orientation and her research interest in differential migration. In the context of that background, for example, I believe one can better appreciate her statistical analyses of evacuee reactions to the "loyalty" registration and segregation programs, where she clearly demonstrated the differential effects of the evacuees' pre–war backgrounds on their registration and segregation decisions. She unfortunately failed to pursue this investigation along the many lines which the data permit, but Thomas' work was important in showing what could be done, and might still be done, with the material.

The Spoilage, too, I believe has been badly undervalued because of a failure to appreciate its neo–positivist intent. Read in the light of the statistical analyses, one can see that the book is an account of how people with a certain kind of pre–war background reacted to the military and WRA programs imposed on them. And if the study is placed in the larger, historical context of Japanese minority experiences before the war, and attention is directed to the sectors of the population which experienced the severest pre–war segregation, *The Spoilage* may be seen as yielding an understanding of a group that otherwise would be forgotten in history.

Notes

1. Peter T. Suzuki, "The University of California Japanese Evacuation and Resettlement Study: A Prolegomenon," *Dialectical Anthropology* 10 (1986), 189–213.

2. George A. Lundberg, *Foundations of Sociology*, abridged ed. (New York: David McKay Co., Inc., 1964).

3. For a detailed analysis of the positivistic view, see Leszek Kolakowski, *The Alienation of Reason: A History of Positivist Thought* (Garden City, New York: Doubleday and Co., Inc., 1968).

4. *Ibid.*, 2–10; see also, Lundberg, *Foundations of Sociology*, 1–50.

5. Dorothy S. Thomas, *The Salvage* (Berkeley: University of California Press, 1952), 3–128 and 571–626; and Dorothy S. Thomas and Richard S. Nishimoto, *The Spoilage* (Berkeley: University of California Press, 1946), 61–63 and 104–12.

6. Dorothy S. Thomas and Associates, *Some New Techniques for Studying Social Behavior* (New York: Teachers College Columbia University, 1929), 1–10.

7. Dorothy S. Thomas, "Experiences in Interdisciplinary Research," *American Sociological Review* 17 (December 1952), 665.

8. *Ibid.*, 667–69

9. Dorothy S. Thomas, *Research Memorandum on Migration Differentials*, Bulletin 43 (New York: Social Science Research Council, 1941); and Dorothy S. Thomas, *Social and Economic Aspects of Swedish Population Movement, 1750–1933* (New York: MacMillan Co., 1941).

10. Thomas and Associates, *New Techniques*, 1.

11. Edmund H. Volkart, ed., *Social Behavior and Personality: Contributions of W. I. Thomas to Theory and Social Research* (New York: Social Science Research Council, 1951).

12. *Ibid.*, 20–22.

13. W. I. Thomas and Dorothy S. Thomas, *The Child in America* (New York: Alfred A. Knopf, 1927), 504–75.

14. W. I. Thomas, *Primitive Behavior: An Introduction to the Social Sciences* (New York: McGraw–Hill Book Co., 1937).

15. Stephen O. Murray, "W. I. Thomas, Behaviorist Ethnologist," *Journal of the History of the Behavioral Sciences* 24 (October 1988), 381–91. Dr. Murray correctly points out that W. I. Thomas shared with his wife a strong disposition toward a behaviorist orientation in sociological research and thus was not a leader of a subjectivist school, as people have presumed. On the other hand, he was a pragmatist in the sense that he felt it important to include subjective factors in sociological research, a feature that Dr. Murray underemphasized. In this respect, W. I. Thomas influenced his wife in her JERS work.

16. Volkart, ed., *Social Behavior and Personality*, 59–69.

17. Thomas and Nishimoto, *The Spoilage*, v.

18. *Ibid.*, v.

19. *Ibid.*, vi. fn.

20. *Ibid.*, vi.

21. Stephen O. Murray, "The Rights of Research Assistants and the Rhetoric of Political Suppression: Morton Grodzins and the University of California Japanese American Evacuation and Resettlement Study," unpublished manuscript, 1–27. To my knowledge, this is the only available, thorough treatment of the conflict between Thomas and Grodzins. I wish to acknowledge my indebtedness to Dr. Murray for making his unpublished paper available to me. In contrast, Peter T. Suzuki in his essay in this volume presents a political interpretation of the conflict.

22. Morton Grodzins, *Americans Betrayed* (Chicago: University of Chicago Press, 1949).

23. Thomas and Nishimoto, *The Spoilage*, 61–63 and 104–09.

24. Thomas, *The Salvage*, 63–128 and "Statistical Appendix," 571–626.

25. Thomas and Nishimoto, *The Spoilage*, 53–83.

26. *Ibid.*, 61–63 and 103–07.

27. Marvin K. Opler, "Review of *The Spoilage*," *American Anthropologist* 50 (1948), 309.

28. Thomas, *The Salvage*, 95–105.

29. *Ibid.*

30. *Ibid.*, 105–08.

31. Thomas and Nishimoto, *The Spoilage*.

32. Opler, "Review of *The Spoilage*," 307–10.

33. Suzuki, "JERS: A Prolegomenon," 189–213.

34. *Ibid.*, 190.

35. Thomas and Nishimoto, *The Spoilage*, 333–61.

36. *Ibid.*, 1–83.

37. *Ibid.*, 84–146.

38. *Ibid.*, 147–83.

39. *Ibid.*, 184–332.

40. Opler, "Review of *The Spoilage*," 310.

41. Suzuki, "JERS: A Prolegomenon," 205.

42. Thomas, *The Salvage*, 95–105.

43. Opler, "Review of *The Spoilage*," 309.

44. Gunnar Myrdal, *The American Dilemma* (New York: Harper and Brothers, 1944) II.

45. Opler, "Review of *The Spoilage*," 310.

46. United States Department of Interior, War Relocation Authority, *Impounded People: Japanese Americans in the Relocation Centers* (Washington, D.C.: GPO, 1946).

47. Suzuki, "JERS: A Prolegomenon," 205.

48. Rosalie Hankey Wax, *Doing Fieldwork: Warnings and Advice* (Chicago: University of Chicago Press, 1971), ix.

49. Thomas and Nishimoto, *The Spoilage*, 370–79.

50. Suzuki, "JERS: A Prolegomenon," 193–94.

51. D. O. Hebb and W. R. Thompson, "The Social Significance of Animal Studies," in Gardner Lindzey, ed., *Handbook of Social Psychology* (Cambridge, Massachusetts: Addison–Wesley Publishing Co., 1954), I, 543–48.

52. Suzuki, "JERS: A Prolegomenon," 194–97.

53. Wax, *Doing Fieldwork.*

54. Suzuki, "JERS: A Prolegomenon," 194.

55. Wax, *Doing Fieldwork*, 155–56.

56. *Ibid.*, 168–69.

57. Suzuki, "JERS: A Prolegomenon," 194–95.

58. Thomas and Nishimoto, *The Spoilage*, 290.

The "Credible" Witness:

The Central Role of Richard S. Nishimoto in JERS

LANE RYO HIRABAYASHI
JAMES HIRABAYASHI

Of all JERS staff members, Richard S. Nishimoto, the only Issei on the project, played the most central role. He joined the staff in 1943 when Tamie Tsuchiyama, another staff member, introduced him to Dorothy S. Thomas, who soon considered him as "one of [her] most valuable observers. . . ."[1] While confined at Poston, Arizona, Nishimoto worked closely with Thomas through active correspondence. Upon release from Poston in 1945, he continued his work at the University of California at Berkeley where he co-authored *The Spoilage* in 1946. He remained on the staff until 1948.

Nishimoto performed multiple tasks for JERS. His many duties included what he personally described as "coordination and evaluation of field reports" and "compilation and analysis of statistical data."[2] As a JERS fieldworker, he also wrote hundreds of pages on Japanese-Americans and Poston camp life in various forms. These included a daily sociological journal, historical and demographic surveys, ethnographic studies, and numerous letters. Besides co-authoring *The Spoilage*, he assisted in the initial preparation of *The Salvage*. He also wrote an extensive manuscript on the pre-World War II economic adaptation of Japanese-Americans.[3]

Even after the termination of his JERS research assistant appointment, Nishimoto continued to serve as a consultant to JERS. Indeed, in 1952 Dorothy S. Thomas recommended him as a critical reader of the manuscript version of *Prejudice, War and the Constitution*,[4] and he meticulously read the manuscript, corrected many errors, and suggested hypotheses to the book's authors. In short, Nishimoto was involved, directly or indirectly, in the publication of all three JERS books.

This paper examines Nishimoto's varied roles within JERS, as well as how he came to establish his credibility as an interpreter of Japanese-American life.[5] We will examine Nishimoto's life history—in particular, his wartime experiences—as it affected his JERS research. On this basis, we also will explore the question of the validity of Nishimoto's research assessments.

We have undertaken this task because, clearly, the present-day utilization of JERS materials must be based on an understanding of 1) how and why that research was produced; and, 2) what constraints and biases may have governed its production. In short, our primary goal here is to delineate Nishimoto's background, orientation, and activities, both as an individual and as a JERS staff member, so that we may properly assess his intellectual contributions to JERS.

Our analysis is based largely on a critical reading of Nishimoto's own written contributions to JERS, supplemented by and cross-checked against as many relevant documents and interviews as we could obtain.[6] We have chosen this approach intentionally. Nishimoto died in the mid-1950s, and, apart from what was deposited in the JERS collection, none of his personal papers were preserved. We have therefore made an effort to convey how Nishimoto, himself, saw his research and role. At the same time, we present another perspective on Nishimoto's character and research, as also revealed by our critical reading of his written contributions to JERS.

Nishimoto's Background: An Issei with the Appearance of a Nisei

Richard Shigeaki Nishimoto was born August 23, 1904, in Tokyo, Japan.[7] He received an elementary school education between the ages of six and 12. After this, he studied at an American Episcopal missionary intermediate school (Rikkyo Chugakko) from which he graduated in 1921. Recalling his middle school experience, Nishimoto wrote that, because he had lived in school dormitories since he was ten, he had grown up basically, apart from his parents, among "a large group of boys of similar age."

Thereafter, at the age of 17, Nishimoto immigrated to the United States in 1921, where he joined his parents who were living in California. At that time, his father was running an export business in San Francisco, and Nishimoto helped out with the business. He also enrolled in San Francisco's Lowell High school in 1921 and successfully completed his studies there in 1925.

After finishing high school, Nishimoto immediately enrolled at Stanford University. He studied there between 1925 and 1929, earning a degree from the School of Engineering. He, like all of the JERS Nikkei staff, did university-level course work in the social sciences, but his transcript indicates that he completed only introductory classes in sociology, economics, psychology, and political science.[8]

During summer vacations, and for an entire year when he took a leave of absence from the university, Nishimoto worked on a large fruit orchard in the Sacramento valley. Eventually he managed this orchard for a while, and once wrote:

> Here I gained valuable experience in associating with and handling thirty to one hundred-and-fifty resident and migrant farm laborers—Japanese, Portugese [*sic*], Spanish [*sic*], Filipino, etc.

In 1929, when he graduated in engineering, it was already the custom for businesses and corporations to come to Stanford to interview members of the senior class. One associate of Nishimoto's told us that all of his Caucasian classmates received job offers after the interviews, but Nishimoto did not. When he asked the reason, he was reportedly told: "Look at your face. It's Oriental. No one will hire you."[9]

This experience reportedly affected Nishimoto very deeply, at both a personal and professional level. He was bitter about being rejected, but also cowed. He never tried to apply for work as a professional engineer again.

After finishing at Stanford, Nishimoto moved to Los Angeles where he engaged in a number of different occupations between 1929 and 1934. According to his resume, his principal means of livelihood was running an insurance brokerage firm, although he offered income tax services on the side. Until civil service status was required, Nishimoto was also "on call" as a Japanese-English interpreter for the Municipal and Superior Courts of Los Angeles.

By 1934, Nishimoto was living in Gardena, California, which was then the site of a small but dynamic Japanese-American farming community.[10] He started out as a partner in a Japanese grocery store, but a year-and-a-half later he became the owner and operator of his own fruit and vegetable market. Nishimoto commented:

> People often wondered why I, a college engineering graduate, was in such a "low down business." To that I used to say "I just learned the art of 'bull session' at the expense of [a] hard earned $5,000."

Removed from Gardena in May 1942, Nishimoto was incarcerated at Poston. He was 38-years old, married to a Nisei woman, and had two daughters, ages eight and ten. That same year he wrote of himself:

> My friends tell me that I have the appearance of a Nisei, and act like one, yet my thoughts are typically those of intelligent Issei.

Poston—The Colorado River Project

The "Colorado River War Relocation Project," as the Poston camp was officially known, was located in western Arizona, near the town of Parker.[11] The largest of the ten WRA camps, it housed some 20,000 residents and was broken into three sub-units. Nishimoto lived in the largest: Unit 1.

Like Manzanar, Poston was first an "assembly center" (referred to as the "Parker Dam Assembly Center"), and was used as an initial site for removal. It later became one of the permanent "relocation centers" for the duration of the war. Thus, Nishimoto stayed at Poston from 1942 until he left camp in 1945.

Another significant aspect of Poston was that the facility was originally placed under the authority of the Office of Indian Affairs (OIA).[12] One of two WRA camps located on an Indian reservation, Poston was actually administered by the OIA until December 31, 1943.[13] This was because the U.S. Army felt that the director of the OIA, John Collier, Sr., and his staff had the necessary expertise to set up and supervise the camp. As a result, institutional policies in Poston were especially complex. In addition to the usual split between WRA bureaucrats (staffing the regional WRA office in San Francisco, in this case) and the WRA staff within the camp, there were distinct WRA and OIA factions within the Caucasian administrative staff.[14] In reports by both Nishimoto and fellow JERS fieldworker Tamie Tsuchiyama, much attention is given to this split because of the constant tension it produced: each faction had its own views regarding the goals and procedures of administering Poston.[15]

Third, Poston was unusual in that its head administrator, Wade Head, tried to maximize "self-governance" in an effort to lessen the effects of alienation.[16] Some of Head's efforts, in fact, were viewed with suspicion by WRA administrators as being divergent from official policy.

Head's efforts notwithstanding, Poston's residents—like those of all ten WRA camps—were seriously divided. Intra-community conflict was, in fact, a major theme in Nishimoto's field journals. Such conflict was reflected in a major strike in November 1942, which was triggered by arrest of men accused of beating suspected *inu*, or informers.[17]

Nishimoto's Multi-faceted Role in Poston

A review of Nishimoto's activities at Poston demonstrates how multi-faceted and complex his roles were.

As mentioned above, Nishimoto was incarcerated along with the rest of the Nikkei inhabitants of Gardena, and thus entered Poston as a regular internee. Immediately upon arrival, he took on a variety of jobs in the Unit 1 division.

Between June and September 1942, he was the foreman of the firebreak gang, a work-group responsible for clearing the grounds as well as other menial tasks.[18]

By early 1943, Nishimoto was elected the manager of Block 45. Later, he became a block councilman, again representing Block 45. By facing and resolving a variety of personnel and interpersonal problems in each of these positions, Nishimoto quickly established his skill in administration.[19]

It should be noted here that Nishimoto's educational background probably influenced his social status favorably. The Issei valued education, and educated men had prestige. Being educated in Japan at a higher level than most Issei, Nishimoto had one of the necessary requisites in this subculture to assume a leadership role. Insofar as the Kibei were concerned, Nishimoto was older and better educated than most. Although he spoke English with an accent, his degree from Stanford meant that he was also better educated than most of the Nisei, even by their own standards. Furthermore, although Nishimoto was among the younger Issei, his status was still that of an Issei, and not of a Nisei, which is significant in a subculture where generational age-grading was an operative dimension of the social structure.

Although he served in official and semi-official capacities, Nishimoto was also an active participant in camp protests from the very beginning. His role in this regard merits some commentary.[20]

On Wednesday, November 18, 1942, Nishimoto was regarded highly enough to be "selected as leader" of a demonstration to be staged at Ward 7 of the hospital. That afternoon, a WRA official was making a presentation to the City Council which was in joint session with the Issei Advisory Board. Although the demonstration was cancelled, Nishimoto was clearly willing to carry out his charge.

Not long afterward, Nishimoto talked the block managers of Unit 1 into resigning "in mass." In doing so, he is said to have argued:

> Don't kid yourselves. The job [i.e., negotiating with the WRA] is too big for us. We have elected representatives whose duty it is to negotiate with Mr. Evans. What we should do is resign and join the movement.

Nishimoto is also reported as having told several "young Nisei intellectuals" who felt uncomfortable about block standards which looked suspiciously to them like Japanese flags (see diagram on opposite page):

> That is a sign of defiance. For example, when you scold a child, he sticks his tongue out at you. If you kick a dog around several times eventually he will bite you . . . This fight against the administration is a result of their incompetency and inefficiency added to the suffering caused by evacuation. We've got to let off our steam sometime. That man in jail is just a symbol and an igniting point. As for the flags they are just made up by a few crackpots with mischievous notions. If they really wanted to signify their allegiance they would have instead put up real flags. They are trying to tease the Caucasians as they have been teased by them so often.

As noted below, Nishimoto used his position as block manager to influence residents to support the strike (albeit, in terms of the view delineated above, and in a way he felt was appropriate).

According to Nishimoto, in the year following the Poston strike, he was involved in a series of political changes which led him to assume a leadership position in the camp as a whole. As Nishimoto told his JERS colleagues at a staff conference in Salt Lake City in 1944, he was able to win political battles and consolidate his power base since:

> [I] held no official position, but had good influence over preevacuation leaders who returned from internment camp or who were afraid to take part in the movement of the extremists. They didn't hold official positions. Orange County blocks, for instance, were controlled by a man named Murata (pseudonym). . . [I] contacted about five of these men. [I] controlled the Orange County, Salinas, Imperial and Los Angeles groups. [I] knew how the preevacuation politics worked . . .[21]

By 1943, many Poston inmates simply wanted order and peace, amidst continually chaotic circumstances. Responding to this mood, Nishimoto maneuvered to gain as much power as possible for the block managers. He believed that since the block managers had an intimate tie to the residents—and that the executive committee of the block managers was, in turn, selected

DIAGRAM #1

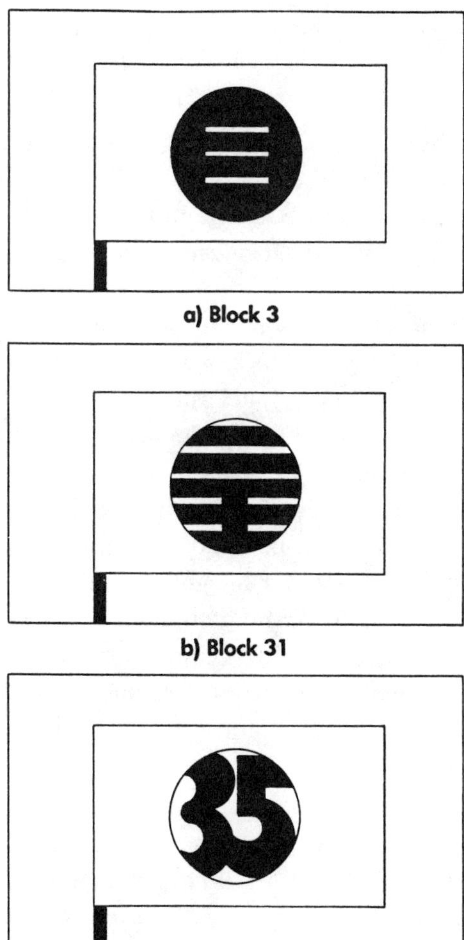

a) Block 3

b) Block 31

c) Block 35

[During the course of the Poston strike] ". . .the banners became more and more conspicuous and came to approximate the Japanese flag as much as they dared. Banners such as these flew prominently from block poles and at a distance of 15 or 20 feet were indistinguishable from the Japanese flag."

(The drawings and the quote are from Tamie Tsuchiyama, JERS J6.24, p. 17.)

by the block managers themselves—this constituted a fair and representative system of self-government. Nishimoto reasoned:

> The residents want to bring their problems where it is (*sic*) most effective. By bringing problems to the block managers their problems are being solved.[22]

By comparison, other formal and informal political bodies in Poston were apparently ineffectual or divided.

In this fashion, Nishimoto was able to influence the council, successfully challenge competing Issei and Kibei leaders, and become a formidable power broker within the camp.

We will outline an example which illustrates how Nishimoto then used his power and position within the block managers' group in order to manipulate circumstances (and even the WRA) in Poston.

In April 1944, the WRA tried to trim down the block staff from five to three-and-a-half. This proposed policy was pushed by an unpopular administrator, Morris Berge, the deputy project director. The block managers met and decided that a cut in staff would cripple operations extensively and leave residents dissatisfied with services. The block managers decided to threaten to strike. Their petition was passed along to Washington, but the WRA officials there rejected it, so the block managers decided to quit *en masse*. Their unhappiness was spread, by the block managers themselves, among the residents. Nishimoto, who was personally involved in fomenting discontent, was approached by anxious WRA personnel.

> Powell, the Assistant Project Director, knocks on [my] apartment. The Community Analyst knocks on [my] door, too. (*I was . . . agitating to cause trouble among the residents.*) [The Nisei Unit 1 Administrator] was instructed [by me] to stay out. Administration has to save face. [I] tell the community analyst that the negotiation committee of the block managers has resigned. Tomorrow the block managers will resign.[23] [emphasis added]

In the heat of this crisis, Nishimoto was made "personal advisor" to Poston's WRA administrators, June 20 through July 25. Nishimoto commented: "[I could carry] anything out." Berge left the camp. Nishimoto subsequently became supervisor of the block managers. He also became a permanent "personal advisor" to the project director (see diagram 2). Nishimoto commented on the broader implications of the block managers' machinations:

> Anything dealing with evacuees, the project director does not act on important matters without consulting [me]. The assistant project directors come to [me]. It creates pressures on the Caucasian hierarchy. When any emergency arises, Caucasians are placed under [me].

DIAGRAM #2[24]

Project Director
Deputy Project Director
Chairman of the Local Council — Richard Nishimoto
Local Council — Executive Committee, Block Managers
Supervisor, Block Managers
36 Block Managers
Block Council
Residents

At the same JERS staff meeting, he even implied that he had negotiated for civil service status and received it. Nishimoto stated that soon after starting out with a CAF-9 ranking, he jumped to a CAF-11.[25] Although Nishimoto's account is clearly self-enhancing, it appears as if he gained a tremendous amount of influence as a result of this power play.

In summary, a variety of characteristics put Nishimoto in a unique position to achieve a prominent leadership position in Poston. It will be remembered that Nishimoto had experience managing labor relations even before he entered Poston. Such a background most certainly affected his ability to become politically active within the Poston setting. Thus, Nishimoto quickly (albeit, carefully, in the beginning) launched a career as a community leader and representative, starting out in his capacity as labor foreman and block manager.

In such roles, Nishimoto's language skills, education, and temperament enabled him to become an able mediator between different interest groups. He was able to communicate with, and understand, the Issei and the Nisei alike. According to his own comments about himself, Nishimoto also used his insights in order to manipulate residents toward what he felt were their true needs and interests.[26]

JERS researcher Tamie Tsuchiyama's account of Nishimoto's efforts to get his block to participate in the November strike effectively illustrates his leadership style and is thus worth quoting at length.

> Inother [*sic*] block the intimidation was more subtle. Thus in block 45 X [Nishimoto] told me that by adroit handling of the first day he was able to bring his indifferent block into line and steer its course the way he wanted without any overt expression of dissatisfaction emerging throughout the ncident. He began his *experiment* [emphasis added] by calling a block meeting on Thursday morning at seven o'clock—the breakfast hour—so that the turn out would be as nearly 100% as possible. At that time he explained that the City Council, the Issei Advisory Board, and the block managers had all resigned the day before and that a general strike had been called by the Emergency Council. He informed them that block 45 had certain commitments to fulfill along with every block in camp [underline included], one of them being supporting the strike 100% and furnishing pickets in front of the police station at all hours of the day and night. He then read off the names of the block people who had participated in the demonstration the day before and asked the audience to show their appreciation of them by clapping. He next assigned pickets to certain shifts and when he arrived at the graveyard shift (midnight to 8:00 a.m.) he stopped momentarily and then resumed quietly: "Now let me read the names of people who volunteered [underline included] for these hours." There were fourteen of them and when he added an extra seven there was no opposition from that quarter. Then cleverly he approached two older men—one, a confirmed invalid, the other a cripple—and requested their cooperation in picketing. When these two acquiesced there was no other recourse for any one but to fall in line and support his program. Only one individual was not approached—Reverend Kitano [pseudonym], the blind Evangelist. But when he came on his own accord, and when X spied him on the highway, [X] went out to meet him and melodramatically led him to the proper campfire to the surprise of fellow block pickets. Through clever intimidation he had no difficulty in securing the fullest cooperation of his block throughout the strike or in suppressing any overt action, e.g., the hoisting of a Japanese flag or the reciting of the loud banzais. Their standard was simply a large white banner with 45 in red letters.[27]

Nishimoto, it is clear, was able to utilize popular issues to consolidate his power base. As a result, he eventually became the supervisor of the block managers of Unit 1, and thus further strengthened his ability to "deliver the goods" in his role as one of Poston's key power brokers. In addition, because of his experience in bureaucratic institutions in the dominant society, and with his interest in management theory, he was able to understand and to deal with WRA administrators (and researchers) as well.[28]

Nishimoto's Role as a Researcher

Now that we have outlined Nishimoto's occupational and political history, it remains to comment on his activities as a researcher.

By June 1942, one scant month after he arrived in camp, Nishimoto was already working as an assistant for the Bureau of Sociological Research (BSR).[29] Presumably he obtained employment because—as an educated and fully bilingual, bicultural individual—he was especially well-qualified to record the impact of relocation. Nishimoto, however, disliked Alexander Leighton, the director of the bureau, so he quit in December 1942.[30]

Tamie Tsuchiyama was also an employee of the bureau. She quit around the same time as Nishimoto because she found Leighton hard to relate to.[31] On the recommendation of her anthropology professors at UC Berkeley, Tsuchiyama was already affiliated with the JERS project, so when she quit BSR, she simply moved into JERS work full-time.

Tsuchiyama was acquainted with Nishimoto, having met him in both San Francisco and Los Angeles before the war. Her older sister was also a friend of Nishimoto's wife.[32] After they renewed their acquaintance, Nishimoto took an interest in her work and was willing to share "inside" information about the November strike and the camp as a whole.[33]

On this basis, Nishimoto was formally hired as a member of JERS in early 1943, largely on Tsuchiyama's recommendation. His initial task was to act as her assistant and help her keep up with her reports at Poston. This summary simplifies an interesting development, and so we present selected quotes from Tsuchiyama's correspondence with Thomas to show how this arrangement evolved.[34]

In early January 1943, Tsuchiyama wrote Thomas that:

> Since the strike I have gained the confidence of X [i.e., Nishimoto], one of the two most powerful figures in camp . . . [He] supplies me with all the

> political intrigues behind the scenes so that I am at present in a better position to analyze camp politics. Frequently he gives me advance notices of certain movements on foot [*sic*] so that I shall more fully appreciate them when they happen . . . [35]

Nishimoto also allowed Tsuchiyama access to his journal, which she cut up and filed, in order to make it available as data for JERS.

In early April 1943, Tsuchiyama, who had a great deal of work and no staff to help her, wrote to Thomas wondering:

> . . . whther [*sic*] there were sufficient funds in the Study to permit me to take X as an Issei observer, just as Bob [Spencer] has Abe [pseudonym] and Hayano [pseudonym] for his assistants. I sounded out X . . . in a round about way and gathered that he would be perfectly willing . . . One of the advantages in "hiring" X is that I can have access to all the official memos sent out by the administration to the blocks. Furthermore he comes in daily contact with a great number of Issei and a certain type of Nisei that it will permit me to focus my attention on that type of Nisei he does not touch. So far I have found his material very reliable . . . [36]

In this fashion, from 1943 to 1945, Nishimoto became a clandestine researcher in Poston for the JERS project.[37] And he made every effort to conceal this fact during the war years. Because he realized that he would have no access to information should his role as a JERS researcher be known, Nishimoto asked that all references to him in JERS materials be coded as "X" to avoid identifying him by name. Although Nishimoto never mentioned fear for his personal safety, it is clear from his own notes that other "researchers" were suspected of being *inu*, or informants, and that such an accusation could place them in physical jeopardy.[38]

The new hire, and the subsequent division of labor, worked well in the beginning. For example, in early August, Tsuchiyama reported that although she was late in turning in a report, the team was sure to succeed:

> I'm sure we'll get some swell data soon since our informants are strategically placed in the segregation set-up in camp. X as undisputed leader of the block managers is frequently consulted by Nelson and has his full confidence . . . [39]

Ultimately, for a variety of complex reasons that we cannot pursue here, Tsuchiyama's relationship with Dorothy S. Thomas (and the JERS project) terminated almost a year later, with bad feelings on both sides. After an exchange of acrimonious letters, Tsuchiyama quit her job with JERS at the end of July 1944.

Nishimoto, however, continued his work in Poston until 1945 and followed Thomas to UC Berkeley after being released from camp. He gained an even more central role in JERS, since the other Nikkei associated with the study either moved on to other things after getting out of camp or, like Tsuchiyama, resigned from JERS because their views differed too much from the director's.

Nishimoto's Role in the JERS Publications

Documentary evidence which would clarify Nishimoto's substantive and conceptual contributions to the three JERS publications is extremely limited. There are no surviving "working notes" for either *The Spoilage* or *The Salvage*, at least not in the libraries or archives of the two universities where these were most likely to be deposited had they been preserved: UC Berkeley and the University of Pennsylvania. Moreover, all of Nishimoto's personal papers were lost (or destroyed) after his death in the mid-1950s.

What remains in the Bancroft Library are two of Nishimoto's letters to Thomas, written in early 1952. Much of the text concerns Nishimoto's "woes in job hunting." Both letters, however, provide the longest available accounts indicating what Nishimoto felt his contributions to the JERS project had been.

Nishimoto began his reflections on *The Spoilage* by noting that it was W. I. and Dorothy S. Thomas who decided to make him a co-author. Nishimoto's satisfaction in being so named was that:

> . . . my conceptualization triumphed over the others'. It concerns the trichotomy—the spoilage, the salvage, and the residue. You are the one who refined and crystallized the concept and gave the most apt names to them. However, if you go back to the first Salt Lake City conference, you'll remember I was toying with the idea . . . [40]

Nishimoto recalled that he had proposed that "the spoilage" segment of the study be completed first, "because the subject matter was more definitive and easier to handle then." Reportedly, everyone on the staff, except for Rosalie Hankey, was against the idea. Nishimoto complained about the "snitching and sniping" on the part of other JERS staff members who opposed him, noting that the latter agreed to go along only after Thomas approved his suggestion.

> So, my pleasure in seeing my name on the cover of *The Spoilage* was perverted. I felt that my original concept was supported by you and that it was the best reply to the critics who said, "What the hell does he know about Sociology? He has no training in the field." [41]

Nishimoto felt that he had contributed relatively little to *The Salvage*, as he confirmed to Thomas: "You are correct in stating that I am not a co-author, nor a contributor as Kikuchi or Sakoda is." Regarding his own economic study and its relationship to *The Salvage*, Nishimoto recalled:

> When I was working on the economic history, I didn't realize it was going to be an important and valuable work. My aim then was to prepare a basis for *The Salvage* for you.[42]

While admitting that his manuscript had many substantive gaps, he also pointed out in retrospect that it was one of only two works that provided a sense of the economic baseline of Japanese-Americans in 1940 (the other being *Removal and Return* by Leonard Broom and Ruth Reimer). Nishimoto stated that: "Although the study was based on a 25 percent sampling, its sources are unique—the almost complete census data of a minority group."

To what extent did Thomas end up drawing from this study? We do not know at this point, since the bulk of it appears to have been lost or destroyed, and no working notes on *The Salvage* are deposited in the JERS collection. Although the study is never directly cited in the book, indirect references (e.g., p. 604) are made to it.

Regarding Nishimoto's editorial services for tenBroek, Barnhart, and Matson for *Prejudice, War and the Constitution*, he worked vigorously on the revision, although he complained in correspondence that the process was exhausting. He agreed completely with Thomas' desire to see tenBroek and associates produce a book that would critique and refute Morton Grodzins' *Americans Betrayed*. On this basis, Nishimoto labored for a number of weeks with all three authors collectively, as well as helping each to correct and sharpen the arguments in their individually-authored sections.[43]

It is clear, in fact, from this same letter, that no effort was spared by either Nishimoto or Thomas to aid tenBroek and his associates. At one level, support meant full access to JERS materials, including published and unpublished manuscripts. At another level, Nishimoto commented that: "if the final form is satisfactory to us, they deserve any and every support you can give them. I sincerely believe they need it . . ." [44]

When the manuscript—submitted to the University of California Press—was turned down, Thomas wrote to the editor, advising him to consult with Nishimoto:

> I should be grateful if . . . you asked Nishimoto to give you his evaluation for he is an unbiased, hard-hitting critic, whose scholarship is of the best, and who is about as "expert" in the matters dealt with as anyone you could possibly find.[45]

Although the editor chose not to follow Thomas' advice, "Chick" tenBroek wrote to Nishimoto a month later (May 7, 1953), asking him to submit an independent evaluation of the work.[46] Nishimoto's letter of May 11, praised the manuscript and concluded: " . . . it would be a serious loss to the world of scholarship if this book were not to be published."[47]

In the end, the manuscript was accepted for publication and was finally released in 1954. In the book's preface, the authors described Nishimoto's contribution in the following words:

> Richard S. Nishimoto, who is as informed about the Japanese in America as any living person, has meticulously read the manuscript; he has corrected many errors, supplied many facts, and suggested many interpretive hypotheses.[48]

The Basis of Nishimoto's Credibility

Now that Nishimoto's personal background and his various JERS activities have been outlined, the issue of Nishimoto's credibility within the project can be addressed in detail.

We have seen how, coming from a family of means, Nishimoto had the benefit of a good education. He had more schooling than the average immigrant Issei, and his education was probably of a higher quality because of its recentness and the fact that all of Nishimoto's schools were located in the capital city of Tokyo.

By the time he emigrated, Nishimoto was old enough to have been quite familiar with Japanese culture and society. At the same time, his middle school experience, sponsored by the Episcopalians, implies exposure to American language, values, and culture. This, along with the fact that he knew he was to join his parents in America, probably resulted in a degree of pre-adaptation to American life. This would account for his success in rapidly completing his studies at Lowell High School, even though he was a new immigrant. Subsequently, it only took him four years in school to earn his baccalaureate degree in engineering from Stanford.

In short, Nishimoto was educationally qualified to record the impact of "relocation" and the incarceration because of his background and education both in Japan and the United States.

In addition, his BSR and JERS reports indicate that Nishimoto was able to record data systematically and that he could be a careful and thorough observer. His early "firebreak gang" study demonstrates that he not only had the ability to lead men; he could also observe and analyze a situation, record it, and arrange the data into a thematic report which included his own socio-cultural analysis.[49]

Regarding his apparent lack of training for his work as a field researcher, it should be noted that even *graduate* course work in anthropology before World War II did not include systematic or comprehensive instruction in ethnographic field methods. As one of the professionally-trained members of the JERS staff pointed out, no one received such training in those days. Fieldworkers were more or less on their own. Thus, sensitivity, insight, and persistence, on the individual level, and the ability to learn on the spot, were key prerequisites, rather than formal training *per se*.

Nishimoto's work as a member of two research teams inside of Poston—the BSR and JERS—was essentially carried out on this basis. It should be noted, however, that as a member of both teams, he was instructed as to the goals and methods of each project, had contact with both directors, and attended BSR and JERS staff meetings and seminars. Thus Nishimoto studied and learned as he went along; his own notes as well as his associates' correspondence suggest that he acquired and read the latest literature, in order to keep up with the social science theories and methodologies of his day.[50]

In terms of his various administrative posts, all tied to the block managers' group, Nishimoto was in an excellent position to carry out his JERS research duties, especially because of his access to information. That is, he had a legitimate reason to know about everything that was going on in Poston. He would also have been able to inquire about anything without exciting too much suspicion. Given this situation, it is not surprising that Nishimoto's journals are rich in data: they contain information that would have probably been denied to non-Nikkei ethnographers or researchers, and that would not have been available to many of Poston's "residents."

For all of these same reasons, Nishimoto was sought out and consulted by many different people within Poston—Nikkei and Caucasian alike. His advice was valued because he had extensive knowledge of the internal "goings-on" of the camp and also knew quite a bit about WRA bureaucracy and policy. He could frame his counsel in terms of both sets of conditions.[51]

At the same time, as a research assistant who was able to produce page upon page of description, commentary, and analysis, Nishimoto was able to impress Dorothy S. Thomas as an energetic, informed reporter, even though he was much more active than a social science researcher would usually be, even as a "participant observer."

In sum, Nishimoto was positioned perfectly to be a researcher in Poston for the JERS project:

1) he was a *bona fide* resident;

2) he was an Issei, educated in Japan and the United States, and had both Japanese and English language skills; he was bicultural; thus, he could offer insights into the motives and views of Issei and Kibei residents;

3) he was a careful observer when he chose to be, was able to record data systematically, and also able to arrange them into thematic reports;

4) he knew all of the key leaders at Poston and had assessed their basic motives and intentions; he was informed about the political set-up in the WRA camps, in general;

5) as "supervisor of the block managers," he had access to diverse kinds of information, as well as the right to pursue information if he ever felt a need to do so.

These same attributes also make up a good part of the explanation for why Thomas came to rely so heavily upon Nishimoto. While Thomas was a highly trained demographer and researcher, she did not speak or read Japanese. She was not intimate with the "ins-and-outs" of the Japanese-American community, its leaders, or its politics. Thomas neither lived in, nor engaged in extensive participant-observation, in any of the camps. In all these areas, Nishimoto's experience, skills, and insights fully complemented those of his boss.

Thomas herself fully recognized Nishimoto's value in this regard. In a letter fragment in our possession (probably written in 1952) to Edward Barnhart, Thomas commented on the inconsistencies between an early draft of *Prejudice, War and the Constitution* and her own research, noting:

> In some instances, I felt that these inconsistencies were due merely to the fact that complete documentation was not available in secondary sources, or in our files, and that gaps would have to be filled in by having an informed, intelligent "insider" review these sections. In this respect, I thought[,] and continue to think, that Nishimoto has unique value. I am therefore deeply gratified that he has turned up at this crucial moment.[52]

Nishimoto's Research Biases: Personal, Intellectual, and Political

Nishimoto's credibility within the JERS project can also be seen from another angle: that is, in terms of how his frame of reference influenced his perceptions and interpretations of data. Furthermore, analysis of his JERS contributions, along with selected interviews, indicate that his biases need to be considered at three different levels: personal, intellectual, and political.[53]

Although Nishimoto's Poston materials exhibit a tendency toward self-enhancement, his research, along with the comments of his contemporaries, indicate that he was a complex individual. One associate assessed him as follows: "...he was an intellectual; he was a marginal person ...[and] he was an internationalist."[54] As such, Nishimoto's diaries also reflect his thoughts on ethnicity and race relations in general, as well as the evolving nature of his own ethnic identity.

A number of times, based on readings in the sociology of race relations of his day, Nishimoto drew explicit analogies in his journal between the situation of the Jews and the Japanese in the United States. Upon reading Louis Adamic's *From Many Lands,* Nishimoto quoted extensively from the book and then made the following comment:

> Evacuation brought a drastic change in my race consciousness...It was different. No longer did it feel that I am "on trial." No longer did I "look at myself in a mirror" if I have chance among the Caucasians, nor did I care. I was resigned to the idea that I am a Japanese and am being treated as such. I began to feel that I am as good as any one of the Caucasians... Should I say that with the evacuation any inward-directed race consciousness was transformed into outwardly-directed violent race consciousness?[55]

This passage shows that Nishimoto's own sense of ethnic identity went through a transition in camp. His sensitivity about racial issues, it will be remembered, was partially a result of his own career experiences. The "evacuation" and "relocation" experiences reinforced his view that racial discrimination was a central aspect of Nikkei life in the United States.

It is also clear that this personal consciousness had an impact on Nishimoto's interpretations of events in the camps. At one point in a JERS staff meeting, he argued against James Sakoda's "labor conflict" explanation of camp rebellions. Nishimoto hypothesized that the general camp pattern (i.e., involving protest and strikes) was not a matter of labor or class conflicts, but rather defiance against a "caste system."[56]

At an intellectual level, in a long letter to Thomas, dated March 1952, Nishimoto reflected on his motives for doing research for the JERS project. Since this letter is the only surviving account by Nishimoto along these lines that we have been able to find, it is worth quoting at length.

> Remember those days in 1942? Many scientists were groping around in the dark. I thought I could help them to their advantage. I knew that I was one of the few experts in the field of resident Japanese problems, as good as any of the recognized authors of the secondary sources then existing. (Hell with "modesty.") I thought I could straighten out a lot of misconceptions about the Japanese, and the Nisei "scientists," too, were not getting anywhere . . .
>
> I never expected that I would be working for you after that period, nor did I anticipate that I would later be coming to Berkeley and would participate in the publication of our findings. You never told me, and I never asked you, how long I would be working at Berkeley. I just kept on with the idea that I would be helping as long as I was needed and my assistance was of any value . . .
>
> My purpose was therefore very altruistic. I knew I was good at the things we were doing, and was fully aware that we were producing something extremely valuable for the science. This "honorable" trait in me was also responsible for Chick's [i.e., Jacobus tenBroek's] group. Yes, it is true that those two factors you mentioned, *viz.*, (1) a "moral" obligation, and (2) a "socialized" desire, were the primary ones that motivated me to help them. But more than these, I saw an unpolished gem in their work . . .[57]

This account, however, appears to be quite idealized so we made a point of asking those who knew him personally if Nishimoto appeared to feel any conflict or guilt over the ethical implications of his clandestine research. One acquaintance replied that a skeptic might argue that he was "greedy for the extra money," or anxious for the "chance to remain in touch with West Coast intellectual life." While Nishimoto's associate was willing to allow the latter point, he also noted:

> I do not remember his discussing the ethics of his own activities, and I think this was significant . . . I think he was fundamentally at peace with his research role and did not feel that it needed discussion [underline included].[58]

Nishimoto, then, did not appear to perceive any conflict between his roles as an active member of the camp community, and that of a JERS staff member. How could this seeming contradiction have been reconciled?

The social sciences of the time rested on the assumption that research is justified because it involved the search for "truth." On this basis, Dorothy Thomas' primary ethical concern was to insist upon confidentiality. JERS staff members, for example, were not supposed to share research data with WRA authorities nor with the FBI.[59]

Although ethical standards concerning informant confidentiality was a dictum of the JERS project, in the actual field situation, things were not clear cut. JERS fieldworkers, it must be remembered, were relatively inexperienced as most of them were still graduate students. For this reason, JERS staff often found their interactions with social science colleagues on the WRA staff intellectually satisfying. In turn, the community analysts, by and large, were of liberal persuasion, and sympathetic to the plight of the community members.[60] Thus, JERS correspondence and journals indicate that friendly interrelationships were often established between JERS staff and WRA social scientists, and that a good deal of information sharing took place.[61]

In addition, from the standpoint of the JERS staff members, the exchange of letters with Thomas indicates that each was under pressure to produce data. There was a "tit for tat" exchange of information in response to this pressure, so that research workers, regardless of affiliation, found it to their advantage to maximize control of information by an exchange of data. Thus, the JERS dictum of confidentiality was more ideal than actual.

Furthermore, Nishimoto's insistence on a clandestine role with JERS had a dual basis. On one hand, he did not wish to have the sources of information, which made him valuable to the project, dry up. Nor, at the same time, was Nishimoto willing to have his ability to operate as a political leader in Poston jeopardized by the exposure of his association with JERS. In the context of the camp, where paranoia prevailed, Nishimoto knew that revelation concerning his role in JERS would curtail his effectiveness as a block manager. Since Nishimoto's simultaneous roles as researcher and leader necessitated secrecy, and since he considered himself a "marginal man" anyway, we conclude that Nishimoto compartmentalized his roles. This allowed him to situationally separate his activities, and carry out both roles without feeling that he was betraying the trust of either constituency.[62]

Turning to other biases, we can say that the evidence at hand supports the view that Nishimoto was a political moderate within Poston. That is, he was not an adherent of the JACL view nor a partisan of the ostensibly pro-Japanese Issei, Kibei or Nisei in camp.[63] There are indications, however, that, while Nishimoto was sometimes Machiavellian, he often carried out his actions for a larger purpose: to make life as tolerable as possible for the majority of the inhabitants of Poston.[64] This helps to explain why he was so intent on eliminating the power base of his Issei and Kibei rivals during 1943. Nishimoto thought that their militancy would only create frustrations that were not really resolvable in the camp setting. Thus, as an activist and a moderate, Nishimoto felt that political extremism interfered with the basic task of survival.

In 1944, when a JERS staff member asked directly about Nishimoto's and his allies' political stance at Poston, another staff member jumped into the conversation to comment: "They're people who could get things done for people." According to the conference transcripts, Nishimoto immediately agreed: "That's the way they're regarded."[65]

On the same occasion, Nishimoto also commented that:

> . . . unless the community is integrated you can't get anything done at all. They can't integrate at either end of the scale . . . it has to be somewhere near the middle. [With] segregation and relocation it's become easier to organize in the middle. A good example is that it is difficult to move flakes of snow in any one direction. After making it into a ball, it's easy to move.[66]

Another bias is, at once, intellectual *and* political in nature. Nishimoto claimed on his resume, after the war, that his degree specialty within engineering had been in "factory management." "Factory Management" was based on the point of view that the social sciences were scientific enough to engage in "human engineering."[67] Although Nishimoto's claims in this regard were not actually true, he was probably exposed to this field while in camp through his contacts with anthropologists like Edward Spicer and Alexander Leighton. At any rate, this orientation would fit well with Nishimoto's approach to the management of fellow internees at Poston. In summary, one interpretation of Nishimoto's initial decision to participate in JERS at Poston is that it presented a way for him to employ a range of intellectual abilities and ambitions which had been completely (and unfairly) curtailed before World War II. In this same sense, as we have mentioned previously, JERS status gave Nishimoto the chance to study his environment, while at the same time recording and analyzing the efficacy of his attempts to try and "engineer" events within it.

Conclusion: Assessing the Impact of Nishimoto's Contributions to JERS

The assessment of Nishimoto's contributions to the Poston phase of the JERS project is full of irony. Nishimoto was "a prime mover" in Poston's Unit I. As an internee involved in camp politics, he influenced much of what occurred there, particularly between 1943 and 1945.

In Nishimoto's case, he was far beyond being a typical participant observer. He was a community leader in Poston. He was even willing to encourage militancy when he thought it would serve his interests and ends as an activist. His field notes and analytic essays contain colorful descriptions of his own activities, using a pseudonym to disguise his identity. Thus, Nishimoto's Poston research must be used with care because he controlled information in order to enhance his political status within the camp community and, simultaneously, his machinations became an important part of his "data"—his contributions to JERS project files.

In short, the fact that Nishimoto was a full-fledged activist and leader in Poston sets him apart from the rest of the JERS researchers. Following from this, Nishimoto's sociological journals can be considered a unique form of "auto-ethnography," informed by Nishimoto's own plans and activities as the supervisor of the block managers.[68]

It is difficult to determine how Nishimoto's Poston research—including his intellectual orientation and biases—affected his subsequent contributions to official JERS publications like *The Spoilage*. To begin with, Nishimoto was never at Tule Lake, and so the issue of Nishimoto's tendency to inflate his own role is not relevant. Also *The Spoilage* is Thomas and Nishimoto's secondary analysis of Rosalie Wax's (nee, Hankey's) field notes. To further complicate matters, no working papers are available which specify which author—Thomas or Nishimoto—was responsible for which ideas or for which thematic sections of the book.

It is appropriate, nonetheless, to note that Marvin K. Opler's review of *The Spoilage* criticized Thomas and Nishimoto's tendency to view political conflict at Tule Lake in terms of a small number of elites, divided into competing factions.[69] It is interesting to speculate whether this bias, which Opler felt might be the result of an over-reliance upon Wax's field notes, was also influenced by Nishimoto's political worldview and leadership style.

Similarly, there is evidence that Nishimoto's attitude towards "extremists" in Poston influenced Wax's interpretations of the "resegregationists" in Tule Lake. Nishimoto and Tsuchiyama visited Wax in Gila during September 1943. Nishimoto disagreed with a statement in Wax's report on the segregation of the "loyal" and "disloyal" internees. She had commented that the white Chief of Police's opinion that the "disloyals" were going to Tule Lake to escape the draft was nonsense.

According to Wax,

> Nishimoto . . . asserted that this remark was not nonsense but the plain truth. I listened carefully while he explained that most of the Japanese had made the decision which categorized them as "loyal" or "disloyal" with sensible or practical considerations in mind, even though many might insist that they had answered the military questionnaires in a spirit of exalted idealism. Most of the WRA staff members believed that the evacuees' decision had been idealistic, and in consequence, they were not able to understand what the evacuees said or did. He added that I was not to feel too bad about this, because most of the members of the study, including Dr. Thomas and the Japanese research assistants, labored under the same limited view. They refused, he said, to see what the evacuees were really like.[70]

Final assessment of Nishimoto's influence may have to await the time when all of Wax's original field notes will become accessible to researchers.

In conclusion, we do not believe that Nishimoto was either hero or villain, oppressor or victim. Nor do we believe that Nishimoto's role should be assessed in terms of the ethical procedures underlying the social science practices of today. Nishimoto was not a trained social scientist. Rather, insofar as he was concerned, and in terms of his duties as a JERS staff member, he appears to have believed that he was contributing to the ultimate understanding of the Japanese-American experience.

Nishimoto was clearly a valuable source of information and ideas for the professionally-trained JERS social scientists. We have outlined here the different bases of his credibility, insofar as his background, skills, and administrative roles made his accounts especially "worthy of belief."[71]

While he manipulated the situations around him to his own best interests and advantage, Nishimoto was essentially used by JERS personnel and then abandoned. In fact, when he wrote Dorothy Thomas in 1952, Nishimoto was resigned to any kind of a job, including that of a domestic, if it was impossible for him to find academically-related employment. Despite his ability, energy, and years of dedication, Nishimoto was never offered access to graduate school or to secure employment as a research assistant by the professionals who relied so heavily upon his expertise.

Like the camp leader described in Wakako Yamauchi's short story, "The Sensei," Nishimoto no longer enjoyed power and prestige after the war because he had lost his community following.[72] He was all but forgotten, and his last job, before he died in the mid-1950s, was that of a night watchman of a small hotel in downtown San Francisco.

Notes

1. Letter, Dorothy S. Thomas to Richard Nishimoto (September 22, 1943), JERS W 1.25A.

2. Richard S. Nishimoto, "Outline of Personal History" [resume] (February 11, 1952). Courtesy of Mrs. Roberta Shiroma.

3. The manuscript was entitled "The Economic History of Japanese on the Pacific Coast, 1885-1941." Unfortunately, only selected chapters are available in the JERS Collection. See JERS A 1.04, A 1.06-07.

4. Letter, Thomas to August Fruge (March 25, 1953).

5. We will not attempt to summarize the roots or intricacies of this approach here, other than to note that it begins with the premise that no position—theoretical or otherwise—is privileged. The main task is to discover how "credibility" is achieved in ethnographic accounts. See James Clifford, "On Ethnographic Authority," *Representations* 1:2 (1983), 118-46; James Clifford and George Marcus, *Writing Culture: The Poetics and Politics of Ethnography* (Berkeley: University of California Press, 1986); and Paul Stoller, "The Reconstruction of Ethnography," Phyllis Pease Chock and June R. Wyman, eds., *Discourse and the Social Meaning of Life* (Washington, D.C.: Smithsonian Institution Press, 1986), 51-74. The assessment of Nishimoto's work in this fashion parallels assessments of the research of social scientists connected to the WRA and JERS. See Peter T. Suzuki, "The University of California Japanese Evacuation and Resettlement Study: A Prolegomenon," *Dialectical Anthropology* 10 (1986), 189-213; Orin Starn, "Engineering Internment: Anthropologists and the War Relocation Authority," *American Ethnologist* 13:4 (1986), 700-20; Richard Drinnon, *Keeper of Concentration Camps: Dillon S. Myer and American Racism* (Berkeley: University of California Press, 1986); Harland Padfield, "The Problem of Cultural Dominance: Spicer and Anthropology for Peoples without History," unpublished paper prepared for the symposium, "Anthropology and Humanity: The Work of Edward H. Spicer," American Anthropological Association meetings, Washington, D.C., December 7, 1985.

6. Nishimoto's contributions to JERS are listed in Edward N. Barnhart, *Japanese American Evacuation and Resettlement: Catalog of Material in the General Library* (Berkeley: University of California, General Library, 1958), 88, 89, 91, 176, 177, *passim*. Lane Hirabayashi corresponded or conducted interviews with a number of persons who knew Nishimoto. He wishes to acknowledge David French, S. Frank Miyamoto, James Sakoda, Roberta Shiroma, and Rosalie H. Wax, each of whom shared reminiscences and information. In addition, Noriko Sawada, Yuji Ichioka, and Glenn Omatsu provided invaluable advice. We alone bear full responsibility for the interpretation advanced here.

7. All of the data in this section were derived from either: (1) Nishimoto, "Outline

of Personal History," or (2) Nishimoto, "The Firebreak Gang," JERS J 6.07.

8. This information is derived from Nishimoto's Stanford transcript, which was found in "Unpublished manuscripts," Dorothy S. Thomas, Papers regarding Japanese Relocation (four cartons), 78/53c, Bancroft Library, UC Berkeley.

9. This information was provided in an interview taken by Lane Hirabayashi, August 27, 1987. In regard to the employment of Stanford's graduates of Chinese descent, Stanford's University Placement Office noted, as late as 1928, that: ". . . it was almost impossible to place a Chinese of either the first or second generation in *any* kind of position: engineering, manufacturing, or business. Many firms had general regulations against employing them; others objected to them on the grounds that other men employed by their firms did not care to work with them." Pao-Min Chang, *Continuity and Change: A Profile of Chinese Americans* (New York: Vantage Press, 1983), 97. We thank Dr. Michael Chang, Stanford University, for this reference.

10. For a study of this community, see Lane Ryo Hirabayashi and George Tanaka, "The Issei Community in Moneta and the Gardena Valley, 1900-1920," *Southern California Quarterly* 70 (1988), 127-58.

11. For maps of Poston's location in Arizona, as well as maps of Poston itself, see Alexander H. Leighton, *The Governing of Men* (Princeton: Princeton University Press, 1945), 56, 57, 59.

12. *Ibid.*, 48-52.

13. Drinnon, *Keeper of Concentration Camps*, 282.

14. Leighton, *The Governing of Men*, 91, 92, 151.

15. See the report to the JERS staff at the Chicago conference, December, 1943: JERS W 1.10, 43; *passim*. Also see the comments of Tamie Tsuchiyama, "The Poston Strike; A Chronological Account," JERS J 6.24, 33.

16. See Leighton, *The Governing of Men*, 50, 102-05, 110-20.

17. *Ibid.* See also Paul Bailey, *City in the Sun: The Japanese Concentration Camp at Poston, Arizona* (Los Angeles: Westernlore Press, 1971); Gary Y. Okihiro, "Japanese Resistance in America's Concentration Camps: A Re-evaluation," *Amerasia Journal* 2 (1973), 20-34.

18. Nishimoto, "Firebreak Gang," JERS J 6.07.

19. This information appears in the JERS Salt Lake City conference notes: JERS W 1.15, December 4, 1944, 1-20.

20. This information and the following two quotes are taken from: Tamie Tsuchiyama, "The Poston Strike," JERS J 6.24.

21. The quote and account come from "Richard Nishimoto on the Political Organization of Poston" (December 4, 1944), JERS W 1.15.

22. *Ibid.*

23. *Ibid.*

24. *Ibid.*

25. An inquiry, October 8, 1987, to the National Personnel Records Center in this regard resulted in a negative response. The center had no "record of the claimed Federal Employment" (November 5, 1987).

26. "Richard Nishimoto on the Political Organization of Poston" (December 4, 1944), JERS W 1.15, 8. See also Nishimoto's "Journal" (March 29, 1944), JERS J 6.13, 8-11, for another classic example.

27. Tamie Tsuchiyama, "The Poston Strike," JERS J 6.24. Here, it is appropriate to note that Tsuchiyama's comments on "X" often appear to be Nishimoto's self-assertions; as such, they reflect Nishimoto's tendency towards self-enhancement. Tsuchiyama's willingness to accept Nishimoto's "data" as fact must be seen in the context of the direct pressure which Dorothy Thomas put on JERS researchers to produce high quality information. For one outstanding example of such pressure, see Letter, Thomas to Tsuchiyama (July 28, 1944), JERS J 6.32.

28. Nishimoto's "Journal" for the month of March, 1944, records his discussions with WRA officials and community analysts, JERS J 6.13C.

29. In one account, Nishimoto asserts that his penchant for ethnographic observations derived from an initial interest in writing fiction. "The writer [i.e., Nishimoto] desired to write stories in Japanese, depicting such exodus and life at a relocation camp for his pleasure. The materials used in this report were originally collected and intended for such purposes—jotted down on little pieces of paper from time to time." Richard S. Nishimoto, "Firebreak Gang," JERS J 6.07.

30. See "Richard S. Nishimoto on the Political Organization of Poston," JERS W 1.15, 11. See also letter, Nishimoto to Thomas (October 22, 1943), JERS W 1.25A; and letter, Tsuchiyama to Thomas (November 2, 1943), JERS J 6.32.

31. Letter, Tsuchiyama to Thomas (November 2, 1942), JERS J 6.32. It is also clear from Tsuchiyama's letter of August 24, 1942, that WRA officials at a variety of levels were fully aware of her identity and mission, both with the BSR and with JERS: *ibid.*

32. Letters, Tsuchiyama to Thomas (December 1, 1942 and March 26, 1943), *ibid.*

33. Letter, Tsuchiyama to Thomas (December 1, 1942), *ibid.*

34. We would like to acknowledge the generosity of Professor Yuji Ichioka in sharing these letters with us. In addition, we would like to note there are complexities to Tsuchiyama's story which we cannot go into here.

35. Letter, Tsuchiyama to Thomas (January 3, 1943), JERS J 6.32.

36. Letter, Tsuchiyama to Thomas (April 6, 1943), *ibid.*

37. Nishimoto was first hired as Tsuchiyama's "Issei assistant" at the rate of $15 a month, letter, Thomas to Tsuchiyama (April 8, 1943), *ibid.* In this same letter Thomas pointed out that the state did not allow direct payments to Issei "but we are allowed to buy their 'product'." Later Thomas indicated that Nishimoto's salary would be raised

to $50 a month, letter, Thomas to Tsuchiyama (June 23, 1943), *ibid.*

38. See Nishimoto's "Journal" (March 13, 1944), JERS J 6.13C, 7, and "Sociological Journal" (February 19, 1944), JERS J 6.16F, 10. See also letter, Tsuchiyama to Thomas (November 2, 1942), JERS J 6.32.

39. Letter, Tsuchiyama to Thomas (August 7, 1943), JERS J 6.32.

40. Letter, Nishimoto to Thomas (March 5, 1952), "Unpublished manuscripts," Dorothy S. Thomas, Papers regarding Japanese Relocation (four cartons), 78/53c, Bancroft Library.

41. *Ibid.*, 10.

42. *Ibid.*

43. Letter, Nishimoto to Thomas (February 27, 1952), "Unpublished manuscripts," Dorothy S. Thomas, Papers regarding Japanese Relocation (four cartons), 78/53c, Bancroft Library.

44. *Ibid.*, 3.

45. Letter, Thomas to Fruge (March 25, 1953). Courtesy of Mrs. Roberta Shiroma.

46. Letter, tenBroek to Nishimoto (May 7, 1953). Courtesy of Mrs. Roberta Shiroma.

47. Letter, Nishimoto to Fruge (May 11, 1953). Courtesy of Mrs. Roberta Shiroma.

48. Jacobus tenBroek et al., *Prejudice, War and the Constitution* (Berkeley: University of California Press, 1970), xii-xiii.

49. Nishimoto, "Firebreak Gang," JERS J 6.07.

50. See Nishimoto's "Journal" (October 1, 1943), JERS J 6.13A, 1-3. See also letter, Tsuchiyama to Thomas (March 4, 1943), JERS J 6.32, 4.

51. Nishimoto's "Journal" provides numerous examples of his day-to-day efforts on behalf of his constituents: e.g., his intervention in domestic quarrels, health, sanitation and police matters, JERS J 6.13A-E. For examples of contact with WRA staff, see his "Journal" for the month of March 1944, which shows that Nishimoto conversed with the likes of Edward Spicer, David French, and John Powell: JERS J 6.13C. See the same "Journal" (June 26, 1944), for a reference to Nishimoto's conversation with Morris Burge, JERS J 6.13D, 1.

52. Letter (fragment) [probably Thomas to Edward Barnhart, 1952]. Courtesy of Mrs. Roberta Shiroma.

53. We use the term "biases" here following Gunnar Myrdal, *Objectivity in Social Research* (New York: Pantheon Books, 1969), 41-56, passim. In this usage, all social science research is affected by explicit and implicit biases. Myrdal argues that analyses become "objective" only insofar as a researcher ". . . expose[s] the valuations to full light, make[s] them conscious, specific, and explicit . . . ," 55-56.

54. Letter from former WRA staff member, July 10, 1986. Regarding the second point, Dorothy Thomas had apparently recommended that Nishimoto read Everett V.

Stonequist, *Marginal Man: A Study in Personality and Culture Conflict* (New York: C. Scribner's Sons, 1937), and Nishimoto had taken the portrait to heart, *ibid.*

55. Nishimoto's "Journal" (September 17, 1942), JERS J 6.13A, 1-2.

56. This comment appears in the notes on the Salt Lake City conference, June, 1944, JERS W 1.15, 83.

57. Letter, Nishimoto to Thomas (March 5, 1952), 6-7, "Unpublished manuscripts," Dorothy S. Thomas, Papers regarding Japanese Relocation (four cartons), 78/53c, Bancroft Library.

58. Letter from former WRA staff member, July 10, 1986.

59. For the original guidelines of the project, see JERS W 1.00 and W 1.20. For comments regarding the ethical guidelines of the project, see Dorothy S. Thomas and Richard Nishimoto, *The Spoilage* (Berkeley: University of California Press, 1946), v-xv.

60. See Orin Starn, "Engineering Internment: Anthropologists and the War Relocation Authority," 700-20.

61. For documentation regarding Nishimoto's contact with WRA analysts and administrators, not to mention one of Poston's Caucasian F.B.I. agents, see his "Journal" entries for March and April 1944, J 6.13C. For documentation regarding the JERS project as a whole, see "Correspondence of JERS Director Dorothy S. Thomas and Staff," JERS W 1.25A-F.

62. It is vital to remember, here, that as soon as Dillon S. Myer suspected that Nishimoto was a JERS staff member, he interviewed Nishimoto first-hand, and then ordered that he be removed from Poston. See Richard Drinnon, *Keeper of Concentration Camps: Dillon S. Myer and American Racism*, 48-49. Nishimoto's presence in Poston would *not* have been a problem for Myer if Nishimoto had simply been an agent for WRA or the U. S. government.

63. See Nishimoto's "Journal" (October 1, 1943), JERS J 6.13A, 1-3; see also "Richard Nishimoto on the Political Organization of Poston" (December 4, 1944), JERS W 1.15, *passim*.

64. Although often manipulative and self-aggrandizing, it is important to note that Nishimoto enjoyed using his power to intimidate Caucasian WRA personnel and making them comply with their duties.

65. "Richard Nishimoto on the Political Organization of Poston" (December 4, 1944), JERS W 1.15, 19.

66. *Ibid.*, 20.

67. According to Spicer's later publications on applied anthropology, factory management theory during the twenties and thirties shifted from "optimum physiological conditions," which would promote productivity, to "work groups of which individuals were a part, both in and out of the factory." See Edward Spicer, "Early Applications of Anthropology in North America," in Anthony F. C. Wallace et

al., eds., *Perspectives on Anthropology* (Washington, D.C.: American Anthropological Association, 1976), 116-41. Interestingly enough, this new perspective, which would be influential in fields such as industrial psychology and business administration, was partially a product of anthropological research, including studies by then graduate students Conrad Arensberg and Solon Kimball, *ibid.*, and F. L. W. Richardson, "Social Interaction and Industrial Productivity," in Walter Goldschmidt, ed., *The Uses of Anthropology* (Washington, D.C.: American Anthropological Association, Special Publication No. 10, 1979), 79-99. Both Arensberg and Kimball would go on to work for the WRA, the former as an outside consultant, the latter as head of the Community Management Division who actually designed the original administrative set up at Poston, Spicer, "Early Applications of Anthropology in North America," 223, 231.

68. See David M. Hayano, "Auto-ethnography," *Human Organization* 38 (1979), 99-104, for a thorough discussion of auto-ethnographies.

69. Marvin K. Opler, *American Anthropologist* 50 (1948), 308.

70. Rosalie H. Wax, *Doing Fieldwork: Warnings and Advice* (Chicago: University of Chicago Press, 1971), 74. We note that there has been heated debate over political and ethical aspects of *The Spoilage*, only some of which is available in print. Further commentary on these matters is difficult here, primarily because there is no evidence as to Nishimoto's substantive contributions in this regard.

71. "Credible" is defined as "worthy of belief" and "entitled to confidence" in *Webster's Third New International Dictionary* (Springfield, Massachusetts: G. & C. Merriam, 1976), 532.

72. See Wakako Yamauchi, "The Sensei" in Shawn Wong and Frank Chin, eds., *Yardbird Reader* (Berkeley: Yardbird Publishing, 1974), III, 245-54.

For the Sake of Inter–university Comity:

The Attempted Suppression by the University of California of Morton Grodzins' ***Americans Betrayed***

PETER T. SUZUKI

For more than three years immediately following World War II, University of California officials attempted to block publication of a manuscript by former JERS staff member Morton Grodzins. The manuscript, a searing indictment of the forces behind the wartime evacuation, was eventually published in 1949 by the University of Chicago Press under the title of *Americans Betrayed: Politics and the Japanese Evacuation,* despite the strenuous objections by University of California officials. Their opposition included repeated attempts to discredit Grodzins' scholarship, an effort to pressure officials of the University of Chicago Press to halt publication of the manuscript, and a campaign to rush into print another book—which became *Prejudice, War and the Constitution*—to rebut Grodzins' main arguments.

At the center of the Berkeley group's objections was Grodzins' thesis: that California and West Coast officials played a major role in the events which led to the removal of Japanese–Americans. Grodzins was especially critical of the wartime role of California Governor Earl Warren, then the state's attorney general, and a close friend of UC President Robert G. Sproul. In the post–war period, Warren had risen to national prominence in the Republican Party.

Elsewhere, in a preliminary analysis of JERS,[1] I briefly described the attempts to suppress Grodzins' book. Unlike that article, this paper is based on unpublished materials at the Bancroft Library at the University of California, Berkeley, and the University of Chicago. It will deal with the principals involved in the attempted suppression, the issues, and the outcomes.

Grodzins' Work with JERS

Morton Grodzins was with JERS from July 1, 1942, to March 31, 1945. In many respects he was the right–hand man of its director, Dorothy S. Thomas. He researched the events which led to the 1942 evacuation and, in this capacity, conducted interviews with numerous public officials and politicians, surveyed newspaper and magazine articles, attended relevant functions, and compiled and analyzed pertinent documents. He was also a doctoral student in UC's Department of Political Science, and in 1945 received his Ph.D. upon completion of his dissertation, "Political Aspects of the Japanese Evacuation."

This dissertation was written under the supervision of Charles Aikin, professor of political science, along with others on his committee. The dissertation itself was withheld as a classified document until at least 1949, the year Grodzins' book *Americans Betrayed* appeared. Although not a government–sponsored project, a majority of the JERS materials were classified and maintained that status many years after the termination of the study.[2]

Difficulties arose for Grodzins when he expressed his desire to Thomas to revise his dissertation for publication as a book, a task he started to undertake immediately after he received his Ph.D. degree. In a detailed letter to Thomas dated August 9, 1945 (but mailed on August 14, "V–J Day"), he cogently stated the reasons for publishing his study as part of the planned series of JERS books. One reason which stood out was that, owing to the war's end, he felt there was no longer any need to withhold information about the forces behind the evacuation.[3]

Thomas was hardly moved by this letter. In her reply, she angrily denounced his dissertation as unsuitable for publication (despite not having seen his revision), stating that it was "excessively verbose" (it was 727 pages long) and included "a number of intemperate and immature judgments about the behavior and misbehavior of government officials." She then informed him that his dissertation would not be "released" until all the proposed publication plans for JERS had been made.[4] (The publication plans included four books: *The Spoilage, The Salvage, The Residue,* and *The Ecology of Loyalty*; only the first two came off the press.[5])

As a compromise, Grodzins then proposed to have his revised dissertation published independently of the JERS series but felt seriously handicapped by what he saw as Thomas' "excess secreteiveness" [*sic*] to the degree that he did not even have permission to show his manuscript to Dean Robert Redfield of the Division of the Social Sciences of the University of Chicago, the institution where Grodzins was teaching. Redfield had done some research on the Japanese in America for the War Relocation Authority. On the other hand, Thomas accused Grodzins of wanting to publish his dissertation for commercial gain. He hotly denied this accusation and offered to donate any royalties from the sales of the proposed book to the foundations which had financed JERS.[6]

Toward the end of 1945 Aikin and Thomas denied Grodzins permission to publish two articles based on his dissertation. Moreover, he was again reminded by Thomas that he was forbidden to do any of the following:

> (a) showing the manuscript [revised dissertation] around, (b) giving speeches based on the materials; and (c) publishing articles, books, pamphlets or anything else.[7]

Undeterred by all the restrictions imposed upon him and the negative reactions from Aikin and Thomas, Grodzins continued to rework the dissertation. He sent copies to Aikin and Thomas. The former reacted by sending a detailed analysis of ten, single–spaced, typed pages, which, although friendly in tone, was critical in nature. In addition to criticisms dealing with technical matters, he warned Grodzins not "to be another Carey McWilliams"[8] (i.e., a liberal, who had used a political and economic interpretation to account for the evacuation in his 1944 book, *Prejudice*) and concluded with the observation that Grodzins' work was partly "propaganda."[9]

Interestingly enough, several years later, Howard Jay Graham, who had received his master's degree under Aikin and who was initially asked by Thomas to revise the Grodzins manuscript, found it to be "extraordinarily well done in many respects—in fact, on the basis of the early chapters[,] Chuck [Charles] Aikin's criticisms seemed unduly severe."[10]

However, so unhappy was Thomas with Grodzins and with his revision that, without his knowledge or consent, she and Aikin asked Milton Chernin, a Berkeley social welfare professor, to "completely rewrite" the Grodzins manuscript and to be the co–author of the final product.[11] Quite understandably, Grodzins was strongly opposed to this plan once he learned about it and felt affronted that he had not been consulted about it prior to the offer to Chernin, an early staff member of JERS who had to resign to assume another assignment. Grodzins suggested to Aikin and Thomas that they abandon their plan because he would revise his manuscript to their satisfaction.[12]

After Chernin backed out of the offer to revise the manuscript, Thomas ignored Grodzins' latest proposal and approached Richard S. Nishimoto. With the help of Thomas, Nishimoto succeeded in revising the manuscript to her satisfaction.[13] Nevertheless, because neither Nishimoto nor Thomas was a political scientist, she felt uncomfortable about the revision,[14] a situation which resulted in seeking out another person, in this case, the aforementioned Howard Jay Graham, an Aikin "protégé,"[15] to do the rewrite job in early 1948.[16]

Graham initially showed interest in the project but then withdrew from it, as stated in a letter to Thomas dated March 8, 1948, which suggested Aikin as the logical alternative for the task.[17] Thomas did not follow his advice, for she shortly thereafter got in touch with someone at the Carnegie Corporation of New York to act as an intermediary to offer the job to another political scientist, Oliver Garceau, who was living in Maine at the time.[18] Garceau, in turn, refused the offer, which included a stipend of $800 for a summer's worth of work, a fairly princely sum in 1948.[19] Garceau did not brush off the offer immediately, insofar as he read over Grodzins' and the Nishimoto–Thomas revision. Regarding the latter, what impressed him was that it was "a mere chronology, inherently very biassed and perhaps more subtle propaganda than Grodzins[']."[20] Yet, this was the same revised version about which Thomas had been so pleased and proud.[21]

Upon receiving word of Garceau's refusal, Thomas asked Jacobus tenBroek of Berkeley's speech department [*sic*] to assume the task of rewriting the much–traveled manuscript, upon Aikin's recommendation.[22] tenBroek was the fifth—and, as it turned out, final—person who got the offer. He then teamed up with Edward N. Barnhart of the speech department for the task. They were assisted by a graduate student, Floyd W. Matson, to write what came to be *Prejudice, War and the Constitution*. For Thomas, 1948 was not only a busy year because of her contacts with Graham, Pendelton Herring of the Carnegie Corporation, Garceau, and tenBroek, but also because she was busy spiking attempts by Grodzins to have his manuscript published:

> . . . Grodzins offered his copy of the manuscript to at least one commercial publisher—Macmillan's, who, after consulting me, declined to consider it.[23]

In this same letter to R. L. Johnson, the administrative assistant to Robert G. Sproul, president of the University of California, Thomas labeled the Grodzins manuscript an "incompetent work" based on "his flagrant use of highly confidential materials obtained in the name of the University," and strongly urged the immediate activation by Sproul of a university committee on the custodianship of JERS materials to look into the matter and to "protect members of the University of California faculty who are now preparing a monograph on the subject. . .[*viz.*, tenBroek, Barnhart, and Matson]."[24]

Three days later, in a letter to the assistant director of the University of Chicago Press as a response to a telegram he had sent Thomas informing her that it was preparing to publish the Grodzins study, Thomas charged Grodzins with having "pirated" California materials and averred that publication by Chicago would mean "an appropriation of materials belonging to the University of California and a breach of trust by Morton Grodzins." To this person—Fred Wieck—Thomas also stated that the manuscript was based on incompetent workmanship and was of "unscholarly character." About the same time, tenBroek informed Grodzins that Thomas was threatening to send "a letter to every publisher in the nation to tell them that a manuscript by Grodzins was a stolen one."[25]

Formation of a UC Investigative Subcommittee

On September 7, 1948, a subcommittee of the University's Library Committee was formed, consisting of Professors tenBroek, Barnhart, Harold E. Jones, Robert A. Nisbet, and Harry B. Wellman.[26] tenBroek was appointed chairman, and when Thomas learned of this, she wrote to him to "avoid quoting the lurid Grodzins–Thomas correspondence . . ." in the subcommittee's work.[27] Among other things, the members interviewed a number of former JERS personnel to get at the facts.[28]

In its final report to Sproul, written by tenBroek and Barnhart, the subcommittee:

> . . . was unanimously agreed that high level negotiations should be carried on *to prevent the publication* by the University of Chicago of the Grodzins' [*sic*] MSS [*sic*], relying primarily on ethical arguments and arguments of *inter–university comity*.[29] [emphasis added]

While these activities were going on at Berkeley, the director of the University of Chicago Press, William Terry Couch, asked tenBroek to send him a copy of the contractual agreement between Grodzins and the University of California in which the latter forbade Grodzins to use JERS materials. Couch received no such copy in response to even his third request to tenBroek, dated September 29, 1948 (the earlier ones were contained in letters dated September 9 and 17).[30] Thomas had to admit to tenBroek: "There is of course no contract in a legal sense." Then she testily added, "They know perfectly well that contracts are not made with research assistants."[31] Around the same time, Sproul had written to Dean Tyler of the Division of the Social Sciences of the University of Chicago about the University of California's position and requested the latter "to consider the matter."[32]

It was in the context of such an exchange that tenBroek was able to state with accuracy that "the big guns . . . [were] being wheeled into place in the Grodzins affair," not only because of communication between Sproul and Tyler but also because a lawsuit in the form of an injunction to stop the University of Chicago Press from publishing the Grodzins book was being considered.[33] Also, the chancellor of the University of Chicago, Robert Maynard Hutchins, was being brought into the case by Sproul's assistant, Johnson.[34]

That feelings on the Berkeley campus ran high against Grodzins can be gathered in the following comments about him made by the person who agreed to revise his manuscript, as stated to Thomas in tenBroek's letter: "If someone had dropped Grodzins in the [San Francisco] bay at the early age of two he would have saved a number of us a lot of trouble."[35] And in a previous letter to her he derisively referred to Grodzins as "our good brother."[36] It should be noted that tenBroek, too, echoing Thomas' line, maintained that Grodzins' work was not scholarly, so "the University of California has an interest in seeing that the data are handled in a scholarly way."[37]

Meanwhile, the Berkeley group was coming to realize that it might not be able to block publication of Grodzins' book. It began to develop another strategy: that of rushing into print its own book to counter Grodzins' study. The basis for this book was the much-traveled JERS manuscript, originating from Grodzins' data, and assigned for rewriting to tenBroek. The shift in strategy is revealed in Aikin's comments to tenBroek: ". . . there would be no harm in having Morton continue with his plans of publishing the materials and having you and Barney [Barnhart] do the really scholarly job here."[38]

tenBroek and Barnhart then worked at great speed to finish their book, as expressed in the former's statements to Thomas and Aikin:

> Barney and I have been forging ahead at breakneck speed on the work.[39]
>
> In any event, Barney and I have given up hoping for a solution in time to make any difference to our work. For the past two or three weeks we have gotten things underway and have been forging ahead. I have developed a scheme of operation and we have now gone far enough with it to justify tentative belief *that a very different sort of book can and should be produced* out of the Grodzins materials plus some others.[40] [emphasis added]

Prejudice, War and the Constitution was finally published in 1954. Although tenBroek, Barnhart, and Matson failed by five years to offset the immediate impact of Grodzins' book, they succeeded in publishing a sanitized and revisionist version under the imprimatur of the University of California Press.

The Basis for the Berkeley Group's Opposition to Grodzins

In its relentless efforts to suppress the Grodzins manuscript, the Berkeley group failed to reckon with the courage and integrity of the one person who stood in its way, William Terry Couch, the director of the University of Chicago Press.

To Couch, the issue of why the University of California did not want the manuscript in print revolved around more than just the excuse that Grodzins was unauthorized to use the materials or that, as a research assistant with JERS, he was not supposed to publish JERS data except through Thomas–approved publications. Couch's insight is revealed in a letter of September 30, 1948, to a University of Chicago colleague:

> The only real question in this matter is that of ownership of the materials. On that question I long alo [*sic*] arrived at certain opinions which I cannot compromise.
>
> If Mr. Grodzins' study had been made under the auspices of a research committee in the Southern United States, if his subject had been the Negro, and if he had then had the same experience that he has had with the research committee in California, I think if I were running my own publishing concern I would go ahead and publish his book, and I don't believe anybody anywhere could stop me. There are certain kinds of materials that by their nature belong to the public, and if public or philanthropic funds are spent in the collection of this material, it cannot honestly be kept indefinitely

> from the public. I would not respect any customs or agreements of any kind whatever, existing in any southern states, designed to keep information concerning southern white treatment of the Negro from the public at large. If this is a sound position to take with reference to the South it is a sound one to take with reference to the West.[41]

Couch was a transplanted Southerner—he had been director of the University of North Carolina Press prior to being recruited by Robert Maynard Hutchins for the Chicago position. From his letter cited above, it is clear that he was acutely aware of the implications of Grodzins' thesis: that California and West Coast officials and institutions had had a definite hand in the events which led to the evacuation. He saw that this consideration was key to understanding the Berkeley group's attempt to suppress the book.

The University of California steadfastly took the position that it owned the research materials used by Grodzins and therefore it had a legal and moral basis for its position.[42] In contrast, the University of Chicago disputed this notion of "property rights." Through all this interchange, others at the University of Chicago, aside from Couch, could not shake the feeling that the University of California was really interested in preventing the manuscript from coming out as a book because it was bowing to pressure from political forces in the state of California, which had had a long history of discrimination against its citizens of Japanese ancestry.[43]

Significantly, as early as the spring of 1946, Thomas learned that the subject of the wartime internment was an extremely delicate issue when publication of *The Spoilage* was opposed by some members of the Editorial Committee of the University of California Press, made up solely of Berkeley professors. The manuscript earlier had been approved for publication by the manager of UC Press. According to Thomas,

> The opposition was, in the main, motivated by the general distrust that the natural scientists [who comprised eight of the 11–member committee] have of social scientists, *but there was also a good deal of worry about the explosive nature of the subject as such in this region* [i.e., California and the West Coast].[44] [emphasis added]

When Sproul was told of this turn of events, he was outraged and had the manager take a telephone poll of the ten members in the Berkeley area. Nine voted to reverse the decision (the tenth abstained in protest against Sproul's intervention).

This incident clearly showed the sensitive nature of the evacuation issue in the post–war period and it compelled Thomas to become ever so mindful of this condition. Thus, the first 23 pages in *The Spoilage*, which deal with pre–evacuation events, although accurate, give an insipid account of what led to the tragedy—an account hardly designed to disturb the California and West Coast power structure.

Preserving the Name of Earl Warren

As for the California power structure, Governor Earl Warren, of course, was a prominent figure and one who had freely expressed his anti–Japanese sentiments in 1942 as California's attorney general. However, in the immediate post–war period, Warren—a Berkeley alumnus and close friend of UC President Sproul—had emerged as a national political figure. At the Republican National Convention of 1948, Warren was nominated by Sproul as the party's presidential candidate. Although he did not win the nomination, he did run as the vice–presidential candidate with Thomas Dewey, forming a team which was considered invincible against President Truman.[45]

Not surprisingly, therefore, in the JERS–Grodzins correspondence, Warren's name appears frequently. For example, in 1945 Aikin advised Grodzins to be as critical of Governor Culbert Olson (who was governor of California in the early 1940s) as he was of Warren,[46] while Graham defended to Thomas what Warren, Fletcher Bowron (mayor of Los Angeles during the same period) and General John DeWitt (the army officer who carried out the evacuation order) had said or done in 1942.[47] On the other hand, in their committee report to Sproul, tenBroek and Barnhart wrote thusly:

> Grodzins has made the charge and apparently has convinced some University of Chicago people of its truth, that the action of Professor Thomas and others in delaying and eventually attempting to prevent publication of his MSS [*sic*] resulted from consideration of University, state or national politics and a desire by suppressing publication of his disclosures to protect the names of certain prominent politicians such as Governor Warren, and to keep from the light of day Grodzins' severe criticisms of certain policies and persons.[48]

This passage was based in part on a letter written to tenBroek by Malcolm Sharp, University of Chicago professor of law and a member of the Board of

University Publications. Sharp had written: "I hasten to suppose—and you know how naive I am—that the question of publication is any way complicated by university, state, or national politics."[49]

What is found in *Americans Betrayed* about Warren is indeed highly critical, yet it is accurate, and Warren himself never refuted its contents. Interestingly enough, perhaps as a gesture of goodwill, the preface in this book contains the words below:

> The segment of history described is accurate . . . but it would be in error to derive a total opinion of an individual's career from examining this segment alone. Thus, to take but one example, Governor Earl Warren of California was (as attorney–general) very prominent in promoting the evacuation; I am informed that in the postwar period he has actively aided Japanese Americans in their efforts to re–establish themselves in American life.[50]

In contrast, what the authors of *Prejudice, War and the Constitution* have to say about Warren is an interesting study in self–deception. Their book goes into quite some detail over Warren's now well–known (thanks largely to Grodzins) utterances but comes to the astounding conclusion that he had no bearing whatsoever on the decision to mass evacuate Japanese–Americans. As noted in an earlier article, this is because they were so intent upon assigning blame to General DeWitt and to deflect blame from Warren, among others.[51]

Much is made by tenBroek, Barnhart, and Matson that Warren had wielded no influence over DeWitt, especially *before* February 14, 1942, the day DeWitt recommended mass evacuation to Secretary of War Stimson. They refer to a Conference of Sheriffs and District Attorneys of February 2, 1942, convened by Warren. Although they probably first learned of this conference through Grodzins' book—and passages from the proceedings are cited in their book[52]—they conveniently ignore the important citation below from his book , which includes a passage from pages 72–73 of the "Proceedings" (they cite only pages 3–7 of this same document in their book).

> On several occasions Mr. Warren spoke of his previous unpublicized work in urging the necessity of evacuation on federal authorities. (At the conference) [h]e referred to his discussions with "ranking" military and naval authorities and at one point said:
>
> *I have talked to General DeWitt*, I have talked to subordinate officers, I

have talked to the Army, I have talked to the Intelligence Unit of the Navy, I have talked to the F.B.I. I have talked to every federal agency that there is. . . . [53] [emphasis added]

The Role of Charles Aikin in Shaping *Prejudice, War and the Constitution*

Aikin's role as molder of the positions of tenBroek and his colleagues cannot be gainsaid, considering his warning to tenBroek when tenBroek assumed the task of rewriting the Grodzins manuscript: "You see, Morton may come out with the old story that he is being suppressed to preserve the name of Earl Warren."[54] Grodzins himself stated:

> I sincerely hope that President Sproul's "investigation" will conclude with his approving publication of my manuscript at Chicago. But I know of Mrs. Thomas's energy: she cannot fail, for example, to let President Sproul know that my book is very critical of Earl Warren, whom President Sproul put in nomination as a Republican candidate for the presidency.[55]

Aikin's hand is also discernible in *Prejudice, War and the Constitution* in its attempt to discredit Grodzins.[56] This is evident in the following advice he gave to tenBroek in the same letter cited above:

> One further thing, I hope you and Barney will go through the Grodzins materials and select every case of misquotation of evacuation material that Grodzins made. . . . You always need more ammunition than you feel is essential for any particular campaign [including a lawsuit].[57]

Examination of the content of *Prejudice, War and the Constitution* shows that the authors dutifully complied with Aikin's suggestion. No effort is spared to attack Grodzins and to try to discredit his research.

Furthermore, Aikin simplistically interpreted actions and events as purely ideological bents.[58] For example, he saw Grodzins' exposure of Warren and other politicians as tantamount to being a "liberal," a grave sin in Aikin's eyes. Thus, the authors of *Prejudice, War and Constitution*, taking a cue from Aikin, early on in the book (page 4) state that it was written as a refutation of the "liberals." "A number of students of liberal persuasion have attributed the principal responsibility for the evacuation to pressure groups and politicians."[59] Accordingly, they set out to disprove the "politician theory"—i.e., that certain powerful figures were responsible—and the "pressure group theory"[60]—i.e., that the evacuation was due primarily to the influence of selfishly motivated pressure groups, among them agricultural groups.[61] Not surprisingly, therefore, at the beginning stage of his research, tenBroek noted with some satisfaction in a letter to Aikin that ". . . the pressure group thesis is untenable," an opinion he expressed to Thomas as well in a letter to her on the same day.[62]

For following the "politician theory" and the "pressure group theory," Grodzins was severely castigated in the tenBroek, Barnhart, and Matson publication.[63] Nonetheless, if the "pressure group theory" had no grounding in fact and the only reason the University of California objected to seeing *Americans Betrayed* in print was because Grodzins allegedly was not authorized to use JERS materials, the following damning evidence must be confuted convincingly by supporters of the Berkeley position.

Three days before 1948 expired, by prior arrangement, Sproul telephoned Grodzins long distance. By pre–arrangement also, Malcolm Sharp was present at Grodzins' home when the call came through at 8:00 P.M. From Grodzins' confidential memorandum to Chancellor Hutchins, we learn the following:

> Before Mr. Sharp took the phone, Mr. Sproul asked (*obviously assuming Chicago publication*) that I do him the favor of omitting from the manuscript all reference to (a) the private papers from Mr. Richard Neustad's office and (b) the names of the officers of the vegetable growers' organizations when these names were attached to letters to Congressmen. He said the use of these with the names attached to them would embarrass his position. I said I would be glad to comply with this request since it would mean no substantial loss to the manuscript. He asked that his remarks be kept strictly confidential. . . .[64] [emphasis added]

A reading of *Americans Betrayed* shows that Grodzins was true to his word: reference to the private papers of Neustad's office is omitted. (Neustad was Pacific Coast Regional Director of the Social Security Board and was with the Office of Defense, Health, and Welfare Services, charged with removing enemy aliens from prohibited areas prior to President Roosevelt's order for mass evacuation). Furthermore, pseudonyms are used for officials of the vegetable growers' associations. tenBroek, Barnhart, and Matson also use pseudonyms for officials of the vegetable growers' associations; but one individual affiliated with such an association is identified by name (Austin E. Anson, managing secretary, Salinas Grower–Shipper Vegetable Association).[65]

Two days after this telephone conversation with Grodzins and Sharp, Sproul wrote to Dean Tyler of Chicago expressing regret that he could not withdraw his objection to the publication of *Americans Betrayed*.[66]

In contrast to the thick file of JERS–Chicago correspondence of 1948, the 1949 file is extremely thin, in large part because in the fall of 1948, Sproul informed relevant Berkeley faculty that all correspondence on the Grodzins matter would go through him. Thus, the 1949 file in the main consists of tenBroek stressing to his correspondents that the situation had come to a "permanent impasse."[67]

Comparing *Americans Betrayed* to *Prejudice, War and the Constitution*

The Grodzins manuscript received highly favorable reviews from outside reviewers for the University of Chicago Press by Eugene V. Rostow of Yale Law School and Sidney Gulick, former solicitor of the War Relocation Authority,[68] and came off the press in July 1949. It was nominated for a Pulitzer Prize.

Of the reviews I found in social science journals, the only one which was critical was by Forrest E. La Violette. However, this is understandable because Thomas had early on enlisted his aid in reviewing Grodzins' first revised version.[69] The other reviews, by Carr of Dartmouth (who described it as "dispassionate" and "scholarly"), Hayner of the University of Washington, and Spicer of the University of Arizona, were highly favorable.[70]

On the other hand, *Prejudice, War and the Constitution* received mixed reviews. Not surprisingly, La Violette endorsed it enthusiastically, because to him it was

> . . . a corrective, an important corrective, especially to the work of Grodzins which was completed, and apparently unchanged, four years prior to publication in 1949.[71]

Henry Graff of Columbia University's history department noted, however, the "angry and repetitious language" of the book.[72] Tempered by an objectivity gained by almost twenty years' distance, another Columbia history Ph.D., John Modell, in 1973 described it as "somewhat tendentious." He then observed:

> The highly argumentative tone of this volume, one suspects, can be explained by the fact that its authors . . . were quite concerned with refuting the argument of Morton Grodzins in *Americans Betrayed*. . . .[73]

As was shown by this writer, *Prejudice, War and the Constitution* was not even planned as a part of the JERS publication series but only came into being to counter the Grodzins book.[74] Although *Americans Betrayed* is not without its fault, the book born of expediency, *Prejudice, War and the Constitution*, falls far short of Grodzins' book in terms of honesty and integrity.

One striking example is its research methodology. In chapter 4 ("Two Theories of Responsibility"), the authors' dubious research method is most evident. This is also an important chapter in that it is their attempt to lay bare the falsity of the theory that politicians and certain economic groups were behind the evacuation, the position taken by Grodzins. Hence, if the authors can find fault with Grodzins here, they can also accomplish the following: discredit his scholarship and the "two theories" and burnish the image of certain politicians and economic groups tarnished in *Americans Betrayed*.

To achieve these ends, the authors sent out a number of letters to various persons, organizations, and agencies—i.e., all those analyzed and discussed in the Grodzins book. From the replies they received, it is clear that the purpose of the inquiries was to find out whether the recipients of the letters had indeed done what Grodzins had claimed they had done, which is to say, come out for the evacuation.

The endnotes to chapter 4 show that 25 replies were received. Of the responses, only three admitted outright that their organizations had come out for the evacuation. These three were the chambers of commerce of Pasadena and Porterville, California, and Tacoma, Washington. Another three mailed back information which was equivocal or on tangential issues. The remainder, 19, or 76 percent, categorically denied having come out for the evacuation. Typical of the answers received are the three examples below.[75]

One correspondent was "sure that the . . . [Grower–Shipper] Association [of Salinas] . . . and its members did not take any official or unofficial action in the evacuation or maneuvers to obtain the evacuation. Any action of representations credited to the Association was done by individuals as individuals."

In another reply, a judge wrote to the authors as follows: "I have no recollection of any actions taken of any of the meetings [of the Association of Oregon Counties] over the past twelve years with reference to the desirability of evacuating the Japanese residents of Oregon during the months following the attack on Pearl Harbor."

Finally, the Secretary of State of California wrote that "We do not have any record of any statement by the Secretary of State of California regarding the evacuation of the Japanese from the west coast."

These replies are not surprising. Shortly after the war, the evacuation was seen by many, including the most rabidly anti–Japanese elements, as a major blotch on American democracy, and Grodzins' searing indictment of it certainly strengthened that opinion. Therefore, what is surprising is that between 1949 and 1951, when the authors received replies as reported in their book, even three had admitted that their organizations had come out for the evacuation. What is *not* surprising is that the overwhelming majority, 76 percent, denied having come out for the evacuation. However, because the authors were so intent in disproving the "politician" and "economic–interests" theories and in discrediting Grodzins, they readily accepted at face value the contents of the letters received as proof that the theories were false and that Grodzins' work was unscholarly.

Additionally, because of the authors' *idee fixe,* they made no attempt whatsoever to do any investigative fieldwork on their own. This is clearly seen in the case of the Secretary of State of California. The authors did not even bother to drive to Sacramento, the state capital, a city within easy driving distance of Berkeley, to examine the public records or to interview relevant officials.

Furthermore, despite the crusading and self–righteous tone of *Prejudice, War and the Constitution,* the book is vulnerable inasmuch as the authors lacked the courage of their convictions. This is exemplified in the three cases cited below.

1) The authors provide this brief background sketch of how *Prejudice, War and the Constitution* came into being:

> Before leaving the University of California and the directorship of the Evacuation and Resettlement Study in 1948, Professor [Dorothy S.] Thomas, together with Professor [Charles] Aikin, prevailed upon Professor tenBroek to undertake the preparation of the present volume. The latter invited Professor Barnhart to participate in the enterprise, and subsequently Floyd Matson was asked to join as collaborator.[76]

This precis passes over in silence the attempts made by the University of California people, including tenBroek, to block publication of *Americans Betrayed* and the fact that *Prejudice, War and the Constitution* was not planned as part of the series of JERS publications. Correlatively, the most scandalous turn–of–events associated with this debacle is unreported in their book. On November 20, 1950, William Terry Couch, director of the University of Chicago Press and tenured professor, was summarily dismissed because he went ahead with publication of *Americans Betrayed,* in the face of what President Ernest C. Cowell of Chicago had told him, *viz.,* that "inter–university comity was more important than freedom of the press." His firing received major coverage in the *New York Times,* among other newspapers.[77]

2) *Prejudice, War and the Constitution* provides only a perfunctory discussion of the status of alien enemies, especially Italians, in contrast to Grodzins' strong condemnation of the invidious treatment of Japanese–Americans. He devotes a section comparing the Italians in America with the Japanese aliens and points out how pro–fascist–Italy the former were, their children's lower level of education, and their higher delinquency rates.[78] Moreover, he points out that then-San Francisco Mayor Angelo Rossi made comments critical of the Japanese in America. In contrast, tenBroek and his colleagues make no mention of Rossi.[79]

This attention to the "Italian connection" is brought to the fore because it has bearing in the following sense: JERS was financed in part by the Giannini Foundation (now known as the Bank of America–Giannini Foundation); JERS was headquartered in Room 207, Giannini Hall, on the Berkeley campus; Thomas' academic title was "Lecturer in Sociology for the Giannini Foundation"; two JERS researchers, Haruo Najima and George Kuznets, were working for the Giannini Foundation; and Professor Harry Wellman, a member of tenBroek's subcommittee who had recommended that the California Press people "get at" the Chicago Press people, was director of the Giannini Foundation. The amount contributed by this foundation to JERS is not disclosed in *The Spoilage,* but most significantly, *Prejudice, War and the Constitution does not mention at all this foundation.* In *The Spoilage,* one comes across this acknowledgment: "Generous financial support was obtained from the funds of the University of California, from its Social Science Institute, from the Giannini Foundation, and from the Columbia and Rockefeller Foundations.[80] Contrast this with the following acknowledgment in the tenBroek book:

> During this time the study received financial support of over $100,000: To assist in conducting the study the University of California contributed $29,554, the Rockefeller Foundation supplied $32,500, and the Columbia Foundation provided $30,000. In addition the Rockefeller Foundation provided $6,250 to help meet the costs of publishing the study's findings and this sum was matched by the University of California. Since 1948 the university has made available additional small amounts for microfilming and travel.[81]

3) Certainly the most egregious and inexcusable omission in a book which putatively examines all of the legal cases surrounding evacuation—this legal facet consumes a third of the book and was written by tenBroek, an expert on constitutional law—is its failure to even mention the case of Ernest Kinzo Wakayama and his wife, Toki. On August 20, 1942, while incarcerated in the Santa Anita Assembly Center, they filed a petition against the U.S. government to obtain release from the camp. The petition was *"one of the first challenges to the validity of group exclusion of the Japanese . . . ,"* according to a government document.[82] [emphasis added]

This startling omission probably had to do with the fact that Wakayama's character was thoroughly smeared—he was even labeled "effeminate" in *The Spoilage* ("Stanley Masanobu Kira" was the pseudonym given to him by JERS)—because Rosalie Hankey, a JERS researcher, despised him the most among a number of other Tule Lake inmates she despised (Hankey eventually turned Wakayama's name over to the FBI). tenBroek, Barnhart, and Matson obviously bought whole cloth what was stated about Wakayama in *The Spoilage* (Hankey was the main author of the sections of this book which dealt with Tule Lake) and in the JERS files.[83]

JERS: A Disaster of Major Proportions

JERS was a disaster of major proportions. The attempted suppression of the Grodzins book was an ignominious effort which, unfortunately, was consonant with other equally questionable features of JERS. For example, major sections of *The Spoilage* (i.e., those dealing with Tule Lake), as intimated by Marvin K. Opler, border on fraud.[84] One of the JERS researchers became an FBI informer who reported on Wakayama.[85] JERS itself was conducted as a covert operation and its subjects were kept in the dark about its goals and activities.[86]

The Salvage, while not excessive in any way, unremittingly piles fact upon fact, unrelieved by any theoretical or conceptual intermezzos, and is similar in this way to *The Spoilage*. The other JERS books planned never even made it to the rough–draft stage. *The Spoilage* and *The Salvage*, then, are the sum and substance of the lavishly funded JERS project. In today's dollars, it was a multi–million dollar undertaking, a project which, according to Grodzins, originally had envisioned eight to ten books as its products.

Prejudice, War and the Constitution, with its faulty methodology, disingenuous research, "angry and repetitious language," and "highly argumentative tone," was a product of an afterthought whose major aim—quoting Modell again—was "concerned with refuting the argument of Morton Grodzins in *Americans Betrayed.*" Not surprisingly, it was also a logical outcome of JERS, a pretentious and arrogant research project incompetently administered by Dorothy S. Thomas.[87]

Although of small comfort, Couch can take some solace in the knowledge that he was not the only victim of JERS. The project made a shambles of the lives of the Wakayamas and Kazue Matsuda (now Violet Kazue de Cristoforo) and her family. Because JERS was a clandestine project, the camp inmates where JERS did its research were also manipulated and victimized. (Clearly, too, an attempt was made by JERS to ruin Grodzins' budding career.[88])

That a world–class university was willing to sacrifice freedom of the press for the sake of "inter–university comity" speaks volumes about JERS, the status of a then-beleaguered racial minority, and the relationship of the academic world to the "real world."

Notes

This is a revised version of a paper which was given at the 30th Annual Missouri Valley History Conference, March 4, 1987, Omaha, Nebraska. This paper is dedicated to William Terry Couch. I gratefully acknowledge the generosity of Couch for having provided me with copies of University of Chicago documents and to Dr. Stephen O. Murray for the same service and his useful comments on earlier drafts of this paper. I bear sole responsibility for all statements in this publication.

1. Peter T. Suzuki, "The University of California Japanese Evacuation and Resettlement Study: A Prolegomenon," *Dialectical Anthropology* 10 (1986), 189–213; see also, "Anthropologists in the Wartime Camps for Japanese Americans: A Documentary Study," *Dialectical Anthropology* 6 (1981):23–60; "When Black Was White: Misapplied Anthroplogy in Wartime America," *Man and Life* 12 (1986), 1–12.

2. Letter, Margaret D. Uridge (head, General Library, University of California), to Jacobus tenBroek (September 29, 1948), Bancroft Library call no. 67/14c, Carton II, "JERS Staff Correspondence: tenBroek, I" (to be cited hereafter as tB–I). Unless otherwise noted, all documents cited will be letters from this collection. Some letters are originals; some are typed copies: no distinction is made between the two in the references that follow (except those which were handwritten). See also, tenBroek to Uridge, n.d. [October, 1948?], tB–I. In 1986, when I visited the Bancroft Library I had to sign a statement to gain access to documents with an asterisk after the call numbers because of their supposed confidential nature.

3. Morton Grodzins to Dorothy [Thomas] (August 9, 1945), esp. 2–3, 67/14c, Carton I, "JERS Staff Correspondence: Grodzins, Morton" (to be cited hereafter as "JERS: Grodzins").

4. Thomas to Morton [Grodzins] (August 18, 1945), *ibid.*

5. Suzuki, "JERS: A Prolegomenon," 189–90. According to Grodzins, Thomas initially planned to publish a series of eight to ten books. See Memorandum, Grodzins to [William T.] Couch and [Ralph] Tyler (October 7, 1948), 6, University of Chicago Regenstein Library, University of Chicago Press Archives. (All University of Chicago Press Archives documents will be cited hereafter as "Regenstein.") *The Ecology of Loyalty* was supposed to be authored by George Kuznets, a researcher affiliated with the Giannini Foundation. For example, see Thomas to O. Lundberg, Chief Accounting Office, University of California (February 23, 1948): "there are two monographs [in addition to *The Spoilage* and *The Salvage*] (written by others, to be edited by me), for which we have agreement 'in principle' of [financial] support," 67/14c, folder, "JERS Correspondence: Foundation Grants"; Thomas to Gordon Sproul (University of California President), n.d. [Summer 1948], 1, *ibid.*, Carton II, "JERS Staff Correspondence: tenBroek, II" (to be cited hereafter as tB–II). In Charles Aiken to Sproul (November 17,

1949), 1, tB–I, Aikin notes: "The study by Dr. Kuznets on *The Ecology of Loyalty* can be completed soon." However, in a letter from tenBroek to Thomas written less than a week later (November 23, 1949), *ibid.*, the former states: "Kuznets has done nothing on his monograph." In her reply, Thomas to tenBroek (November 30, 1949), 1–2, *ibid.*, Thomas informed him as follows: "A new application for funds will have to be submitted to the [Rockefeller] Foundation, but obviously that should not be done until we have a completed manuscript at hand. As you know, we also have a Gentlemen's Agreement for funds to be allocated to the publication of monographs—meaning yours and Kuznets'." See also footnote 26, below, on Kuznets.

6. Grodzins to Aikin (October 12, 1945), 2, "JERS: Grodzins."

7. Thomas to Morton (December 6, 1945), *ibid.* This prohibition to publish articles is also in a letter from Thomas to Grodzins (June 6, 1945), Bancroft 78/53c, Carton II, Folder "Grodzins, Morton."

8. Aikin to Grodzins (December 15, 1945), 2, "JERS: Grodzins."

9. *Ibid.*, 8; for Thomas' criticisms, see Thomas to Morton (December 6, 1945), *ibid.*

10. Howard Jay Graham to Thomas (February 28, 1948), tB–I (handwritten).

11. Thomas to Morton (July 24, 1946), "JERS: Grodzins." In this letter, Thomas wrote: "Charles Aikin and I have had several discussions about ways and means of bringing the preevacuation material into publishable form. We have decided that the only possible solution to the problem is to take your manuscript as the basis for the monograph, but to have it completely rewritten by the most competent scholar we can find here on the campus [Berkeley]. This scholar will, of course, appear as joint author with you. . . .

"We have asked Chernin to undertake the job, on a joint authorship basis. . . . There are few men whose names we should like to see on publications of the Study as much as Chernin's. His scholarship is the best, and his early association with the Study makes it more than usually appropriate to ask him to undertake the preparation of the monograph."

12. Grodzins to Thomas (July 27, 1946), *ibid.* See also Grodzins to Aikin (August 22, 1946) and Aikin to Grodzins (August 19, 1946), *ibid.* Apparently a second revised version by Grodzins was submitted to Aikin and Thomas. Aikin found it just as unsatisfactory as the first because Grodzins "drew little from [Aikin's] long series of criticisms [listed in Aikin to Grodzins (December 15, 1945), *ibid.*]," Aikin to Thomas (August 1, 1945), *ibid.* In point of fact, it is clear that Grodzins did incorporate a number of changes suggested to him by Aikins as presented in the latter's letter to Grodzins of December 15, 1945.

13. Thomas to Graham (March 2, 1948), 2, tB–I.

14. *Ibid.* On this same point, Thomas wrote: "Nishimoto's revisions came about as follows: Chernin would do nothing [about revising the Grodzins manuscript] and we

decided we would write it up. The organization [of the manuscript] was Dick's, with my advice. I was to do the rewrite job, and [some] . . . of the pages of the manuscript are mine. Both of us felt we couldn't do justice to the matter since we weren't political scientists." Thomas to tenBroek (December 10, 1945), 3, *ibid.* (handwritten).

15. See Thomas to "Pen" [Pendelton Herring of the Carnegie Corporation] (March 11, 1948), *ibid.*, on Aikin's "protégé." On Thomas' request to Graham, see Thomas to Graham (February 11 and March 2, 1948), *ibid.*

16. At the time, Graham was Ordering Librarian, Los Angeles County Law Library, Los Angeles.

17. Graham to Thomas (March 8, 1948), 1, tB–I (handwritten).

18. Thomas to "Pen" (March 11, 1948), *ibid.* Garceau was to assume a position at Bennington College in the fall of 1948; he taught there ten years.

19. *Ibid.*

20. Garceau to Thomas (April 4, 1948), *ibid.*

21. Thomas to Graham (March 2, 1948), 2, *ibid.*: "Nishimoto has done an excellent job in checking sources (Grodzins was sloppy about that sort of thing) and his manuscript can be trusted in that respect. . . . Also, he has used the 'tact and prudence' you found lacking in regard to direct quotations, etc." See also Thomas to Graham (November 2, 1948), *ibid.*, for the same tenor.

22. Aikin to Thomas (May 17, 1948), Bancroft 78/53c, "Dorothy S. Thomas Correspondence," Carton 4, Folder, "Robert G. Sproul": "I urge you to sign him [tenBroek] up if possible. . . . Don't think for a moment that I am suggesting tenBroek as a last resort." tenBroek confessed to Grodzins that he was in a "peculiar and even embarrassing position: I was engaged by the Director [Thomas] . . . to rework the data collected by you before it was known that there was any real prospect of your publication. After discovery of the Chicago Press and other publication information and after Dorothy's departure from the University [of California for the University of Pennsylvania] I was made chairman of the committee established to continue responsibility for the affairs of the Evacuation and Resettlement Study." tenBroek to Grodzins (October 1, 1948), 1, tB–I. However, from various other correspondence it seems quite clear that by the time tenBroek had agreed to assume the task of rewriting Grodzins' manuscript, he knew that there was a very distinct possibility that it would be published by some firm, if not Chicago.

23. Thomas to R. L. Johnson (August 25, 1948), 1, tB–I.

24. *Ibid.*, 1–2. See also, Thomas to Robert G. Sproul (President, University of California), n.d. [1948], 2, *ibid.*

25. Thomas to Wieck (August 28, 1948), *ibid.*; Grodzins to "Chick" [Jacobus tenBroek] (September 1, 1948), 1, *ibid.*, regarding Thomas' threat.

26. On the formation of this committee, see tenBroek to Thomas (September 9,

1948), 1, *ibid.* Wellman made it possible for George Kuznets, a researcher who was supposed to write *The Ecology of Loyalty*, the fourth volume in the JERS series, to be assigned to the Giannini Foundation while doing research on the book; see Thomas to Sproul, n.d. [Summer 1948], 1, tB–II. The Kuznets project was never completed. tenBroek reported to Thomas as follows regarding the committee's first meeting: "Wellman had a number of suggestions which, in the end[,] were adopted by the committee. One was that an attempt should be made through the California Press to get at the Chicago Press people. A second, that some attempt should be made to discover and if they exist contact faculty personnel at Chicago who might be on a committee of the press. Third, that if the Chicago Press gives an unfavorable answer we should then ask Dennes[,] now Dean of the Graduate Division [Berkeley], to write to his counterpart at Chicago rather than seeking to involve the two presidents. All agreed that a notice should be sent out to all departments of the University and all former research assistants of the study [JERS]." tenBroek to Dorothy (September 9, 1948), 1, tB–I.

On this subcommittee, see also Donald Coney (librarian, Berkeley) to R. G. Sproul (October 4, 1948), 1–2, *ibid.*, in which he advises the president of the university to make the subcommittee into an administrative committee, "making it responsible for continuing all affairs of the Study, for advising you or acting for you in the Grodzins' [*sic*] problem, and for controlling access to the Study materials. . . ." He also advances the recommendation that Sproul write to Dean R. Tyler of Chicago to inform the latter of the new lines of communication. "The President [Sproul] wishes all future correspondence on the Grodzins affair with the University of Chicago officers to be directed through his office . . ." Memorandum, Coney to Members of the Library Sub–Committee on the Evacuation and Resettlement Study (October 20, [1948]), *ibid.* (handwritten).

27. Thomas to Jacobus (September 25 [1948]), *ibid.* (handwritten).

28. On Thomas' recommendations to tenBroek to collect testimony from Mrs. Mary Wilson, former JERS secretary, who had helped type Grodzins' dissertation, see Thomas to Jacobus (December 10, 1948), 2, *ibid.* (handwritten) and December 12, 1948, 1, *ibid.* (handwritten).

29. tenBroek and Barnhart, "Report on the Grodzins' [*sic*] Affair" (November 3, 1948), 8, *ibid.*

30. Couch to tenBroek (September 9, 17, and 29, 1948), *ibid.*

31. Thomas to Jacobus (September 25, [1948]), *ibid.* (handwritten).

32. Couch to tenBroek (September 29, 1948), 1, *ibid.*

33. tenBroek to Dorothy (October 7, 1948), *ibid.*

34. tenBroek to Dorothy (October 15, 1948), *ibid.*; and tenBroek to Aikin (October 15, 1948), 2, *ibid.*

35. tenBroek to Dorothy (November 6, 1948), 1, tB–II.

36. tenBroek to Dorothy (September 9, 1948), tB–I.

37. tenBroek to Morton (October 1, 1948), 1, *ibid.*

38. Aikin to Chick (October 11, 1948), 1, tB–II.

39. tenBroek to Dorothy (November 6, 1948), 1., *ibid.*

40. tenBroek to Chuck (November 6, 1948), 1, *ibid.* That JERS was producing a volume which had not been in the proposal to the Rockefeller Foundation, which was funding its publications, was not a minor concern to tenBroek and Barnhart. This is evident in the passages below in two tenBroek letters, one to Thomas and the other to Aikin, both written October 15, 1948 (tB–I). He wrote to Thomas: "But there is one angle of the problem on which we would like to get some reassurances. It has to do with the publication subsidy. Your gentleman's [*sic*] agreement with Rockefeller may or may not have been specific as to the political aspects volume [i.e., what was to be *Prejudice, War and the Constitution*] of the whole study [JERS], but in any event it was made long before there was any prospect of two more or less duplicatory volumes [i.e., tenBroek's and Grodzins'] on the same subject." And he asked: "What is your feeling about this matter? Could you now reapproach Rockefeller to find out whether Grodzins' prior publication through the University of Chicago Press would affect their willingness to subsidize the publication of Barney's [Barnhart's] and my work by the University of California Press?" He wrote to Aikin: "After talking with Farquhar [of the University of California Press], it seems to us quite clear that the press will only publish a second volume if a subsidy is forthcoming. Dorothy [Thomas] says that she has a 'gentleman's [*sic*] agreement' with Rockefeller to supply the subsidy. However, the gentleman's [*sic*] agreement probably doesn't specifically apply to a volume on the political aspects and certainly was made long before the possibility of two more or less duplicatory studies on those aspects."

41. Couch to "Sam" [last name unknown] (September 30, 1948), tB–I; on the recruitment of Couch, see Hutchins to Couch (July 18, 1945), "Regenstein."

42. tenBroek to Morton (October 1, 1948), 1, tB–I; Coney to Sproul (October 4, 1948), 2, *ibid.*

43. Malcolm Sharp (law professor and member, University of Chicago Press Board of University Publications) to Chick (October 29, 1948), 1–2, tB–II. For an analysis of this letter by Sharp, see tenBroek, "Analysis of Professor Sharp's Letter of October 29, 1948," *ibid.* For a lengthy letter (eight, single-spaced, typed pages)—equivalent to a legal brief with numerous citations to legal cases—see Sharp to Chick (November 27, 1948), *ibid.* See also, tenBroek to Morton (December 1, 1948), 1, *ibid.*, in which tenBroek describes California's legal position, noting that, "on the legal side, Malcolm [Sharp] and Ed[ward] Levi are, of course, wrong." (Levi, also a Chicago law professor, was later named U.S. Attorney General by President Ford.)

44. Thomas to Joseph H. Willits of Rockefeller Foundation (June 11, 1946), 1,

Bancroft 67/14c, Folder, "JERS Correspondence: Foundation Grants." The editor of the University of California Press thereafter suggested to Thomas to sharply revise certain aspects of the manuscript dealing with the pre–evacuation events, which obviously she did. David R. Brower to Thomas (June 17, 1946), tB–I.

45. On the nomination and the Warren–Sproul friendship, see Agnes R. Robb, "Robert Gordon Sproul and the University of California," Oral History Project (Berkeley: University of California, 1976), 78–81.

46. Aikin to Morton (December 15, 1945), 8, "JERS: Grodzins." On this point, Aikin was quite correct.

47. Graham to Thomas (March 26, 1948), 1, tB–I.

48. tenBroek and Barnhart, "Report on the Grodzins' [*sic*] Affair" (November 3, 1948), 6, *ibid.*

49. Sharp to Chick (October 29, 1948), 2, tB–II. tenBroek wasted no time in attempting to disabuse the Chicago group of this notion, as seen in his prompt reply to Sharp: "Incidentally, as to the motivation of the people who have handled the case out here, don't believe the fairy tale that there have been considerations of university, state and national politics or a desire to suppress the conclusions expressed. In varying degrees, practically everybody who has had a hand in the affair out here is sympathetic to the major conclusions stated in the Grodzins manuscript. The University might still have a reasonable interest in maintaining the integrity of its research project and of reasonable standards of scholarship in the statement of its results." tenBroek to Malcolm (November 2, 1948), 1, *ibid.* See also tenBroek, "Analysis of Professor Sharp's Letter of October 29, 1948" (November 4, 1948), *ibid.*: "Sharp and apparently everybody else at Chicago has accepted Grodzins' fairy tale about the motivation of the University of California (Cf. reference to '. . . university, state, or national politics.')"

50. Grodzins, *Americans Betrayed*, xi.

51. Suzuki, "JERS: A Prolegomenon," 199; see also, tenBroek *et al.*, *Prejudice*, 200–01 (1968 edition). On Warren, see 83–84, 93, 95, 102, 138, 203, 267–68.

52. tenBroek *et al.*, *Prejudice*, 83–84.

53. Grodzins, *Americans Betrayed*, 95. According to one federal officer who was at the conference, "In his opening remarks Mr. Warren cautioned against hysteria *but then proceeded to outline the [Japanese–American] situation in such a fashion as to encourage hysterical thinking . . .*" [emphasis added]. Roger Daniels, *The Decision to Relocate the Japanese Americans* (Philadelphia: Lippencott, 1975), 40; original insertion in brackets; original ellipses. tenBroek *et al.*, *Prejudice*, 84, attempt to exonerate Warren's extreme statements at this conference by noting the following statement in parentheses: "(It should be emphasized, however, that the public report of the conference called only for removal of enemy aliens—*not*—of all Japanese Americans." [emphasis in original]

54. Aikin to Chick (October 11, 1948), 1–2, tB–I.

55. Grodzins, Memorandum to Couch and Tyler (October 7, 1948), 19, "Regenstein."

56. Cf. Suzuki, "JERS: A Prolegomenon," 207.

57. Aikin to Chick (October 11, 1948), 1, tB–I. On a possible lawsuit, see Ino. U. Calkins, Jr. (attorney for the Regents of the University of California) to tenBroek (November 10, 1948), *ibid.*: ". . . I felt it proper to advise Dr. Sproul that we could likely maintain an action at law or in equity with some hope of success."

58. Aikin to Morton (December 15, 1948), 8, "JERS: Grodzins"; Aikin to Chick (October 11, 1948), 1, *ibid.* In both citations, Aikin criticizes "liberals."

59. Suzuki, "JERS: A Prolegomenon," 198. For an analysis of the simplistic notion of seeing the evacuation in terms of a conservative or liberal ideology, see 200 ff.

60. tenBroek *et al.*, *Prejudice*, 4.

61. *Ibid.*, 185; for agricultural groups, see 189–92.

62. tenBroek to Chuck (November 6, 1948), 1, tB–II; tenBroek to Dorothy (November 6, 1948), 1–2, *ibid.*

63. See Suzuki, "JERS: A Prolegomenon," 198–99.

64. Grodzins, "Memorandum to Chancellor [Robert Maynard] Hutchins, "Telephone Conversation with Robert Gordon Sproul, December 28, 1948, 8:45 P.M., Confidential, With Note by Malcolm Sharp Confirming the Conversation" (December 28, 1948), "Regenstein." Several sentences have been omitted. In this same conversation, "Mr. Sproul told me that, despite this formal position he was forced to take, he wanted to reaffirm the statement he had previously made to me in Chicago: that he hoped the University of Chicago would be able to publish the manuscript. He said he wanted to let me know, informally, that he expected Chicago would publish. I asked him if he would put this in an informal note to me. He responded that his position would not let him commit his view in writing. I asked if he were able to give his statement verbally to Mr. Sharp. Mr. Sproul said he would be glad to do this, and Mr. Sharp's note on his conversation with Mr. Sproul is given below."

65. tenBroek *et al.*, *Prejudice*, 387 n17; see also, 190 and 264 for the statement he made.

66. Sproul to Ralph W. Tyler (December 30, 1948), tB–II.

67. tenBroek to Dorothy (January 14, 1949), *ibid.*; tenBroek to Edward W. Strong (chairman of the Library Committee) (February 3, 1949), *ibid.*; tenBroek to Sproul (February 3, 1949), *ibid.*

68. Anonymous reviews of Grodzins' manuscript by outside reviewers (hectographed) are also deposited at Bancroft, "JERS: Grodzins." Others who were favorably impressed with the MS were: Hans Morgenthau, professor of political science, Chicago; Robert Redfield; Dillon S. Myer, former director of the War Relocation Authority; and Norman Thomas, Socialist. All had written to the University of

Chicago Press; their testimonials are in "Regenstein."

69. La Violette, review of *Americans Betrayed*, *Pacific Affairs* 22 (1949), 442. On La Violette's role, see Thomas to Grodzins (July 24, 1946), "JERS: Grodzins."

70. Robert K. Carr, review of *Americans Betrayed*, *American Political Science Review* 43 (1949), 1042–043; Norman S. Hayner, review of *Americans Betrayed*, *Annals of the American Academy of Political and Social Sciences* 267 (1950), 241–42; Edward H. Spicer, review of *Americans Betrayed*, *American Journal of Sociology* 55 (1950), 603–04.

71. La Violette, review of *Prejudice, War and the Constitution*, *American Sociological Review* 20 (1955), 490.

72. Henry Graff, review of *Prejudice, War and the Constitution*, *American Historical Review* 60 (1955), 925.

73. Suzuki, "JERS: A Prolegomenon," 199.

74. *Ibid.*, 189–90, 207.

75. The 25 letters are cited in the following in tenBroek *et al.*, *Prejudice*, 372 n22; 373–74 n28; 374 n41; 374–75 n44; 375 n46, n47, n49; 376 n50, n57; 377 n67; 378 n73, n75; 379 n83, n84, n85; 380 n95, n101, n102; 381 n102, n106. On the three who admitted espousing the evacuation, see 375 n46, n47; 378 n75. On the Grower–Shipper Association reply, see 374 n28 (original ellipses). On the judge's reply, see 380 n101. On the California secretary of state's response, see 379 n83.

76. *Ibid.*, x.

77. Suzuki, "JERS: A Prolegomenon," 198–99, citing *The New York Times*, "Ousted Chicago Man says Book Cost Job" (December 15, 1950), 27, col. 4. The phrase "inter–university comity" was used against Couch when he was fired, for which, see The Council of the University of Chicago Senate (March 7, 1951), "Regenstein." This phrase was first coined by tenBroek and Barnhart in their report of November 3, 1948, to Sproul (see note 29) and was picked up by Chicago administrators. On Couch's status as tenured professor, and for other aspects of this case, see Weldon B. Brown, Napier Wilt, and Paul C. Hodges, "Summary Report of the Subcommittee on the Couch Dismissal, Exhibit A" (n.d.), "Regenstein." On the attempted suppression, see also "Extract from Minutes of the Board of University Publications, October 27, 1948: Reports, Morton Grodzins' *Americans Betrayed* Approved for Publication July 14, 1948," by Elizabeth T. Pattullo for the Secretary of the Faculties (November 8, 1948), "Regenstein"; "Extract from Minutes of the Board of University Publications, November 29, 1948: Morton Grodzins' *Americans Betrayed*," by F. Joseph Mullin, secretary of Faculties (n.d.), "Regenstein." See also, Joseph Fichter, *One–Man Research: Reminiscences of a Catholic Sociologist* (New York: John Wiley, 1973), 54, on the attempted suppression (I thank David Southern for this reference). On Couch as director of the University of North Carolina Press, see David Southern, *Gunnar Myrdal and Black–White Relations* (Baton Rouge: LSU Press, 1987), chapter 4. Even while at North

Carolina, Couch had been a critic of the treatment of the Negro in the South, and this indignation over racism—and what he perceived to be the University of California's position on the Japanese–American—accounts for his letter of September 30, 1948, to a University of Chicago colleague, cited in Note 41 *supra.* On the publication of *Americans Betrayed* as the proximate cause of Couch's dismissal, see Couch to Council of the University of Chicago Senate (March 7, 1951), "Regenstein." See also Couch, "A Case History in Book Publishing," *Scene* 3:1 (1951), 17–19; Frank Hughes, "How to Fire a Professor," *The Freeman* (December 3, 1951), 145–48.

78. Grodzins, *Americans Betrayed*, 172–73. Grodzins in his index (see page 427) has this heading as one of the entries: "Alien enemy groups other than Japanese compared with resident Japanese, 144, 172–73, 322," showing his concern over the invidious treatment received by the Japanese. Cf. tenBroek *et al., Prejudice,* 399, under "Alien enemies."

79. Grodzins, *Americans Betrayed*, 110, on Rossi. Cf. Suzuki, "JERS: A Prolegomenon," 213 n128 on Rossi and Italians.

80. Dorothy S. Thomas and Richard S. Nishimoto, *The Spoilage* (Berkeley: University of California Press, 1946), xiv. On the Giannini Foundation, see also Dorothy S. Thomas, *The Salvage* (Berkeley: University of California, 1952), vii.

81. tenBroek *et al., Prejudice,* ix. Cf. Suzuki, "JERS: A Prolegomenon," 207, 213 n128, on foundations and research grants; see also, "Philanthropy, Patronage, Politics," *Daedalus* 116:1 (Winter 1987), entire issue, in addition to the literature I have cited. According to information in the letters from Thomas to Sproul (July 1, 1942) and Thomas to Wellman (August 5, 1942), Bancroft 67/14c, Folder, "JERS Correspondence: Foundation Grants," the Giannini Foundation contributed $5,900 to JERS; but Thomas in "Suggested Letter [to Willits of the Rockefeller Foundation]," n.d., attached to July 1, 1942, letter to Sproul, was going to request $10,000 per annum from the Giannini Foundation.

82. Suzuki, "JERS: A Prolegomenon," 210 n47, citing Western Defense Command.

83. *Ibid.,* 194–97, on Wakayama and Hankey (Wax); also, Cf. Suzuki, "Anthropologists in the Wartime Camps," on these two individuals. Even months after the war had ended, Hankey wrote a letter to Thomas which contained derogatory remarks about "our friend Kinzo Wakayama" and "dear Kinzo," as reported in Hankey to Thomas (March 3, 1946), 67/14c, "JERS Staff Correspondence: Thomas, Dorothy Swaine and Staff," Carton 2, #2. The incident covered in the letter is related in Rosalie H. Wax, *Doing Fieldwork* (Chicago: University of Chicago Press, 1971, paperback edition), 169.

84. Suzuki, "JERS: A Prolegonemon," 205–06.

85. On Hankey's ruinous role in the lives of another Tule Lake family, see Violet Kazue de Cristoforo, "A Victim of the Japanese Evacuation and Resettlement Study

(JERS)," Salinas, California, 1987, unpublished manuscript. On the dubious research methods used by Richard Nishimoto, see the article by the Hirabayashis in this volume.

86. This point was brought out by a former JERS researcher on the panel, "Part II; Reassessment of the Japanese Evacuation and Resettlement Study (JERS)," held on September 20, 1987, at the JERS conference in Berkeley, California.

87. *Prejudice, War and the Constitution* was the recipient of the Woodrow Wilson Prize in Political Science for the best book in 1954. However, obviously the details regarding how the book came into being and other aspects of the book as discussed in this article were not known at that time. As for Thomas' ineptness, in addition to what has been brought out in this paper and in my previous publications, a most telling case is how she dealt with Rosalie Hankey. In 1944, while Hankey was at Gila Relocation Center, Arizona, Thomas wrote these revealing passages to her (Thomas to Hankey (n.d.) [1944], 1–2, Bancroft 78/53c, Carton 2, Folder, "Rosalie Hankey"): "You are, it seems to me, over–identifying yourself as part of the 'core of the Japanese community.' You are showing an excessive 'Einfühlung' [empathy] in connection with the Issei; an excessive degree of skepticism about the ability of any Nisei or Caucasian to achieve any degree of 'Einsicht' [insight]. Now, Rosalie, you can never become a Japanese or instead of 'never,' let us say at least not in time to do the study [JERS] any good." And Thomas added: "If you lose your naturalness and become too 'devious,' you are sure to be discovered. You can, however, carry this too far even with the general population, many of whom will be very quick to detect a 'phony assimilation'."

While still at Gila, Thomas reported thusly on Hankey in Thomas to Nishimoto (August 11, 1944), 2, Bancroft 67/14c W1.25): "I had lunch with Mr. [Robert B.] Cozzens [West Coast Regional Director, War Relocation Authority] yesterday, and he told me that [Leroy] Bennett [Director, Gila Relocation Center] and others at Gila had been complaining bitterly about her [Hankey]. They claim that she is 'against all government' and has been inciting the evacuees to anarchy. I was pretty disgusted, but also a little bit worried."

Despite this kind of knowledge about Hankey's undisciplined behavior as a researcher, Thomas nonetheless dispatched Hankey permanently to Tule Lake, where events were much more volatile and political, with *disastrous* consequences for JERS and the inmates of Tule Lake. (Richard Drinnon, *Keeper of Concentration Camps* (Berkeley: University of California Press, 1987), 283, cites part of the Thomas–Nishimoto letter but unfortunately fails to realize the significance of the information received by Thomas.)

88. Grodzins fared better than the others mentioned. To mute further criticisms—after Couch was dismissed—including criticisms from the American Association of University Professors (which was a powerful organization on matters of

academic freedom in those days), the University of Chicago appointed Grodzins as Couch's successor to the University of Chicago Press, despite the fact that his only previous experience in book publishing had been with student publications while at the University of Louisville. Then, two years later, at age 36, he was appointed dean of the Division of Social Sciences, one of the most prestigious positions at a university whose history and tradition in the social sciences had been unparalleled among American institutions of higher learning. On Grodzins' appointments, see C. Herman Pritchett, "In Memoriam [Morton Grodzins]," *American Political Science Review* 58 (1964), 504; on the AAUP's criticisms, see "Couch Dismissal Scored," *New York Times* (November 30, 1950), 41, col. 3; Cf. Suzuki, "JERS: A Prolegomenon," 211 n59.

PART II

Resentment, Distrust, and Insecurity at Tule Lake

S. FRANK MIYAMOTO

This is a study of attitudes which were observed among the evacuees at the Tule Lake Relocation Center in 1942 before it became a segregation center.[1] The study focuses on resentment, distrust, and insecurity because these were among the most widely observed attitudes in this period and had the greatest influence on behavior. Resentment was virtually universal among evacuees, as might be imagined, but the degree of distrust directed at white people and American society and the amount of insecurity felt about the circumstances varied a good deal. One objective of this paper is to show how resentment in combination with distrust and insecurity became a source of protest behavior.

Relationship of Attitudes to Collective Behavior

It seems obvious that in order to understand the evacuees, it is important to understand their attitudes, yet there is today surprisingly little to be found in the research literature bearing on these attitudes. A brief technical discussion of attitudes is needed to explain the paucity of attitude studies. An *attitude*, as the term is used by social psychologists, may be defined as: a tendency of action toward a class of objects. Thus, a racial attitude would be an attitude ranging from prejudice against to liking for some racial group; a political attitude might be an attitude of conservatism, liberalism, or radicalism; and an attitude toward abortion might be an attitude of support for or opposition to abortion. Because an attitude is a tendency that exists before an action occurs, a person's attitude, if accurately determined, is considered an important means of predicting how he will behave, and of understanding why he behaves as he does.

There are several reasons why studies of evacuee attitudes were not undertaken. Attitude studies are commonly done with the use of questionnaires or personal interviews, but for understandable reasons evacuees resisted speaking openly about their attitudes to strangers, and the resistance became especially strong as a fear of the *inu* (informers) spread in the centers. Moreover, to ensure that the attitudes reported were representative, it would have been necessary to carry out an appropriate sampling of the respondents, but the use of a sampling procedure was almost certain to arouse hostility and risked the danger of foreclosing all research. For these reasons, formal attitude studies were never attempted in our research. Instead, indirect means were employed to get at attitudes as circumstances permitted. Nevertheless, the lack of attitude studies was a serious defect, for in their absence there was little basis for judging the "inner feelings" of the residents.

To circumvent the difficulty, I later devised a method of inferring attitudes from the evacuees' collective behavior. A brief discussion of the logic of this method is needed. *Collective behavior* is a technical term applied to the behavior of such collectivities as crowds, panics, riots, rock festivals, religious cults, and revolutions. It refers to the concurrent action of large numbers of people who are acting toward a common goal, but whose actions are not regulated by institutional or conventional controls.[2] Thus, collective behavior is the opposite of *institutional behavior*. For example, a large number of people attending a regular Sunday church service, whose behavior is largely regulated by church customs, would be involved in institutional behavior; but if a fire broke out in the church and the assemblage tried in a panic to escape the fire, the latter action, which is no longer controlled by standard church conduct, would be called collective behavior. Because the WRA centers were all newly created communities where institutional controls were weak, the circumstances were favorable for the occurrence of collective behavior.

But how can the study of collective behavior reveal anything regarding the attitudes of a group? There is substantial evidence that collective behavior generally occurs only where a favorable attitude toward such behavior already exists.[3] For example, lynchings of black people occurred where strong prejudices against Blacks pre-existed.[4] Similarly, rumors are most easily generated in circumstances where people are already disposed to believe them.[5] We shall state it as a principle, therefore, that if some form of collective behavior occurs, a predisposing attitude must have existed. And if this principle is accepted, it then follows that wherever a case of collective behavior is observed, it should be possible to infer the predisposing attitude.

Given the unstable conditions of life at Tule Lake in 1942, instances of collective behavior abounded. They occurred in many different forms, but here special attention will be given to one particular type which we call *collective preoccupations.*[6] The term *preoccupation* refers to a mental state of being engrossed in a subject. A collective preoccupation, therefore, refers to a tendency of a large number of people to be absorbed in the same subject matter. Because people have a tendency to talk about any collective preoccupation, persistent discussion of the subject tends to be one of its characteristics. For research purposes, this is a great advantage, for the preoccupation then is identifiable and directly observable.

In summary, the method of inferring attitudes from collective behavior presupposes that wherever collective behavior occurs, a predisposing attitude or set of attitudes was present. Methodologically, this use of collective behavior has two great advantages. First, because a large number of people is observed who are engaged in very similar behavior, the question of sampling biases tends to be minimized. Second, because collective behavior necessarily involves significant and directly observable behavior of many persons, it also minimizes the problem, often encountered in attitude studies, of identifying the attitude and validating it.

The Anti–JACL Sentiment

We turn now to a study of some of the most prevalent attitudes observed at Tule Lake. Perhaps it goes without saying that the most general attitude of the evacuees was one of indignation, resentment, and embitterment at being singled out for exclusion and removal. The resentment was universal because every evacuee, whether young or old, generally lost things of significant value as a result of the forced uprooting.

Resentment was most commonly directed toward General John L. DeWitt, the *keto* (derogatory for "Whites"), the Wartime Civil Control Administration (WCCA), and other persons and agencies connected with the evacuation. But these were distant or abstract objects against whom no direct action could be taken. The bitterest resentment therefore came to be redirected toward the Japanese American Citizens League (JACL). There were in that period interminable discussions of why and how the evacuation had come about, and one of the most persistent *collective preoccupations* focused on how the JACL had contributed to its occurrence. An analysis of this anti-JACL sentiment will aid in a basic understanding of the evacuees' reactions to the evacuation.[7]

For more than a decade before the war, the JACL had been the Nisei's leading organization, and following the decline of Issei authority after Pearl Harbor, it assumed primary organizational leadership in the Japanese-American communities. The JACL's problems during the wartime period began with its leaders' appearance before the Tolan Congressional Committee Hearings in February 1942. As presumptive spokesmen for the Japanese minority communities, the JACL leaders opposed the evacuation and argued against it; but when asked if Japanese–Americans would show their loyalty by cooperating with an evacuation if it were deemed a "military necessity," the leaders pledged their readiness to "cooperate."[8] Saburo Kido, then president of the JACL, later issued a widely publicized statement to the press that declared: ". . . we are going into exile as our duty to our country because the President and military commander of this area have deemed it a necessity. We are gladly cooperating because this is one way of showing. . .our loyalty."[9]

At the assembly and relocation centers, critical comments regarding the JACL's role in the evacuation snowballed. The negative reactions varied between simple criticism of the JACL position to active hostility toward its leaders. There was, for example, the general criticism that, although no Japanese–American group perhaps could have prevented the evacuation, it was hypocritical for JACL leaders to say that Japanese–Americans would cooperate willingly and naive to believe the evacuation was required because of military necessity.[10] The harsher critics focused on the JACL leaders' alleged collaborationist role and their presumed cooperation with the Army for reasons of self-protection and personal gain.[11]

Other JACL actions exacerbated the hostility toward the organization. Perhaps the most important was the JACL's assumption at the assembly centers of administrative and leadership roles when called on to do so by the WCCA, the civilian branch of the Army which administered the centers. Because of the many inherent deficiencies in the assembly centers, those administering or helping to administer the centers, especially JACL leaders, were bound to become targets of criticism from the resident population.

Measured against the actual damage which JACL leaders may have inflicted on their fellow evacuees, however, the reaction against them seemed disproportionately hostile. There probably existed some real bases for the evacuees' hostility toward the JACL. Charges were heard that JACL leaders turned in to U.S. intelligence services the names of Issei and Kibei who were considered to be security risks, which I understand did in fact occur. But in 1942 I knew of no one at Tule Lake with hard evidence of JACL's complicity in such activity. Furthermore, much of the collective preoccupation I refer to above revolved around criticisms of JACL's failure to protest the evacuation more effectively and vigorously. But even in 1942 it appeared doubtful that JACL statements could have materially affected the ultimate decision regarding evacuation.

The other frequent topic of discussion concerned alleged instances of JACL graft and corruption for personal gain at the assembly centers, but there was never any evidence of JACL misconduct in this regard. Generally speaking, collective behavior is initially provoked by some real grounds for reaction, but often the degree of reaction is out of proportion to the conditions which first instigated a reaction. If the hostility against the JACL was indeed disproportionate, there are reasons to suspect that the organization's behavior inflamed an underlying disposition of the evacuees that was ready to be ignited.

The damage the JACL inflicted on the evacuees was more symbolic than objectively real, but it was the symbolic effect which made it especially painful. In brief, the JACL's policy and conduct provoked resentment because they violated the self-image which evacuees wanted to project of themselves. Resentment, too, it should be noted, is fundamentally a symbolic phenomenon. In a two-party relationship, resentment occurs when the second party treats the first as being less desirable, less worthy, and due fewer rights than the first party feels entitled to. That is, the source of resentment is a discrepancy between two conceptions of one's self: the first, a person's own self-conception, and the second, his conception of how another person apparently sees him, erroneously and unfairly. For example, we resent prejudice against us because the prejudiced person obviously views us as being less worthy than we believe ourselves to be. It goes without saying that evacuees resented the evacuation because they found their rights being disregarded, and because they were subjected to humiliation and indignities—in short, because their selves were assaulted.

When the self is thus assaulted, the tendency of any human, except an utter degenerate, is to protect the self, to fight back. For the evacuees, unfortunately, the evacuation and incarceration left them with an acute problem of self-respect. They had failed to resist the evacuation, yet as a matter of self–respect they keenly felt the need to have stood up to the white man.

The JACL's policy of cooperation with the evacuation aggravated the evacuees' problem of self-conception in two ways. First, although the evacuees felt they had been helpless to oppose the federal action individually, they felt the JACL, as the leading Nisei organization, should have resisted much more aggressively than it did. Worst of all, the JACL, with which the Japanese-American minority necessarily identified, adopted what was felt to be a most unseemly submissive posture, and thereby depicted the group in a most undesirable image. Second, the JACL's continued policy of cooperation with the Army, the WCCA, and the WRA throughout the evacuation process sustained an image of submissiveness which the evacuees wanted to shake off. In brief, the evacuees felt an intense resentment of the evacuation, but because the real objects of their resentment, such as General DeWitt and white people as a whole, were relatively inaccessible, the resentment was redirected against the JACL.

Distrust of White People and Insecurity

Distrust of white people was a second major attitudinal factor that significantly influenced evacuees at Tule Lake. The degree of distrust varied a good deal among the evacuees, but that it was a substantial influence on behavior was later demonstrated by the relatively high percentage of Tule Lake people who chose "No–No" responses at the time of the "loyalty" registration. The distrust of white people was reflected in two very persistent preoccupations of the Tule Lake residents.

The first was a recurrent rumor (I call it "The Arkansas Traveler Rumor") which alleged that Tule Lake was only a temporary center for the evacuees, and that its residents would soon be moved to Arkansas.[13] The Project Director repeatedly denied the rumor, both orally and in print,[14] and there was never any evidence supporting the story. Still, the rumor kept recurring month after month.

The reasons given to justify the rumor changed with shifting events. Probably the initial reason was the fact that Tule Lake, being located in California, was within the military zone from which all persons of Japanese ancestry were excluded. Moreover, Manzanar, the only other WRA center in California, was at the outset called a "reception center," connoting a staging area for evacuees rather than a permanent WRA center. And reports that new centers were under construction in Jerome and Rohwer, Arkansas, quickly brought Arkansas into focus as the presumed destination for the Tuleans.

Some residents found a more elaborate basis for the rumor in news stories of Japanese military successes in the Pacific in the summer of 1942. The Japanese Army and Navy, they claimed, were gaining overwhelming dominance in the

Pacific, the American forces were suffering enormous casualties, and Tule Lake therefore was being prepared as a base hospital for the large number of wounded American sailors and soldiers who were already arriving at West Coast ports. Support for this idea was found one day in a story that spread rapidly through the encampment alleging the arrival of freight cars full of crutches at the center railway siding. The "crutches story" was soon dispelled by the revelation that the presumed crutches were, in fact, wooden laundry racks for evacuee households, but other stories quickly replaced it to sustain the rumor.

The listing of events which again and again provoked this particular rumor does not explain why it persisted. There must have been an underlying, unresolved tension that caused its recurrence. To begin with, it should be noted that not everyone believed the rumor. Compared to the Issei, more Nisei were disbelievers, and compared to the less educated from rural areas, the sophisticated were likewise disbelievers.

It was probably not accidental that the rumor of a further transfer of Tule Lake residents focused on Arkansas as the presumed destination. Among Tuleans, those from California had originated from rural communities located in the Sacramento Valley, which was no more than 200 miles from Tule Lake. To such California Japanese, Arkansas was a barren and unknown wilderness that must have connoted a semi-tropical Siberia.

The Arkansas Traveler Rumor revealed something deeply embedded in the thinking of many evacuees, namely, an abiding distrust of white people and a persistent insecurity about the future. The believers assumed, for example, that whites were basically hostile toward Japanese-Americans and only awaited a suitable opportunity to rid themselves of the group. They assumed that as the war went on, conditions would get progressively worse for the evacuees, and that every further move imposed on them would lead only to a worsening of their condition. The safest course, therefore, was to resist every effort of the government to force them out and to stay as long as possible at Tule Lake. The fact that Tule Lake was located in California no doubt added greatly to the feeling that the people should resist any further forced migration.

By the fall of 1942, the WRA began emphasizing the unhealthy effects of detention on the evacuees and the desirability, therefore, of relocating them into non-exclusion zones as rapidly as possible.[15] With the first mention of this proposed policy, the Arkansas Traveler Rumor again surfaced, and a stubborn resistance to the relocation program developed. A few months later when the "loyalty" registration was started, a related "requirement" that evacuees should simultaneously apply for leave clearance was added. Many residents saw this as another WRA attempt to force them out of Tule Lake and California. It is difficult to judge how much the leave clearance question ultimately contributed to the high rate of negative responses to the "loyalty" questions at Tule Lake, but it unquestionably was an important part of the registration debate.

Another widespread collective preoccupation, the persistent and heated discussions about the canteens, casts further light on the evacuees' distrust of white people.[16] Tule Lake had five general merchandise stores, called canteens, distributed at suitable locations around the encampment. Each was set up to provide food, clothing, and other household necessities which might be required by the evacuees. The canteens were initially established in the community enterprises division of the WRA with a white director, but the understanding was that in due course he would work himself out of his job and that control of the stores would be transferred to the evacuees under a consumer cooperative system with its own board of directors. Although most evacuees probably felt it necessary to have a general merchandise store in the center, there was also a very vocal group that strenuously objected to the canteens.

The antagonism was evident in reactions observed at a costly fire at the Ward 3 canteen in the summer of 1942. Some among the large crowd of onlookers were overheard expressing pleasure that their ward was now rid of the canteen, and others conjectured as to whether someone might have set the fire deliberately.[17] The antagonism was even more clearly evident in an election held on a proposal, developed under canteen sponsorship, to finance a project movie theater at an estimated total cost of $8,400, the cost to be amortized by admission charges of 15 cents for adults and 5 cents for children. Of almost 9,000 residents 16–years of age and older who voted on the referendum, 72 percent rejected the proposal.[18] The voting outcome seems surprising, for there were many, especially among the young people, who hungered for entertainment that would relieve the monotony of the center; but as one community leader said, the 15 cents admission charge represented one–third of an evacuee's daily earning, an amount they could ill afford.

There were at least two reasons for the hostility. First, the canteens were seen as a temptation to the residents, especially the young people and children, to spend without regard for the grave financial problems evacuees would have to face later. Second, many evacuees felt that since the government had deprived them of their means of livelihood, it therefore had the responsibility of providing evacuees with everything they needed. The evacuees' purchases at the canteens were seen as relieving the government of this responsibility.

There was even a concern that the government did not intend to maintain subsistence support for the evacuees. A rumor spread that the food stored in the center warehouses was diminishing rapidly, and that food shortages at the messhalls would develop soon. Some residents thereupon began saving left-over rice from the messhall tables, drying it, and caching it along with canned foods purchased at the canteen. Such purchases contradicted the anti–canteen sentiment, but the fear that the government was, in fact, about to cut the evacuees' supplies proved the more dominant concern.

There were, of course, real grounds for concern about economic security in the future, and likewise for food shortages inasmuch as shortages of supplies at the warehouses seem to have occurred during the early months. But there were others who laughed at those whom they regarded as "rumor mongers" and "food hoarders" and who considered the concern about the canteens to be excessive. As we mentioned in analyzing the hostility toward the JACL, collective behavior is generally impelled by genuine grounds for reaction, but the collective reaction may develop into a form that some people would regard as out of balance relative to the instigating condition. The question of interest here is, what accounted for the difference between the believers and disbelievers of the rumors, and the pro–canteen and anti–canteen advocates?

The difference was the degree of distrust felt toward white people and white society. Among the most distrustful, a strong suspicion existed that white people had no intention of dealing fairly with the evacuees and would treat the Japanese–American minority in whatever way convenience dictated. The WRA's interest in encouraging the evacuees' eastward relocation, it was assumed, simply reflected that agency's desire to rid itself of a difficult and expensive operation. The white society into which evacuees would be thrown, on the other hand, could not be trusted to deal fairly with the evacuees. The safest recourse was to remain entrenched at Tule Lake and carefully husband one's savings as a safeguard against an uncertain future.

A word of clarification is needed regarding those whom we refer to as the relatively trusting. In the light of the evacuation, it may be doubted that any evacuee fully trusted all white people. On the other hand, those who had little hesitation about re–entering white communities, whether for the purpose of seeking temporary seasonal work, attending college, or relocating permanently, made assumptions about receiving fair treatment in white communities which the distrustful were unwilling to make. They also needed to assume that the long–run prospects within white society for employment and fair treatment were reasonably good. In short, the relatively trusting and the distrusting differed significantly with respect to their assumptions regarding the intentions of white people and white society toward the Japanese–American minority.

The degree of trust had a direct effect on the evacuees' sense of security, for the evacuation took away their capacity to control their own destiny and transferred it to white people: the Army, the WRA, and white society. Once they lost control over their own lives, many evacuees came to regard the WRA centers as a point of security. Therefore, when the WRA began promoting a new policy of resettling evacuees outside the centers in the fall and winter of 1943, evacuees again were confronted with the issue of security and the related question of how much white people should be trusted. Basically, there were two main choices: trust the white people, relocate, and take the chance that job opportunities would be available; or distrust the whites, refuse to relocate, and wait out the war until the situation clarified itself.

Relationship Between Distrust and Protest

Given the universal resentment harbored by evacuees, one might have supposed that protest behavior against white authority would also have been a universal reaction among evacuees, but this was not the case. Some evacuees clearly were protesters, but others were equally clearly non-protesters. What caused the difference?

To understand protest behavior, a brief digression into sociological theory is needed. When a minority group comes into conflict with the majority group, there are theoretically three policies of action which the former may adopt toward the latter: protest, accommodation, or withdrawal.[19] *Withdrawal* implies that the minority group tries to sever its relations with the majority group. Since this was not common among the evacuees, we will discuss only the two alternatives of protest versus accommodation.

In situations of conflict, protest and accommodation may be seen as polar extremes on a continuum of attitudes which a minority group may hold toward the majority group. *Protest*, in its extreme form, refers to a militant, aggressive, uncompromising refusal to accede to the views of the majority group, while *accommodation* refers to a willingness to temper one's demands and grant concessions to the majority group. In real intergroup conflict, the attitudes of most people fall at intermediate points on the continuum, so there may be moderate protesters as well as moderate accommodationists. And the largest group may be found in the middle among those who decline to commit themselves to either orientation and who may be called the "uncommitted middle." Finally, because attitudes are changeable, positions on the continuum are not fixed. Over time moderates may become extremists, or vice versa.

At the Tule Lake Center in the summer of 1942, less than three months after the center was opened, a series of conflicts erupted between the evacuees and the WRA administration. Those who adopted the protest, or the accommodationist, orientation in these conflicts were by no means the same people at all times. Depending on the issue, the composition of the two groups varied. Nevertheless, as in the case of party politics, where party members show relatively predictable differences of behavior, there also were recognizable protest or accommodationist tendencies among different categories of center residents. This difference became clearest during the "loyalty" registration crisis of early 1943.

Carried out jointly by the WRA and the Army, the "loyalty" registration had two ostensible purposes: register all evacuees for leave clearance and reinstate the Selective Service draft for citizen males.[20] This program was initiated because the WRA judged that continued detention of the evacuees was undesirable, that they should be permitted to reestablish themselves as rapidly as possible in American society, and that reinstatement of the military draft was a desirable step toward returning the people to normal status. The registration had two crucial questions: Question 27 asked if respondents were willing to serve in the armed forces of the United States, and Question 28 asked if respondents would swear allegiance to the United States and foreswear allegiance to the Japanese emperor (or, for alien Japanese, if they would swear to abide by the laws of the United States).[21]

Of the male population at Tule Lake 17–years of age or older, 49 percent of citizens and 42 percent of aliens responded negatively to these questions or refused to answer them.[22] The events leading up to these responses, which were critical in determining the way people responded, are too complex for discussion here.

Our interest lies in pointing out that a strong, sometimes violent, protest movement developed in the Tule Lake population in opposition to the registration program, led by those who ultimately gave negative or no answers at all and who may be identified as protesters. On the other hand, those who answered the questions positively—slightly more than 50 percent of the Tule Lake population—may be identified as accommodationists.

Thomas and Nishimoto, in *The Spoilage*, have presented a statistical analysis of those who responded negatively to the "loyalty" questions or refused to answer them. Highlighting the background characteristics, they wrote:

> The most striking relationships are in factors manifesting variations in acculturation or assimilation; religious preference for the Occidental patterns of Christianity or agnosticism versus the Oriental pattern of Buddhism; biculturalism in training and education, the extremes being the "pure" Nisei, educated only in America, and the Kibei returning recently after years of education in Japan; origin in certain areas of California, where economic and social segregation from the majority group was pronounced, as against origin in the more tolerant Pacific Northwest; occupation in non-agricultural pursuits, where, on the whole, contact with and accommodation to the majority group occurred to a greater degree than was true with the farming element.[23]

Those who Thomas and Nishimoto have described as the relatively unassimilated, then, were the strongest and most vocal protesters during the registration crisis at Tule Lake. Their analysis offers a basis for explaining the relationship of distrust to protest behavior. In brief, their data show that protest at Tule Lake was, on the average, strongest among those who had in the years before World War II experienced the greatest amount of discrimination, who had been most segregated in the pre-war years, and who therefore had the least experience of associating with white Americans.

Summary

In this article we used *collective preoccupations*, subject matters about which center residents developed intense and persistent interest, as a means of identifying widely held attitudes at Tule Lake during the early months. We interpreted the widespread preoccupation with the failings of the JACL as reflecting the evacuees' deeply felt resentment of the evacuation and their anger at the

JACL for failing to represent that resentment more aggressively. And the preoccupations with the rumor of WRA's alleged intent to impose a further forced migration on the Tule Lake residents, the rumor of food shortages, and the effect of the canteens in depleting evacuee savings were interpreted as reflecting the residents' concern for future security and deep distrust of white people. However, the latter set of preoccupations proved a serious concern to some but of much less concern to others. Thus, the question was posed, what accounted for this difference of attitude between major segments of the same population? Using statistical analyses developed by Thomas and Nishimoto, we showed that those most acutely concerned about their future security and most distrustful of white people were evacuees who in the pre–evacuation years had been subjected to the greatest amount of discrimination and segregation.

These attitudes proved to be predictive of the stormy protest that later developed at Tule Lake over the "loyalty" registration. In the same sense that virtually all evacuees resented the evacuation, protest of the "loyalty" registration was similarly widespread. But out of all those who did protest, those who proved most uncompromising in their protest were those who earlier had shown the strongest concern about being forced to leave Tule Lake and about their future security. In short, non-compliance with the "loyalty" registration was largely explainable as the joint effect of resentment and distrust of white people. By comparison, those who were less distrustful of whites were clearly more accommodative in response to the registration.

Notes

1. S. Frank Miyamoto, "The Career of Intergroup Tension: A Study of the Collective Behavior of Evacuees to Crises at the Tule Lake Relocation Center" (Unpublished Ph.D. dissertation, University of Chicago, 1950). The present study is extracted mainly from chapter 4 of this dissertation.

2. Herbert Blumer, "Collective Behavior," in A.M. Lee, ed., *New Outline of the Principles of Sociology* (New York: Barnes and Noble, Inc., 1946), 168.

3. Hadley Cantril, *The Psychology of Social Movements* (New York: John Wiley and Sons, 1941), 14–21.

4. *Ibid.*, 85–93.

5. Tamotsu Shibutani, *Improvised News: A Sociological Study of Rumor* (Indianapolis: Bobbs Merrill, 1966), 150–53.

6. Miyamoto, "The Career of Intergroup Tension," 100.

7. *Ibid.*, 100–15.

8. U.S. Congress, House of Representative, Select Committee Investigating National Defense Migration, *San Francisco Hearings, Feb. 21 and 23, 1942*, H.R. 113, Part 29, 77th Congress, 2d Sess. (Washington, D.C.: GPO, 1942), 11148.

9. *Oakland Tribune*, March 9, 1942.

10. "Miyamoto Field Notes," June 19, 1942.

11. *Ibid.*, September 8, 1942.

12. Dorothy S. Thomas and Richard Nishimoto, *The Spoilage* (Berkeley: University of California Press, 1946), 49.

13. Miyamoto, "The Career of Intergroup Tension," 139–42.

14. *Tulean Dispatch*, September 25, 1942.

15. Dorothy S. Thomas, *The Salvage* (Berkeley: University of California, 1952), 53–56.

16. Miyamoto, "The Career of Intergroup Tension," 131–39.

17. Tamotsu Shibutani, "Field Notes," August 13, 1942.

18. Miyamoto, "The Career of Intergroup Tension," 132.

19. Gunnar Myrdal, *An American Dilemma: The Negro Problem and Modern Democracy* (New York: Harper and Brothers, 1944), II, 720–67. Myrdal was one of the first to classify these three types of reactions which occur among minorities in conflict. See also Alexander H. Leighton, *The Governing of Men* (Princeton: Princeton University Press, 1945), 263–74.

20. Thomas and Nishimoto, *The Spoilage*, 53–83.

21. *Ibid.*, 53–83.

22. *Ibid.*, 62–63.

23. *Ibid.*, 105–06.

Reminiscences of JERS

S. FRANK MIYAMOTO

I am writing these reminiscences of JERS for the purpose of providing researchers a basis for assessing my contributions. To accomplish this purpose, I believe I need to explain not only what I did on the project but also the influences which shaped me as a social researcher.

When I was in high school, literature interested me greatly, and I aspired to become a writer. But my father, whose judgment I respected, thought literature was very risky for a Nisei, and recommended that I choose a more utilitarian field like engineering. Although my father died before I got to college, I took his advice when I entered the University of Washington in 1930 and started in engineering. I stuck with it for two years.

This was in the depth of the depression. In 1932 I dropped out of school for a year because I was short of funds. During the interlude, I decided that I really was not happy with engineering, that I was more interested in people than in machines, so when I returned to college, I registered in liberal arts courses. One thing I took away from engineering was an appreciation for mathematics and science.

Sociology and psychology attracted me from the first. A major influence that drew me to sociology was the interest that Professor Jesse F. Steiner, chairman of the department, took in me. Steiner had taught for several years in a mission school in Sendai, Japan, which no doubt was a reason for his cordiality toward me. He also encouraged me to go on to graduate study in sociology, although, interestingly enough, he too suggested that I get training in a "back up" field such as foreign trade. When I proposed a study of the Seattle Japanese community for my M.A. thesis, he again encouraged and advised me.

The local Japanese community interested me because it was so thoroughly organized. When I was in the second grade, our family moved into a white, middle–class neighborhood where I spent much of my everyday life during my elementary and high school years. I later came to realize that the Japanese community was very different from the white community, and that it functioned under a much more structured system of relationships. I observed its strong kinship and *kenjin* relations, extensive joint activities for all kinds of occasions, emphasis on concepts like *on* (*o*bligations), and seemingly endless etiquette and formalities. When I began shopping for an M.A. thesis, I decided to examine this highly organized community more closely.

Because the Issei still dominated the community in the mid–1930s, I concentrated my study on them, and thereby neglected the emerging Nisei. But allowing for the latter deficiency, I believe I depicted the Seattle Japanese community with reasonable accuracy. Dr. Steiner thought that the thesis, which I titled "Social Solidarity among the Japanese in Seattle," was good enough for publication, and he arranged to have it published by the University of Washington Press.

In this study of the Japanese community, I had both an insider and outsider perspective. My father owned a business in the Japanese district where he maintained extensive contacts, and we also had relatives and many friends there. These associations gave me an insider view. On the other hand, we lived in a white community so that I also felt I was an outsider looking in. These two ways of looking at a community is typical of social research, especially if one is a participant observer. One is an actor within a drama and feels the forces which shape it; but one is simultaneously an outsider, a member of the audience, who observes the drama as it is played out by others.

As a sociologist, one is habituated to shifting one's perspective from actor to outside observer, back to actor, and so on. Growing up at the margin of two communities influenced me, I feel, toward a disembodied way of looking at the social world. I mention this because, although I was a JERS participant observer, I know that my observations were affected by the depersonalized way in which I sometimes conducted myself.

Growing up in a white neighborhood gave me another type of experience. I had many friends at school, but outside this circle there also were strangers and "gang" members who now and then would take it upon themselves to harass the "Jap" family in their midst. So I learned to be sensitive to prejudice, much more, I think, than if I had grown up exclusively within an ethnic enclave. But I can't say I learned to fight back against prejudice, although I don't believe I was cowardly about it. It was always difficult to fight back without the support of a group. Through my own encounters with prejudice, I gained, at the least, some sense of how prejudice and discrimination may historically have affected the Japanese immigrants in the United States.

One other background influence deserves to be mentioned: my two years of doctoral study at the University of Chicago from 1939 to 1941. My mentor was Professor Herbert Blumer, who at the time was developing two bodies of theory which eventually had a major influence on American sociology. First, Blumer was elaborating George H. Mead's social psychology into what has come to be known as "symbolic interactionism."

Second, he was formulating his collective behavior theory based on the earlier work of Robert E. Park. It was this collective behavior theory which I applied to my JERS research. At Chicago I also became acquainted with Professor William F. Ogburn, who had been Dorothy S. Thomas' mentor. Ogburn may have played a part in recommending me to Dorothy at the time the JERS staff was first being recruited. I completed my preliminary examinations in the spring of 1941 and left Chicago with only my dissertation to finish.

I received my first faculty appointment at the University of Washington. Professor Steiner again was my guardian spirit. He was instrumental in getting me an appointment that started in the fall quarter of 1941. The position was at the lowest rung of the academic ladder, appropriate for someone who had not yet finished his dissertation. I was delighted with the appointment.

Thus, I had barely embarked on my professional career when the war broke out on December 7, 1941. At the time, my wife and I were not yet married, but as soon as the war started, we decided not to wait any longer and were married during the Christmas break. A little over two months later, when General DeWitt issued his general exclusion orders on March 2, 1942, we briefly considered evacuating voluntarily to Chicago where I had friends, but we quickly dismissed the idea because of the problems which would arise if we left our families.

I believe it was late in March that Dr. Steiner informed me of a call he had from Dorothy Thomas asking about my possible interest in joining a project she was organizing for a study of the impending evacuation. If I was interested in her project, she suggested that I promptly apply to the Social Science Research Council for a pre–doctoral field fellowship, which she felt quite sure I would receive. My wife and I discussed the possibilities with our respective families, and despite all the uncertainties, everyone felt that this was a chance I should not pass up. I called Dorothy Thomas to tell her that I was interested. This is how I became involved with JERS.

I am sure Dr. Thomas would not have thought of me if my M.A. thesis had not been published. Moreover, I knew people who were her friends: Dr. Ogburn of Chicago, her onetime mentor; Dr. Steiner, my mentor; Dr. Calvin Schmid, a demographer at Washington whom she knew well; and others. Thus, my personal background played a significant part in drawing me into JERS.

It was in early May 1942 that we were evacuated to the Puyallup Assembly Center. The sight of hundreds of people assembled with assorted baggage, lined up to board the buses at the embarkation point, with rifle–bearing soldiers standing around as guards, is still imprinted in memory. And I can still remember the acute sense of embitterment, humiliation, resentment, anger, depression, concern, and other mixed feelings which I felt as we rode the 30 miles to the Puyallup Fairground. The miserable facilities at this assembly center compounded these feelings.

Dorothy Thomas had told me earlier that she probably would ask my wife and me to transfer to the Tule Lake Relocation Center where the main JERS staff members were being assembled. The evacuees at Puyallup were scheduled to be sent to the Minidoka Center in Idaho, but when, as it happened, a call was issued for 200 people to go to Tule Lake as an advance crew to open that center, my older sister and her husband, my other sister, and my mother decided to join this crew. So they preceded us to Tule Lake.

Our transfer orders arrived in June. The train trip from Puyallup to Klamath Falls, Oregon, the station nearest to Tule Lake, was something of a momentary lark. A WRA staff person met us at the station. We quickly drove out from the beautiful, wooded mountains surrounding Klamath Falls and entered an increasingly desolate, semi–desert countryside. And then we finally came upon the row after row of grim–looking, black, tar–papered barracks laid out across a broad, dusty, treeless, dried–out lake bed, surrounded by guard towers and barbed wire fences. I recall the sense of depression that momentarily engulfed me at the sight of all this, and the business of being checked through the entrance gate by armed sentries did not help my mood. As we drove up to the administration building, however, my spirit rebounded. I saw my brother–in–law waiting for us. We went through the registration procedure and received our apartment assignment. Since we were assigned to the same block as the rest of my family, we had a happy family reunion.

As I think of it now, this was not the right way to arrive for a researcher who was going to study the evacuees. To be sure, we traveled from Puyallup to Tule Lake under the eyes of a police escort, but he was friendly enough and did not make us feel like prisoners. There is no doubt that I felt the impact of being incarcerated, but riding through the gates of Tule Lake in a passenger car was not the same as arriving at the railway siding on "cattle cars," being marched through the gates like prison inmates, and having to stand in long check–in lines. There were differences between being an evacuee researcher and being just another evacuee. I often had to check myself to ensure that I was aware of the differences.

The immediate problem at Tule Lake was to get settled. Our apartment was small and bare of any furnishings, except for a large cast–iron stove and two canvas cots. There was no closet, no table or chairs, no shelves. And no lumber was available to make the needed furniture. Leftover wood from the camp construction lay in a large scrap pile in a firebreak. New arrivals scavenged like a flock of seagulls at a dump through the scrap pile for usable wood. I joined them and got enough wood to make a primitive closet. Activities of this kind took time away from doing fieldwork, but through such activities I gained an appreciation of the problems of camp life.

Tule Luke was laid out in a flat, checkerboard pattern, with nine residental blocks (3 x 3) joined into a ward. Seven wards spread across the encampment divided by wide firebreaks. We lived in Block 5 which, fortunately, was centrally located within the entire camp layout. The fact that my family lived in the same block not only allowed me to keep in touch with everyone easily, but also gave me access to the news and gossip which they had heard. Some friends from Seattle also lived in our block, while other friends from the Northwest were scattered throughout the camp.

Tom Shibutani and his wife, Tomi, lived in Block 4, and Haruo Najima (whom we called "Harno") also lived there. Tom was just finishing his B.A. at Berkeley under Dorothy Thomas. He had been instrumental shortly after Pearl Harbor in getting her interested in studying the increasingly difficult problems of the Japanese minority. Harno was a Berkeley graduate who, as I recall, had begun his graduate study in agricultural economics. He became one of the foremen on the farm, the single most important WRA project at Tule Lake, and he thus served as a significant source of information about the farm crew. Kay Hisatomi, who also worked on the farm crew, and his wife, Keiko, who was another Berkeley student, lived in Block 42 some distance from us. We all quickly became close friends. Tom and I saw each other everyday to discuss research questions.

The other JERS fieldworker was James Sakoda. He too had studied with Dorothy Thomas at Berkeley, and like Shibutani, had started taking field notes on Japanese–Americans soon after Pearl Harbor. Jim lived in a separate part of Tule Lake, so we saw less of him. But because his contacts and interests were different, we found it useful to compare observations with him from time to time.

The only white staff person was Robert Billigmeier, also a Berkeley graduate student. He kept us abreast of developments in the WRA administration. His wife, Hani, who was a teacher, kept us informed on the Tule Lake schools. We had a fair amount of contact with the Billigmeiers. We also had contacts with Harold Jacoby, a sociologist who was the head of Internal Security, and his wife, Joyce.

As a researcher, I became involved in two different roles: one, as an external observer; and, two, as a participant observer. In my earlier study of the Seattle Japanese community, I had assumed the same two roles and anticipated no problems with them. But the situation at Tule Lake proved far more complex than anything I had previously experienced.

By an external observer, I mean a role in which the researcher maintains himself as an outsider in relation to the persons and activities he observes and writes up his observations from the perspective of an outsider. The external observer may actively participate in the group he is observing, but always does so at the invitation of its members. For a social researcher, the most important first step is to gain acceptance from those he hopes to observe. In a community study, one gains acceptance by publicizing one's research project and by obtaining the approval of community officials and institutional leaders. Dorothy Thomas received approval for her research project from the Tule Lake Project Director and his staff, and, as I recall, an announcement about the project appeared in the *Tulean Dispatch*. But the critical legitimation needed was acceptance by the evacuees. This was a very touchy problem.

Immediately after Pearl Harbor, many Issei were arrested by the FBI and sent off to internment camps in Montana, New Mexico, and elsewhere. In all the centers there was considerable fear of investigations which might lead to additional arrests. This concern was especially reflected in the widespread fear of *inu*, or informers, who were thought to be spying on the evacuees and passing on damaging information to the authorities. There were said to be $100 *inu*, $150 *inu*, and so on, the different figures representing the alleged bounties paid by the FBI to the informers. When a beating was inflicted on an evacuee, it was often justified on the ground that the person was an *inu*.

The fear of *inu* unquestionably put a damper on our research, for if we were ever labelled as *inu*, our whole research project was in jeopardy. I even worried about the amount of time I spent at the typewriter. Since the barrack walls were flimsy, sound traveled easily to adjoining apartments or to the outside. I was not particularly worried about our neighbors because they were people I knew, but I was afraid that others must be wondering why I spent so much time at the typewriter.

I avoided being labelled an *inu* by concentrating on observational situations. My presence at public meetings or crowd activities required no explanation. As for observations of organized activities such as meetings of the Community Council or the Consumer Cooperative, permission was easily obtained. When I needed an informant relationship with a specific individual, I proceeded carefully toward establishing a base of confidence before seeking interviews. But the *inu* problem unquestionably made me cautious about approaching people for information, and definitely hampered the research. In hindsight, I feel I was too sensitive about the problem, that I could have accomplished much more if I had conducted the research more openly and aggressively.

The participant observer role refers to carrying on observations of a group in which the observer is considered a member. A participant observer ideally should forget about his research purposes while functioning as a group member. His aim should be to understand the members' experiences by full personal involvement in their problems and activities. Ultimately, however, he must record his observations as an external observer would, but do so while recalling how he felt as a group member.

As an evacuee researcher, I found that the method of participant observation presented special problems, especially at Tule Lake where conflicts between the evacuees and the administration seemed almost endemic. The feelings in the community were often intense and divided. Thus the participant observer faced the problem not only of participating in the conflict and feeling as keenly about the situation as the evacuees felt, but also of assuming the different perspectives held by opposing evacuee factions. Furthermore, although the participant observer must from time to time step out of his participant role and analyze his observations from the standpoint of an external observer, this was difficult to accomplish in the relocation center because the evacuee role was so all–encompassing. For example, if Dorothy Thomas or other Whites visited my apartment to discuss what I had learned as a participant observer, I had to be aware that having frequent white visitors could affect the attitudes of other evacuees toward me. There were many problems of this kind which arose from the fact that my evacuee role and research role were inextricably tied together.

The research difficulty that bothered me most was the persistent feeling that JERS lacked focus. I frequently wished that Dorothy Thomas would specify our research problems more sharply. Dorothy and W. I. Thomas visited Tule Lake soon after our field staff was assembled. I was deeply impressed by these distinguished sociologists whose works I had known for a long time. Dorothy struck me as an attractive, very intelligent, and energetic woman. Curiously, one of the things about her that sticks most firmly in my memory is the habit she had of chain–smoking mentholated cigarettes. She never drew deeply on a cigarette, but pecked at it in short, quick puffs. The image sticks in memory, perhaps, because she was a good listener. She listened, and she smoked. Of course, she made comments and discussed our ideas, but more often she sat behind a haze of smoke with her sharp eyes fixed on the speaker. It seems strange how this picture still remains clear, while I recall relatively little of things she said. One trouble with her visits and conferences, I felt, was that she did not talk enough. I wished she would tell us more about her own sociological orientation, indicate the kinds of problems which interested her, and guide us more specifically on how she wanted the research carried out. But she gave us relatively little direction.

I was also surprised that W. I. Thomas did not participate in the discussions more. He too was a good listener. One of the things about his visits which my wife and I clearly recall, with amusement, likewise concerned his smoking habit. He rolled his own Bull Durham cigarettes, and perhaps because his aging fingers were no longer nimble, he spilled a fair amount of tobacco as he rolled them. He would sit on our quilt–covered, steamer trunk that served as a seat, roll his cigarettes over our makeshift coffee table, and finally carefully brush the spilled tobacco back into his pouch using the edge of a notepaper as a scoop. But after his visits, the cracks in the rough, shiplap flooring where W. I. had sat were invariably filled with spilled tobacco. On each occasion my wife and I spent some time digging out the tobacco from the cracks, but because W. I. was such a down–to–earth, grand, old man, who counseled us with pithy remarks and entertained us with droll stories, we actually enjoyed the small chore of digging out the tobacco he left behind.

I now realize why the Thomases gave us so little research direction. More theoretically–minded sociologists would have expounded freely on hypotheses regarding the evacuees and the center which deserved investigation, but both Thomases were empiricists who placed little faith in hypotheses and theories which were not well grounded in facts. For them the empirical groundwork needed to come first, and so we spent much time at our meetings talking over the nuts and bolts of what was happening in the center. I believe this is the reason I remember so little of what was discussed.

I understand Dorothy Thomas' mode of research better today than I did at Tule Lake. During the first summer, she sent us a detailed outline of the topics she thought should be covered. She wanted, first, a general historical account. But the bulk of the initial effort was to be directed toward giving a structural picture of the Tule Lake community: its political, economic, religious, family, educational, and recreational organizations. Each of us was assigned a set of subjects we were to investigate and write reports on. My assignment included social structure, and political, economic, and recreational organizations.

During my first months at Tule Lake I was kept busy investigating my assigned topics. Yet I was uncertain about the aims of our research and felt frustrated by the uncertainty. My difficulty was that I was trained under a different research tradition than Dorothy's. All through my graduate training, I was taught to first delimit the subject area for research, examine theories which bore on that subject, state significant research problems derived from the theories, and outline a plan of research and methodology designed to resolve the problems. Dorothy's procedure, by contrast, was to carry out preliminary studies in a broadly defined empirical area, and on the basis of the data determine the significant problems of research. Considering that we were investigating a phenomenon regarding which there was little prior research experience, I now believe hers was the better approach. But at the time her line of attack left me feeling we were not studying important issues bearing on the evacuees, and I felt uncertain and uncomfortable with what I was doing.

In mid–August 1942, an event occurred that suddenly gave focus to my research, and substantially reduced my concern about the lack of research direction. Very early on the morning of August 14, there was a loud knock on our door. Tom Shibutani was there, and he told me that a strike of the large farm crew was developing at the dispatching station in Block 12. He said we should rush over to see what was happening, and suggested we wear work clothes so as not to be obviously out of place. Later, Harno told us that we stuck out like sore thumbs in our improbable work clothes. In any case, we hurried across the quarter mile distance to the dispatching station.

Trucks used every day to transport the farm crew to the farm seven miles up the road were standing in a row, but no one was boarding them. As we turned the corner and approached the dispatching shack, we ran into a large crowd of hundreds of workers, clustered in several groups, loudly discussing their complaints. Some workers milled around, while others lined up against the barracks and glumly watched.

The foremen were gathered in their own group debating what to do. Someone shouted at them, "We had only tea and toast for breakfast, but farmers can't work on a breakfast like that." Others shouted that their breakfasts were no better. Still others began yelling out a list of other complaints: the delay in wage payments, the reneging on promised work clothing, the lack of soap to wash clothes, the lack of proper machinery to do work, and on and on. The foremen retired to an empty room to decide on a course of action. Crowd leaders pushed forward to tell the foremen what they should do.

After what seemed an interminable time, a foreman came out and announced that no one had to work that day (Friday), that a committee was being formed to negotiate the complaints with the WRA administration over the weekend, and that a meeting of the farm crew would be announced later to inform the workers about the results of the negotiation.

All of the following day, Saturday, there was tension in the community as people everywhere talked about the strike. Then, late Sunday morning, an announcement circulated that a public meeting would be held at the outdoor stage at eight o'clock that evening to discuss the results of the negotiations. That evening, well before the appointed time, a large crowd began to assemble at the outdoor stage. This was a Sunday evening, and some Christian church group was using the stage for their service. The surly crowd stood away from the church meeting, but could be heard threatening to take over the stage if it was not vacated soon. Still others crowded around angry protest leaders who were expounding their views. Loud exclamations, such as "*Ware ware wa Dai–*

Nipponjin da zo! Keto no yatsu ni doko made mo oshitsukerareru mon ja nai zo!" (We are people of Imperial Japan! We're not a people to be forever pushed around by the damned Whites!), were heard from the speakers.

The Christian group hurriedly ended its service. The foremen prepared to proceed with the strike meeting. Because of the poor lighting on the platform, a Nisei foreman stepped to the public address microphone and said, "Will someone see if we can't get more lights on the stage?" Someone yelled back from the assembled audience, *"Koko wa Nippon da zo! Eigo wo tsukau mon ga aruka?"* (This is Japan. Who dares to speak English here?) An approving roar went up from the crowd. The atmosphere was electric.

I have since learned from sociological theory that the attitudes toward the majority group within a minority group in conflict typically range between the two poles of accommodation and extreme protest. The two scenes I witnessed at the outdoor stage that evening, the Christian Sunday service and the crowd of angry workers, seemed like successive tableaus of the two poles. Retrospectively, I feel that this event tells us a great deal about human nature, Japanese immigrant history, and minority social movements. When the evacuees voiced extreme protest, they invariably identified themselves as Japanese.

A slender, gray–haired Issei, apparently a foreman, skillfully chaired the meeting that night. Without interruptions, the negotiating committee reported that the WRA had agreed to look into the food problem and all other problems within its control. The chairman, then, closed the meeting without allowing time for discussion. As the meeting started to break up, cries of dissatisfaction arose from men standing near the stage. They demanded something more than dubious promises, and speaker after speaker walked up to the microphone to urge a continuation of the strike until the administration gave more substantial evidence of good faith. But the lateness of the evening brought the meeting to an inconclusive end.

On Monday morning, a large mass of workers again gathered near the dispatching station, and again protest leaders angrily urged that the strike be continued. As the workers milled around uncertain of what to do, the slender, gray–haired Issei chairman of the night before stepped forward and in a quiet but clear and firm voice declared, "The administration has promised to meet our demands, but they need time to work out their problems. In the meantime, if we strike, our families won't get even the small wages we bring home from our work. Let's go to work, see if the administration meets our demands, and if they don't, we can strike at that time." Several men shouted, "*Sansei! Sansei!*" (Agreed! Agreed!), others joined the chorus, and the workers rushed to board the transport trucks. The protest leaders tried to stop them, but to no avail.

This was a wildcat strike with no organizational base. It ended as suddenly as it had begun. The farm workers did not strike again. But their strike had the effect of elevating the protest temper of the community. In the next three months, nine major rebellions, including six other strikes, shook the community. It was an exceedingly tense period. In those three months, I learned more about collective behavior and more sociology than I could ever have hoped to learn in graduate school. It was not a pleasant way to learn sociology—the tension was hard to bear—but it was a very effective way. I have always felt a little guilty that it was from the injustices and adversities experienced by my fellow Japanese–Americans that I learned my sociology.

I have been asked about the reliability of the field notes, reports, and other materials which we collected at Tule Lake. I find there is no good way in which to answer this question. If ours had been a survey research project in which we had drawn a random sample of the Tule Lake evacuees and had interviewed the residents with well–tested questionnaires, I would be able to give a clear, comprehensive answer. I could discuss the representativeness of the sample that was drawn, the reliability and validity of the questionnaires used, and the specific methods of analyses employed. But since ours was not a survey research project, I have no straightforward, obvious answer.

In a sense, we employed an anthropological methodology, and the justification of the material we gathered would not differ greatly from the way anthropologists justify their observations. To be sure, ours was a much more complex community than the preliterate groups which anthropologists typically study, but we at least had the advantage of written documentation and statistical information to supplement our field observations.

In defending the reliability of the data I gathered, I should first point out that I had no reason to misrepresent the events and situations I observed. Trained as I was in American schools, I am sure I had a pro–American and an anti–Japanese political bias, but I doubt that my observations were seriously affected by the bias, for I felt as much aversion toward one–hundred–percent Americanism as toward any strong pro–Japanese nationalism. Moreover, my studies of the history of Japanese immigration to the United States gave me a more solid basis, than less informed persons had, of believing that the evacuation was a product of the history of anti–Japanese prejudice against the Japanese minority on the Pacific Coast.

I believe my training in sociology also helped me to maintain objectivity. In all the methodology courses I ever took, the primary concern was the question of controlling observer biases. Also, I was thoroughly schooled in a basic principle of sociology which holds that every person tends to see the world differently than anyone else, and to understand people's behavior, one needs to understand the different background influences which shaped each person's behavior. Sociologists become habituated to the practice of trying to see things from others' perspectives.

Dorothy Thomas had us concentrate on studies which did not involve methodological issues of representative sampling and personal interviews. For example, one of my assignments was to investigate political organizations. The principal political body at Tule Lake was the Community Council which was made up of a citizen (Nisei or Kibei) representative from each block and which met once a week. I regularly attended Council meetings, received copies of minutes, and interviewed councilmen. In addition, I regularly attended the block meetings in our block and kept notes of the discussions. Through discussions with councilmen from other blocks, I gained some sense of how other blocks functioned. Later, when an Issei political body, called the Planning Board, was established, I was able to carry on similar observations of that group. Political organizations were things I could observe, and observe quite accurately by attending meetings, listening to discussions, and reading minutes and reports. My observations of political organizations gave me a structural sense of the community. Admittedly, I failed to observe informal political groups and individual attitudes.

Structural accounts, however, fail to give a sense of the dynamics of a community, a serious flaw for Tule Lake where changes were a dominant feature. After the wildcat strike of the farm workers, however, I shifted my research focus to observations of collective behavior, a field I had specialized in at the University of Chicago. Collective behavior—which concerns crowds, riots, strikes, rebellions, and social movements—was developed around questions of basic processes in social change, so it was ideally suited to investigating the dynamics of change at Tule Lake.

The observations of collective behavior are relatively defensible. First, because collective behavior refers to phenomena in which large numbers of people participate, questions concerning the representativeness of the data are less critical than in observations of individual persons. Second, because the observations are of spontaneous behavior, there is much less doubt about their reliability in contrast to observations of non–behavioral responses such as attitudes and feelings. Third, because events such as strikes and rebellions generated documentary evidence, I was able to check my own observations against such data. Fourth, because large–scale collective behavior affected the history of the community, the sequence of events needed to make historical sense.

Finally, the predictive power of our data is another good measure of reliability. The widespread resistance that developed at Tule Lake against the "loyalty" registration was the climactic event in the center's turbulent history. All the JERS evidence indicates that the main reasons for the resistance were the residents' concern for their future security, their resistance to any further forced migration out of Tule Lake, and their distrust of the WRA and of white people generally. All the data we collected before the registration crisis portended a strong resistance to any program that might provoke these underlying concerns. In sum, I believe the data we collected at Tule Lake reflected the events there and reactions accurately. But the best advice I can give to current researchers is that they should compare our data against other sources and reach their own conclusions.

Personally, the "loyalty" registration undermined my capacity to continue as a participant observer. Extremists began a vigorous anti–registration campaign, urging everyone either to refuse to register or to answer negatively on the "loyalty" questions. Their speeches were filled not only with denunciations of the bigoted keto, but also with flaming expressions of pro–Japanese nationalism. The main underlying reasons for resistance to the registration had little to do with pro–Japanism, but the extremist views were often heard at block meetings. At the height of the resistance, Kibei leaders drafted a resolution which they wanted all residents to sign. The resolution pledged every signee to refuse to register. At a meeting in our block one evening, a Kibei spokesman gave an impassioned speech calling for a block vote in support of the resolution.

I was disturbed, not only by the nationalistic tone of his speech, but also by the idea that everyone should be compelled either to refuse to register or to register negatively. I was also upset because the chairman of the meeting, a

Kibei councilman whom I respected very much, was being harassed severely for trying to forestall the vote on the resolution. I finally stood up and voiced my personal opposition to the resolution, arguing that registration was a matter of individual choice. As I sat down, I heard a Kibei say, "*Kono yatsu wa fukuro tataki shite mizo no naka ni horikonde yaro!*" (Let's bag this guy, beat him, and roll him in a ditch!). But I was pleased to note that my councilman friend used my remarks as cause for adjourning the meeting.

That night my wife and I made sure the door was locked securely, and we even propped a barrier up against it. And when we went to bed, I placed a hammer near me. It was the only weapon I had. As we lay there wondering what might happen, we heard footsteps at our entry followed by a quiet knock on the door. We had the wildest thoughts of what was about to happen, but much to our relief we heard my mother's voice calling my name. She had come through the dark of the night with a pan of hot water in one hand and a long knitting needle in the other to see if we were still safe. A month or so later, my wife and I left Tule Lake for Chicago to do research on the resettlers.

Gila in Retrospect

ROBERT F. SPENCER

World War II is ancient history, events occurring almost a half century ago. In the years following, the United States has developed a different mood, one reflected in the unsuccessful Korean and Vietnamese wars and in the emergence of such preoccupations as racism, feminism, and in the changing national administrations. Not too many are left whose recollections of the Pacific and European theaters of war are first hand. Yet it is against the background of World War II that the Japanese–American experience must be seen.

It is sometimes forgotten that the forced removal of Japanese–Americans from their West Coast homes took place in a setting directly bound up with the war. At the time, the American population at large achieved a sense of unity and common purpose that has not since been duplicated. True, the events of the war came to touch every American intimately. There was the military draft, to be sure, but the development of new skills and employment connected with the war effort, a response to the depression years of the 1930s, went far beyond the military. There was rationing, what with the shortages of meat, coffee, canned goods, gasoline, all of which came close to home. But far more than this, there was the sense of anxiety, a pervasive awareness of doom and impending destruction, an ethos of disaster. The attack on Pearl Harbor caught the majority of Americans flat–footed. Added to this were the ensuing Japanese successes in the Pacific, at least in the first two years of the war, and there were the German victories all across Europe. The future seemed indeed bleak; at the start, at least, the outcome was wholly unpredictable. There was little sympathy left over for the plight of the Japanese ethnic minority.

To be sure, there were those who felt strongly that forced removal was unjust, totally morally wrong. As events proved, it was. But voices in protest were few and weak. Evacuation became an established fact. It cannot be justified but it is understandable as an exigency of war. Given the realities of the mass evacuation, the extent to which an objective view may be taken poses the difficulty of resolving conflicting opinions. But it is absurd to employ the criteria of today and to apply them to a circumstance long past. Sentiment aside, how may one look objectively at the occurrences of 1942–1945?

It was with some notion of dispassion and with the ostensible sense of objectivity derived from the social sciences as they were then that Dorothy S. Thomas conceived the idea of JERS. She sought to take advantage of an academic trend just then coming into being, a cross–disciplinary and multi–disciplinary approach. Locating herself in sociology, she drew in political scientists, economists, and ultimately, field anthropologists. Within weeks of the announcement of the expulsion of Japanese–Americans from the West Coast, Thomas had obtained funding and went ahead with the support of senior colleagues to engage a staff of research assistants representing the several component disciplines. As is well known, she was able to employ Nisei as well as a Caucasian contingent, all of whom were to report on various aspects of the evacuation and adaptation process. Thomas' project took off early in 1942 and continued for the several years following.

As mentor of JERS, Thomas saw the field of sociology as focal. When appointed to the University of California staff, she was located in the department of agricultural economics, there being no sociology department at the university at the time. Indeed, for various reasons, it was not until well after the war that sociology was represented on the Berkeley campus. But an appointment in agricultural economics suited Thomas' major interests as a demographer and statistician. Her claim to a somewhat more formal and classical sociology lay largely in her marriage to the famous W. I. Thomas. If Dorothy S. Thomas' place as a sociologist is acknowledged, it is largely through the influence of her husband. True, she had collaborated with him in a study of the child in America, but it was the philosophical and theoretical influence of W. I. Thomas which underlay much of the orientation of JERS.

W. I. Thomas, although interested in the structure of contemporary social situations, has to be placed as a social philosopher, more European than American. His uses of ethnology and his evolutionary concerns place him pretty much with the British and French thinkers of the turn of the century. It is true that his best–known work relates to the problems of adaptation and change. This was his collaboration with Florian Znaniecki with whom he assembled the five–volume study of the Polish peasants in Europe and America. It was in this opus that Thomas developed his concept of the "four wishes," a formulation still quoted in various social science classes. He introduced a social psychological dimension and stressed the interplay of societal and individual elements. Thomas proceeded from analysis of behavior, such as could be gleaned from the ethnographic literature, to a recasting of Durkheimian principles. Space is lacking here to detail the contribution of W. I. Thomas to his wife's perspectives but it is worth stressing that Dorothy S. Thomas owed to his influence her perception of the Japanese–American problem. Throughout the years of research, W. I. Thomas remained in the background, not contributing directly perhaps, but making his theoretical position felt both by his wife as well as by her assistants. The compilation of life histories, those to be found in the second volume of the JERS summary, *The Salvage,* finds a parallel in the case studies of Polish peasants.

I joined the JERS staff in April 1942. Dorothy S. Thomas had enlisted the interest of the renowned social anthropologist, Professor Robert H. Lowie, and had suggested to him that he name a graduate student with ethnographic experience to live at one of the so–called relocation centers as an observer. Access to selected centers was, not without difficulty, granted Thomas by the newly–created War Relocation Authority (WRA). One of these was the Gila River Relocation Center in the Arizona desert, some miles south of Phoenix. Two years previously, I had undertaken a study of one of the Native American languages in the Rio Grande valley, "fieldwork" carried on into 1941. As an undergraduate, I had a college year of the Japanese language. On both counts, I was selected to undertake the field studies at Gila for JERS.

My primary association was with Lowie, with whom after joining JERS, I discussed the problems which he, as an ethnographer of great experience, might envision in the relocation center "field." And indeed, it is here that the problem issues arose. What actually did Dorothy S. Thomas want from her field staff, what kinds of analytic methods might one employ, and what was to be the ultimate result? Professor Lowie confessed that he did not know. Thomas herself made the point that she saw my role as that of an observer, one engaged in "empirical" research. Or, to put the matter another way, one was simply to let events shape themselves and report one's findings. The consensus appeared to be that here was a unique opportunity to observe social and cultural dynamics at first hand.

Although Thomas kept a multi–disciplinary focus in mind, the role of the anthropologist, especially of one trained in the Berkeley school, was far from clear. This was because the University of California anthropologists, under the tutelage of Lowie and A. L. Kroeber, had always stressed attention to cultural–

historical phenomena. To "do" anthropology was to embrace history, however much the field today has parted company with that orientation. I confess that I still see myself as an historian of culture, much more interested in Japanese systems as they were shaped by influences from China and Korea beginning in the fifth century, A.D., than in sociological analysis. Hence, to be put into a situation which was primarily synchronic, one in which applied aspects were implicit, ran rather counter to my training and interests.

In the field of anthropology at the time, stress was beginning to be laid on the historic processes of acculturation, i.e., the interaction of two contacting cultures with consequent modifications in the patterns of either or both. As I prepared to go into the field at Gila, it was with the idea of an acculturation study, an examination of the elements of Japanese culture which were carried over by an immigrant generation and persisted in the American–born second generation. This was a topic of great interest to W. I. Thomas and it was one of which Dorothy S. Thomas takes note in the introduction of *The Spoilage*. As a field problem, acculturative process seemed reasonable and appeared to satisfy the project director. But it is fair to say that Thomas herself did not, in these initial months, have a clear idea of either the compilation of data or of their eventual analysis. We of the staff were expected to discover an ultimate focus.

So it was that I went to Gila in August 1942. After a brief contretemps in Phoenix, resulting in my going to the wrong camp—"You want the concentration camp," said the Greyhound bus agent, not realizing that some forty miles away was the empty camp for German prisoners of war; no one in Phoenix seemed aware that the Gila camp for Japanese–Americans was in the process of building—I arrived at Gila. This was at a time when the Gila center was just being filled, the evacuees brought to the camp from a railroad siding some seven miles distant and bussed to their barrack quarters. The population was drawn largely from the assembly centers in the San Joaquin valley. I soon became aware of the horrors of the evacuee situation. Report the observations I could make was all I could do. What emerges from this period is a pure and simple journalism, a recounting of the evacuee experience in day–to–day terms.

The "camp," as may be guessed, was anything but ready for the 13,500 detainees it was eventually to receive. The site had been chosen, so it was said, by one Harvey Coverly, an executive of the WRA in April of that year. Why it was chosen remains unclear. Artesian wells were possible and it was said that with irrigation some agricultural focus could be developed by the farm–

oriented evacuees. By August, the barracks had been erected and the two segments of the Gila center were pretty much filled. Again, why two segments? There was the original section, Canal Camp, while some three miles away was the larger Butte Camp, designed to hold some 8,000 persons. I never learned why the two segments were created, nor in fact was the administration able to shed any light on this. An effect of the division was to separate groups of evacuees, especially since travel between the two sections became at times impossible, what with the heavy hand of the military guards.

By August, the heat of the Arizona desert was in full swing. A flat, riverine plain, marked by scattered buttes, beautified to an extent by the presence of giant saguaro cactus, provided the ground level on which the barracks were erected. To the population, the area seemed a forbidding wasteland. Above all, the heat remained oppressive, reaching, at times, 120 degrees Fahrenheit. Small children and the elderly were particularly adversely affected. Deaths were not uncommon among these groups but they, along with illnesses, often digestive and abdominal disturbances, were given little administrative attention. Cremations in Phoenix mortuaries were the rule.

Present in any case by WRA sufferance, I was asked to offer a *quid pro quo*, performing various tasks for which adequate WRA personnel were lacking. I was asked, for example, to act as escort for a Nisei grape farmer whose mother, too aged to be evacuated, died in a nursing home in Fresno. And again, I drove a Buddhist priest to a barrack quarters to return the ashes of an infant to its mother. Both were touching and moving experiences. The infant's mother asked me if I were Mr. Smith, the project director. When I told her I was not, she begged me to appeal to the WRA for release for her and her family. "My other children will die too," she insisted. But there were many other, no less moving experiences. In time, I was able to dissociate myself from the WRA administration, at least in the eyes of the evacuees. I stated frankly what I was doing and that I represented the University of California. Given the Japanese–American respect for education, the university association was accepted.

But it is hardly necessary to emphasize the problems of a large population suddenly forced to confront inadequate housing, furnishings—cots were borrowed from the prisoner–of–war camp nearby—food, sewage disposal, medical care, and a score of related problems. In short, the center was not yet ready to receive so large a group. It was this beginning phase which I reported, sending my data to Dorothy S. Thomas at Berkeley. Given so tragic and horrendous a situation, it was difficult to remain objective. It speaks well for the resourcefulness and adaptability of the Japanese–Americans that within a few short months, they were able to create the semblance of a community, however questionably integrated.

My own role remained essentially anomalous. I was not a member of the WRA staff and my presence was at times resented by the bureaucrats. A paranoid attitude prevailed among the administrators as it did, of course, among the evacuee population. At first I was obliged to live in barracks provided for the WRA staff, moving to an isolated barrack some distance away later on. But, of course, I had to take meals with the WRA people. I was sometimes accused of being "pro–Japanese" in the war or of spying on the administrators. Despite the rapport I was able to develop with various Japanese–American individuals and groups, I was still a *hakujin*, a *keto*. The fact that I could frame a sentence in Japanese, however haltingly, put me in an invidious position *vis–a–vis* the bureaucracy. In the main, it was a difficult situation. Fortunately, at the beginning, I had previously been acquainted with Eastbourne Smith, the project director, and his wife, Dr. Nan Cook Smith, herself an anthropologist. My way was smoothed by them and it was with great regret that Smith, finding the situation intolerable, resigned within a few months only to be replaced by administrators of questionable competence.

But to return to the question of what was to be accomplished. I persisted in my wish to examine acculturative aspects. It was a poor choice for several reasons. The state of acculturation studies at the time did not allow for in–depth analyses. It was rather that changes in material culture and in societal institutions were overtly visible but lacking was a penetrating awareness of the more deeply rooted patterns present in the group. The subsequent years have defined for anthropology an infinitely more penetrating perspective. The field can treat the concept of culture with an understanding that was essentially missing in 1942, especially for one like myself with historical interests. It seems fair to ask whether contemporary modes of analysis had been applied, the JERS contribution might not have been of a higher order. Or, if the same situation were to occur today, what might we of the JERS staff, not to mention the social scientists hired as community analysts by the WRA, have done differently?

For myself, going back all these years, I plodded along, observing and interviewing, regularly sending journalistic reports back to Thomas in Berkeley. This was evidently what she wished, the assumption being that these raw data were to be subjected to scrutiny later on. I reported, for example, on the beating of one Takeo Tada in Canal Camp, the first instance of overt trouble and dissension among the evacuee population. It is this occurrence which Dr. Arthur Hansen so brilliantly reconstructs many years later.[1] Aside from the factors which evoked this aggressive behavior, Thomas demanded that I probe as deeply as possible into what she saw as incipient disorganization. Actually, it was this, the area of resistance and retaliation, that so attracted Thomas' interest. Yet, despite the documentation I was able to secure, not to mention the reports filed by Joseph Omachi, a Nisei lawyer whom I brought into the project, this "grassroots" happenstance was never explored or aired further.

Students of the anthropology of law have made much of so–called "trouble cases," meaning that legal principles may be elicited from events which depart from a social norm. If Dorothy S. Thomas was concerned with the structuring of the relocation centers, as indeed she was, it was in the areas of trouble that she began to find her sense of problem. At Gila, after the initial outburst against Tada, the community developed along fairly serene lines. To be sure, there were resentments and many cases of aberrant and unacceptable social actions, not to mention instances of psychic disturbance. Not until the issue of the "loyalty" oath and the prospect of the military draft arose in early 1943 did serious troubles appear with the consequent sequestration and relocation of so–called rebels. These prompted the development of the isolation camps at Leupp and elsewhere, and ultimately gave rise to the segregation at the Tule Lake center. Perhaps more could have been done with these instances in terms of analysis, but I should consider them to be secondary rather than primary events because they obscured the underlying issues. Thomas' stress on the "trouble case," however much it should have led to a more precise realization of the nature of the evacuee communities, their structure and organization, shifted the emphasis. Not until later in the development of JERS, at a time when I had left the project, did Thomas and her associates begin to move in the direction of more precise and focused community analysis. But even here a question arises. The broader problem of the mood, the ethos, the climate and tone of the various relocation centers, or of the evacuee population at large, was neglected in the published JERS accounts.

I believe, as I review the writings covering the initial period of evacuation, that W. I. Thomas began more and more to assert his influence. This, as has been noted, appears in an increased emphasis on life histories and personal documentation, points which W. I. Thomas so distinctively used in his Polish study, and which Dorothy S. Thomas introduced in *The Salvage.* I recall conversations with W. I. Thomas in which he asserted that singular events ought to be put aside in favor of a holistic, structured formulation. Obviously, this reflects the influence of the French social philosopher, Émile Durkheim. Yet, as is well known, Durkheim rules out psychology in favor of his "collective representations," the forces emanating exclusively from the societal. In his Polish study, W. I. Thomas introduces a social psychology which, combined with a Durkheimian perspective, becomes his particular hallmark. And it is this amalgam of social psychology and sociology which provided a groundwork for Dorothy Thomas' concerns. It is perhaps worth noting that at the outbreak of the war, prior to any concern with the Japanese–Americans, W. I. Thomas was compiling data on the Yiddish–speaking peoples in Poland, the Ukraine, and New York. He had taught himself Yiddish and read widely in the ethnic press, covering personal letters and the agony columns. Personal documentation underlay this proposed study as it did for the Poles.

But this aside, a proper study should have taken into account the impact of the WRA administration. Charles Kikuchi and I attempted to detail the internal administrative structure in reports to Thomas, and no account of the community itself could be complete without this consideration. The WRA staff, at Gila and elsewhere, consisted of varying shades of occupation and ability. Some exhibited great sympathy for the plight of the Japanese–American population, others were frankly and openly hostile. Little purpose is served here by detailing the activities of the staff whose presence in any case was often only temporary, many being lost to the military. But, of course, directives from the central WRA authority in Washington guided policy and activity. What emerged from the staff presence was a marked sense of colonialism, an attitude to the effect that the various relocation centers were made up of subject peoples, those essentially unable to make choices of their own advantage but who required direction. It was, in fact, the strong sense of decisions made by higher authority that tied the hands of the settlers and perhaps more than any other factor imposed limitations. With colonialism comes a paternalism; it was this which set the tone. The WRA perpetuated the social consequences arising between a dominant and submissive population.

But all such matters can do no more than set a stage. Putting them aside, the major questions still arise as to what was left undone. Alexander Leighton in his *Governing of Men* does a rather better job of defining community than do any of the Thomas staff. JERS did not convey a sense of societal integration as this applied to any of the various relocation centers. Rather than give attention to elements of disorganization, however much such may have been anticipated, a greater emphasis might have been laid on cohesion and on the structured interaction which characterized the Japanese–American population in so tense a situation. Had this been more effectively done, a more pointed awareness of the societal composition might have been reached and might have led, in turn, to a deeper understanding of the problems of an immigrant group and its descendants.

But, of course, part of the difficulty lay in the existing perception of the time. Disunity was striking; unity was not. The observer brought with him/herself an already biased view of the peculiar composition of this and other centers. Given the nature of the immigration process as it applied to people stemming from East Asia and confronted with inhibiting American laws, the Issei–Nisei split was always assumed to apply. We had been told again and again that the American–born descendant of immigrants inclines to repudiate the values and symbols of the parental generation. As a result, the generational division was never questioned. The view was that the Nisei tended to *be* Americans; for most, a command of the Japanese language was minimal, remaining essentially on the level of the childhood experience, while aims, standards, and goals were couched in those of the dominant culture. To be sure, they related to their parents through affectional ties, but they were ostensibly American and not Japanese. Here was a cause of intra–familial conflict. The literature of the time laid bare the "melting pot" theory; the descendants of ethnic groups would assimilate totally the American mold. How wrong this theory was, yet it dominated the thinking of the 1940s.

But this immediate, apparent generational division was rendered infinitely more complex by other, non–familial associations. There were the Kibei, American-born, but with experience and education in Japan, always a group standing apart by virtue of language and cultural orientations. Further, there were urban–rural differences, suggesting that life in America had created class interests dependent on economic activity. And there was the choice of Buddhism as against Christianity. It was inevitable, I suppose, that one pay attention to these and other features which militated against group cohesion and solidarity. In any case, the term "ethnicity" had not yet been invented.

Aware of the literature, and having steeped myself in such accounts of the culture and society of Japan as were then available, I can say, *mea culpa*, that I lacked both knowledge and experience to apply them effectively. Like Thomas, I saw divisiveness. And like Thomas, too, I became aware of the inevitable tensions and troubles of the Gila population. These issues tended to becloud any more subtle or in–depth analysis. If it may be assumed that the problems of acculturation still had validity as a focus, then it followed that I looked for elements carried over from the traditional culture and society of Japan. Among the Issei, these were easily enough found and lay in such overt aspects as Japanese food, etiquette, tea, aesthetic gardening, and many others which began to evolve as the barrack housing became momentarily "home." I joined the sumo club and was made welcome by the mainly Kibei, who formed the teams. Injured in a match, I jokingly referred to my mishap as reflecting a failure of my *Yamato damashii*, the "Japanese spirit." This statement was immediately reported by someone to the project director and nearly led to my expulsion from the center. In sumo, of course, the ritual element is primary and while overt Shinto practices were forbidden, there was considerable latitude for individual and small group attention to them. Similarly, I regularly attended the Shinshu Buddhist services in a barrack assigned to the Buddhist congregation. My own interests led me into the domain of religion, Buddhism particularly, what with Zen and Jodo–Shin well represented at Gila. But this is all relatively superficial. Such descriptions, as I was able to provide, were simple statements in which the immediate aspects of behavior and belief were cited. In other words, the work of JERS, my own included, was oversimplified.

What then was lacking? From the vantage point of forty and more years later, it is easy—and really foolish—to say what we might have done and failed to do. But even in the light of social science theory of the day, too many features were missed. It may be worthwhile to consider some of them. Here I must confine myself to anthropology and its theoretical directions. I was not a sociologist and, indeed, had no background in that discipline. In consequence I was left to "do" an ethnography. As an aside, I might stress that it was this which Professor Lowie requested. I recall being asked by a philosophical friend at the time of my joining the JERS staff what it was that I expected to do. I commented on group and class issues, on familism, religions, the many institutions I expected to encounter. "You sound like an introductory textbook in sociology," he said. Well, yes, it was this which Thomas told me to look for. I took my friend's comment to heart, but I still did not delve with sufficient depth into a potentially exciting situation.

My own predilection for historicism, this in any case being the anthropological watchword of the time, was reinforced by my training with Lowie and Kroeber and eclipsed a more pointed perspective. Concepts of structure and function were just then coming into being. But Lowie himself found much to criticize in the theoretical positions occupied by the famous Malinowski or his functionally oriented rival, Radcliffe–Brown. I recall seminars in which Lowie took the members of the so–called British School of Anthropology to task and, of course, Lowie's own writings were strongly opposed to a strictly synchronic position. It was not until later, in fact, that my own training made Durkheimian and Malinowskian points of view more intelligible. Yet it would have been this, rather than a reconstruction of history, which could have been more profitably directed to the Gila situation. The Kroeberian focus was one of cultural analysis, culture itself being the principal contribution of anthropology to the social sciences then as now. I had assimilated the concept of culture, recognizing that there were distinctive and essentially relativistic features which made each culture and society distinct. Dorothy S. Thomas, of course, was indifferent to this kind of theorizing.

As an example of the kind of problem to which only minimal attention was given and which might have been much more deeply explored, the organization of the Japanese–American family might have been selected. Japanese society, as all sources agree then and now, is primarily family–centered. It might have been predicted that this basic kinship institution would carry over from the Japanese homeland, as indeed it did. But it is difficult to discuss the Japanese family as against that of the West in the sense of discovering distinctive and immediate differences. The Japanese lack the elaborations of familial extensions, such as characterize the Chinese or Koreans. Later, when I did a preliminary analysis of kinship in Japan, it was at once clear that the stress was on nucleation rather than on extensions of kinship.[2] The differences were far more subtle. Applied to the relocation center, it is easily said that nuclear families were primary. It was essentially this overt similarity to the family systems of the West which never suggested to the WRA administration that here might be something a shade different. Thus, husband, wife, and children were allocated space in one of the barrack segments. But missing was an awareness of the depth of emotion and vitality and strength of the social ties pertaining to the Japanese family. To be sure, there were those conservative evacuees who kept a Buddha self, *butsudan*, along with the tablets, or *ihai*, of recently deceased family members. But this again was only superficially observed. Obviously, the elements of structure and the psychological depth of family feeling were not considered. I can say that at this level I made a mistake.

The majority of the Nisei, those defined as a group leaning toward the West and western institutions, seemed not to share directly in the patterns of Japanese familism. Yet this is not correct, given the fact that deference toward age, obedience to the paternal and maternal figures, and a sense of belonging were features which in themselves touched the members of this second generation most closely. In the all important question of marriage, for example, or in the heart–rending decision of some to leave the center and resettle somewhere in the permitted zones, the strength of the family tie made itself felt in prolonged deliberation and discussion and, quite generally in conformity to the wishes of the parental generation. While there was ostensible freedom of choice and while the mating–dating complex of the West touched the Nisei, arising so often from romantic Hollywood films, there were those conservative families which still insisted that as a contract between family groups (and not individuals), marriage should be properly arranged. I was, in fact, asked to serve as a *baishakunin* on two occasions, meaning that my role was that of marriage go–between, one assuming responsibility for overseeing the wedding gift exchanges, the marriage ceremony itself, and ultimately, for the eventual success of the marriage. I was not asked, as might be the case in Japan, or indeed, in rural America, actually to locate an appropriate marriage partner for a daughter or son, but I was named as a principal in the unions. (I should note that both the marriages in which I was more deeply involved ended in divorce—I failed in my role.) On the one hand, the situation reflected a pattern of acculturation, but on the other, I was given a perspective on the depth of Japanese institutions.

But putting the structural and psychological issues relating to the family aside, there was the problem of the community itself. The relocation centers were communities by default; elsewhere I have suggested that they were colonies. At this level, Dorothy S. Thomas' demographic analyses came to the fore. Age, sex, migration, provenance, occupation, and so through a host of interesting but fairly bland statistics, suggest composition of Gila and other centers. But whether the Gila population was urban or rural, whether its residents were drawn from San Joaquin valley farmers or from entrepreneurs from the Monterey peninsula, made little difference. One might expect that those of rural, somewhat socially isolated background, would be more conservative but the issue was not demographic. It was rather how the center settlers representing different areas and thrown together by circumstance succeeded in creating community reality.

It is here that the cultural side of evacuee life again comes to the fore. If the population in question had been made up of Chinese, Koreans, or Vietnamese, it might have been predicted that alliances were formed between those caught in a web of kinship. But, as has been noted, this was not the case with the Japanese. A significant element in the relocation was one much more intimately related to Japanese culture than to the American. Because of the nucleated family, even if a stronger emphasis is placed on collateral and affinal kin than is true of the United States at large, there was the need to consider the kinds of associations which were developed both in the pre–war period and in the centers themselves. One should have been aware of them more pointedly than proved to be the case. Indeed, even in the then available literature on Japanese social structure, much is made of the patterning of associations, clubs, cooperative systems, and other formally structured groups. This general model of association was carried over to America. People from the same prefecture in Japan, those with the same occupation, those with local neighborhood ties, or those with the same general interests formed a starting point. But the development of formally aligned social ties went far beyond the circumstance of merely being thrown together. What is suggested is that the native Japanese inclination toward the forming of extra–familial self–interest units created groups whose presence militated against a community solidarity.

From the perspective of my year–long residence at Gila, I must regard the rise of the various kinds of associations and political interest elements—not in the sense of community governance, but in terms of more immediate group goals—as the most striking aspect of the community. To be sure, there were at the center, block organizations, a community council, elected officials of one or another kind. But these, while overtly discernible, never assumed deeper significance; they were often ephemeral and evoked minimal allegiance. The WRA, operating in the context of Anglo–American patterns, imposed constitutional organization, not unreasonably, it may be supposed, thinking to instill American ideals of democratic procedure. I should not wish to convey that the more formal political institutions, those sanctioned by the WRA, were ineffective but their role was clearly ancillary to less well–defined and yet perceptible groups which reflected more cogent and immediate interests.

Actually, the Nisei were rather more inclined to organize with the benefit of the whole community in mind. On the Nisei side, the Gila Young Peoples' Club (essentially ineffective because of too varied a set of programs), the church and temple clubs, or the various recreational outlets were among those which followed the lines of Nisei interests, pretty much reflecting American patterns. The community services section of the local WRA lent a paternal hand in assisting the development of such organizations, setting forth requirements for elected leadership and constitutional sanction. But even here, there was a lack of unity. An example of tension may be seen in the continuing controversy over support for or against the Japanese American Citizens League (JACL).

Fragmentation was more apparent in the Issei and Kibei groups. Lines of communication were more difficult with the result that some Issei clubs were sanctioned; others were not. Apart from various overt groups, such as men and women's organizations, the *go–shogi* (or chess) clubs, the sumo teams and their supporters, there were the stronger "study clubs," whose presence was less immediately discernible, but which exerted a considerable political strength. Again, these were sometimes sanctioned, but in the main they served as a focus for both Issei and Kibei. These study clubs organized ostensibly for "community benefit," but it was clear that they arose to serve the interests of the more articulate Issei as well as groups of Kibei.

It was, in my view, this fragmentation which served to minimize the effectiveness of community organization. Loyalties went to the association and not to the center at large. The WRA administration inadvertently supported divisiveness. Given the Japanese penchant for organizing along associational lines, the results were perhaps inevitable.

Structure–functional theory assumes a basis for cohesion. The anthropologist who investigates, for example, a tribal society somewhere in the world, thus an essentially small enclave with sets of common understandings and a shared system of culturally defined principles, inclines to seek the elements creative of unity. The assumption is that a human social unit exists as a whole and that there are factors which operate to perpetuate it. In other words, the quest is for bases of integration, points around which the system constellates. Since human societies differ and since their cultural roots stem from varying historical circumstances, it may be expected that the component institutions will function variously so as to create a predictable system. In some societies, as is well known, religion may serve this purpose; in yet another, the political developments; family and kinship in still another. Obviously, this is an orientation drawn from Durkheimian theory, a simple basis for analysis in 1942, infinitely more sophisticated and complex today. But the question emerges—what relevance does such theorizing have for an appreciation of the Japanese–American situation? Or more pointedly, going back to the relocation center, what were the factors creating an integrated community, or indeed, was there a community at all?

In the main, the relocation demand threw together people of differing backgrounds, interests, classes, levels of achievement. To be sure, they were all of Japanese extraction and to a degree shared the same culturally defined understandings. But how far beyond this basic element did the situation go? Most regarded the relocation center as temporary solution to the problems of war. While, as Dr. Sakoda has pointed out, there were those, Issei especially, who appreciated the leisure which the center experience allowed, most evacuees thought of resettlement on the West Coast when the war ended, or they aimed for a location somewhere east of the Rockies. Loyalty to so ephemeral a community was eclipsed by the presence of such associations as could be momentarily established and which worked for not so much individual as family advantage. The result was that the immediate solution to the problem of social needs could be met in the array of extra–familial associational ties. If there was any basis for thinking of Gila as an integrated community, or to find in it a strong front against the outside, the element of the association must be treated in depth. The effect of it was not community solidarity but rather the perpetuation of special interests.

However significant these findings may have been, they were on the whole missed by the JERS staff. We went ahead and spoke of political pressure groups, reported on the activities of the various clubs, religious, social, recreational, but the overall picture eluded us. We lacked the sophistication to see the expansion and contraction of the diverse entities making up the center population. And by failing to deal with this appropriately, we fell back on journalistic reportage, a description of dissension, day–to–day anecdote. We missed the core of meaning. To look at one more major issue, again one reflecting the need to search deeply, there was the pattern of friendship. In the main this relates to the domain of the individual. In Japan, as is well known, dependency relationships stemming from the presence of age and school mates involve a deep emotional tie. Indeed, the fact that the immigrants were often unable to recreate in the pre–war period the close associations with a friend, noting that it was usually one friend, not a group, meant that there was emotional deprivation and individual isolation. Among the Issei this pattern was especially marked. Nisei friendships, again tending rather to follow the prevailing pattern in American society, were more often group–centered. As such, they tended to follow the essentially ephemeral relationships characteristic of friendship among Euro–Americans. In short, such friendships held a minimal depth of commitment. Dependency relationships were apparent among the Kibei, those more in harmony with the old–world background. The Nisei thus tended to find a variety of social outlets; the Issei and Kibei did not. The result was a covert dissension and again an element inhibiting community solidarity. Regrettably, the JERS staff never thought to look into patterns of social intimacy and into the domain of supportive relationships.

The element of friendship had to be contrasted with yet another feature, for which again there is minimal information. This is the problem of leadership, true, of course, in any human enclave, but by stepping back from the designation of formal leaders as such, there remains the problem of the assertion of power. Social classes, group leadership, and elected officials aside, these being relatively easily discernible, there was the sense of the manipulator, the dominant figure working behind the scenes. Given associations organized in ways congenial to the WRA staff, the emphasis was on democracy. But what of the institutions of the Japanese which allow latitude for the expression of power? This proved to be a knotty issue, especially when it is reflected that the native Japanese social system is implicitly hierarchial and the pattern is reinforced by etiquette and honorific usage. It is true that at Gila the population was largely rural and agricultural in its orientations. This being the case, it became possible for the person with greater sophistication and wider life–experience to assume an elite role. They might harangue, exhort, always within the realm of acceptable politeness, and they might employ a moral suasion and offer an ostensibly detached evaluation of center events. Given a following, they gained an informal domination.

In my own experience, I think of several such individuals who could direct the course of events simply by an exertion of force of personality. I hesitate to name them; their activities were always aside and *sub–rosa*. Generally congenial, but demanding of proper deference, these powerbrokers made their presence felt in virtually all decisions affecting the population at large. I sat at the feet of several such men, imbibing innumerable cups of tea, listening to the rumors which they often generated. I think it safe to say that the observer learned more from them than from a scrutiny of overt community events. Each man, and they were always men, became a kind of *daimyo*, a feudal lord, always with a following and always with a finger on center happenings. They never emerged publicly and always avoided the limelight. In regard to the war, those I knew were neither pro–Japanese nor pro–American; they appeared to find satisfaction in the exercise of such informal power as they could gain. Involved was a system of reciprocity. News was fed to them by a select group of informants—one inclines to say henchmen—while they, in turn, delivered sardonic, often tongue–in–cheek pronouncements. They held the evacuee population in contempt and claimed for themselves high social status, whether in Japan or in the United States.

The upshot of such hidden machinations was that no study of the relocation center could have been adequate which failed to take these power roles into account. But neither the WRA nor JERS were sufficiently alert to evaluate the place of these informal yet vital figures. In the main, I believe that JERS never reached the kinds of conclusions which might have lent strength to its analyses. Dorothy S. Thomas hit on one such figure in Richard Nishimoto. She co–authored her first volume with him without, I believe, having precise insight into his ultimate community role.

Conclusion

In these few remarks, I have tried to bring back recollections of 45 years ago. My own objectivity at the time was tempered by the tense and often anxious circumstances of evacuation and life in the Gila center. As I have written the above, I recognize, really for the first time, that I have been obliged to take stock of the JERS contribution. I do not believe that the data compiled were useless or that the enterprise was a failure. As Dr. Miyamoto has said, there is a treasure–trove of raw data still to be examined. My only wish is that we could have gone so much further than we did and could have done so much more in understanding and interpreting the patterns of a population living under great stress. I think it a remarkable tribute to the Americans of Japanese ancestry that they did so well and weathered so adverse a time in their lives.

Notes

1. Arthur A. Hansen, "Cultural Politics in the Gila River Relocation Center, 1942–1943," *Arizona and the West* 27 (1985), 327–62.

2. Robert F. Spencer and Kanmo Imamura, "Notes on the Japanese Kinship System," *Journal of the American Oriental Society* 70 (1950), 165–73.

PART III

Through the JERS Looking Glass:

A Personal View from Within

CHARLES KIKUCHI

Looking back on the Japanese–American generation I knew 45 years ago is not easy. The dwindling numbers who went through the American concentration camps all had a different experience in the post–war years. They resettled with a damaged Japanese heritage left by aging Issei parents, who had been stripped of pre–war social and economic stability. In contrast to the much–acclaimed Nisei soldier, the vast majority of Japanese–Americans less dramatically made their way into the mainstream of American society. The several thousand who resumed college education had a less traumatic adjustment. However, most Nisei were reasonably successful economically; and on the troubled social level, they did pave the way for the Sansei. Some did fall by the psychological wayside in their search for cultural identity. Perhaps the Japanese–Americans were not a "model minority," since racism is still around in the American fabric. But we did achieve an unprecedented success against very heavy odds. We found answers to the confusion of the wartime years in many individual ways and had a shared memory of this past even though many did not choose to talk about it with those who came after. It is up to the contemporary scholars to explore whether the Nisei gave up too much cultural heritage to achieve post–war acculturation in American society.

My own memory of those years is distant, but it is not one of rejection or bitterness. I have not consciously felt any nostalgic attraction for the reality of our wartime rejection. Part of the reason was that my post–war life on the East Coast engaged my full attention. I was too far away to attend any of the internment camp reunions to refresh my distant memory. The vernacular press was not available to me, although I did read several books about the internment in later years. I was able to accept my ethnic identity in a positive way in this less hostile environment.

But back in the 1940s, JERS gathered enormous data on our collective past. Some contemporary scholars might conclude that the JERS collection is suspect because of some faulty research techniques, out–dated sociological concepts, or researchers' over–identification with the subject under study. However, the body of raw, social data collected by a dedicated staff of 35 Nisei, Issei, Kibei, and Caucasian scholars would seem to far outweigh these very real questions. JERS concentrated upon the human qualities of the Japanese–American experience at a crucial time.

For many years I did not even think of JERS as more than a historical curiosity, as my lifestyle in New York kept me at a distance, physically and emotionally, from the events of those times. Although not deliberate, it became part of my "buried past." My almost total concentration in the post–war years was with the present and the future. These concerns crowded out the anger and painful scars of the 1940s. Over the years, much of my personal confusion and conflict about "who I am" became less stormy. I felt comfortable and happy living in New York City with my immediate family, and my situation was relatively free of negative social and economic confrontations. It never occurred to me that the wartime experience and my activity with JERS were a therapeutic contribution to my process of becoming an emotionally balanced Nisei, capable of coping with occasional, overt racism and the wider social problems of American society. But I never lost my ingrained pattern of being a social rebel, even though my psyche became less threatened as the years passed. I compensated for the contradictions of mainstream life by working as a clinical social worker, doing individual and group therapy for the Veterans Administration over 23 years. I worked under my own guidelines, without departmental supervision, in lieu of administrative advancement. It was a meaningful activity, and I felt that I had made a contribution to an imperfect system.

My Identity as a Nisei

Thus, for me, the JERS experience was not a step in the academic direction followed by many of my co–workers. My involvement had a far more significant, personal value, as it helped me to identify myself as part of the Nisei generation. This process seemed to be acute and threatening because I did not have any exposure to the Japanese–American community until after college graduation. When I attended San Francisco State College in 1939, there were only about six Nisei students because most went to UC Berkeley. Prior to this time, personal family circumstances had kept me isolated from the Japanese–American community. But in 1940 I became a direct part of the "Nisei Problem" by moving into San Francisco Japantown, called *Nihonmachi*. It did not take long before I became acutely aware of the effect of racism and economic and social discrimination upon the Nisei personality. Our generation was just coming of age, and the Japanese–American community could not absorb us. There were few jobs, professional or otherwise, available to us.

It did not take very long before I became acutely aware of the consequences of this kind of rejection upon the Nisei personality. My energy in this community was directed toward immediate survival. A college degree was not useful when I was confronted with the reality of those confusing times. The Nisei were the victims of racism, and at the same time we were being blamed for the disruption of the larger society's economic structure. The Nisei inherited the one hundred–year–old burden of the "Yellow Peril." Some Nisei blamed the Issei for not doing more to combat discrimination. At the same time, I was confronted with the reverse bias of the ingrown Japanese–American community. For most of 1940 and 1941, I was an unwilling participant in this "Nisei Problem," and I was often angry and resentful but also confused when confronted with all these internal and external pressures. There were few successful Nisei role models to follow.

Without the emotional or economic support of the community, I floundered through a two–year period of personal disorganization. I faced the Nisei dilemma of widespread social and economic dislocation, while at the same time wondering how the growing threat of America's conflict with Japan would compound our problem. I had no alternative but to follow the dead–end occupational route of many others who left the city to work in the rural areas of Central California. The depression was still on, and a flood of migratory workers came from Oklahoma and Arkansas to join the Mexican, Filipino, Chinese, and Japanese competing for seasonal jobs.

It was not easy for me to adjust to stoop labor at low pay, but it became a part of my post–college education. I worked in the orchards and fields all over Central California following the crops. I went to Alaska and worked briefly in the fishing industry, but I did not have the stamina of others. I picked apples in Washington and Oregon. I worked in the fruit and vegetable stands in Southern California, but I was not able to tolerate real and imagined insults by the public. Nor did I have the talent to make those beautiful fruit stand arrangements made famous by the Japanese–Americans. I picked grapes with the Armenians near Fresno. I worked briefly on Grant Avenue in San Francisco as a low–paid salesman until I forgot to make the courtesy bow to the Issei employer. I worked on the railroads with the Mexicans in Nevada. I tried to organize Filipino field workers cutting celery, and I got fired by the Nisei foreman whose father had bought the farm in the son's name because of California laws which denied this right to the Japanese immigrant. I worked in a Chinese gambling house for a while. I never earned more than 25 cents an hour in my many jobs. But I did make a lot of friends, many Nisei. On rare days off, many of the Nisei summer workers headed for the red–light district in a Chinatown on the Sacramento delta "to improve race relations," we said, in sharp contrast to our almost puritanical behavior on the college campus.

Somehow I survived, until I got a temporary job with the California State Employment Service at 40 cents an hour to do a survey on the Nisei in the San Francisco job market. At the same time, this agency was turning away over–qualified Nisei from defense jobs, which were opening up to all but the Asian–American. My job was my entry card into the inner life of the Japanese–American community. I became acquainted with many levels of social groups, I met business and professional Nisei, I found out about the social distance between the Buddhist and Christian Nisei. I learned about the distinction between the urban and rural Nisei. I met Nisei who were doing schoolboy jobs and working as domestic workers. I got some idea of how the light of educational goals still burned brightly among unemployed Nisei. I learned about the power of social class in the community, the status of agencies and organizations directly linked with Japan. I met many Nisei businessmen who saw a future tied to companies from Japan. I roomed for a while with a college–educated Kibei who worked for the Japanese Embassy, and we discussed which country offered the best hope for the Japanese–American. I was invited into Japanese–American homes for the first time because I held a "professional job." I was able to get a taste of the many layers in the community.

I also followed closely the activities of a loosely–knit street corner gang of Nisei. Due to bitterness about unemployment, they acted out frustrations by engaging in petty crimes and gang wars, mostly in Chinatown. They were few in number but an embarassment to community leaders, who preferred to ignore them. Most members of this group eventually went into military service and compiled a fine record. Others became small businessmen in the post–war

Japanese–American community. Two died of alcoholism, and another jumped off the San Francisco Bay Bridge in despair. One changed his name to a Chinese name and left for the East Coast and eventually gained fame as a singer and actor in a TV police show. They were all a part of the "Nisei Problem."

A Growing Cloud of Pessimism

Over all of these individuals and groups there was a growing cloud of pessimism, which they sought to escape within the narrow framework of the pre–war Japanese–American community. The vernacular press and many organizations tried to divert this sense of futility by placing a disproportionate emphasis upon sports and social activities. They were more or less successful, as there was an active community life, which leaders attributed to the "Japanese spirit" and strong family ties.

By the fall of 1941, I concluded that the Japanese–American community held little promise for my economic salvation and that I would have no future any place without a graduate degree. I enrolled in the social welfare department of the University of California with a goal of working one day with ethnic groups and the disadvantaged of our society. In those days anyone with adequate college grades could register in Berkeley as long as he had $26 for registration fees. There were only four Asian–Americans in the graduate school that year, and we had been individually forewarned that there would be no social welfare jobs available afterward. We persisted in the face of the myth that Japanese– and Chinese–American families did not get welfare, so that Asian–American social workers were really not needed. The immediate struggle was to get a fieldwork assignment with this ethnic limitation. I ended up one semester in the San Francisco Welfare Department, where I had one Japanese–American family on my caseload out of the dozen in the agency. An added strain was my concern about how the political impact of Japan's aggressive actions in Asia would affect the fieldwork placement.

The undergraduate Nisei understandably shielded themselves from the outside world by plunging into studies and the closed social life of the Japanese–American student clubs. I remember the acute concern about the economic future, and overall gloom which prevailed, when over one thousand Nisei college students from all over California attended a weekend conference at San Jose State College, which had for its theme, "Whither Nisei?" There were a few, half-hearted attempts to continue these discussion meetings on the Berkeley campus, but the majority of Nisei rejected the idea in favor of campus social activities and a return to individual study patterns. They believed that education was the only way to succeed.

My practical reason for going to one of these discussion meetings, upon arrival in Berkeley, was to find a room. This was far more difficult than getting registered for classes. Berkeley in those days was less liberal, and there was growing concern that the wave of Nisei students would soon overrun the housing resources of the city. I met Warren Tsuneishi, who had hitchhiked from UCLA that day, and we became the roommates of Kenny Murase in a house filled with other poor Nisei students who each paid only $5 a month for rent. It was here that I eventually met some of the Nisei who later became involved with JERS. Most had been sent to college by parents who sacrificed due to intense belief that education would solve all problems. The Nisei responded with an intensity which was unique to Asian-American students, and they filled the library every evening. Some were so poor that *ochazuke*, or rice with tea and Japanese pickles, was a standard meal.

I was still unwinding from my disorganized pattern, so I felt justified in October 1941 to go down to Stanford to take money from the empty fraternity houses during the "Big Game," so that I could cook up a huge pot of stew to sell to those poor students at ten cents a plate. But they quickly boycotted my gesture when they found out the source of this bounty. It was then that I learned how honest these Nisei students were. My impression now is that about 90 percent of them went on to get Ph.D.s.

Learning about the Nisei Personality

The larger lesson for me in those pre–Pearl Harbor weeks was that the Nisei students were driven by the same inner drive which their immigrant parents had brought from Japan. I learned a lot about the Nisei personality. They did not act out their resentment about racism, and they tended to be politically passive. Only a few joined left-of-center political groups. They did not seem to react negatively to the more patronizing faculty members they frequently encountered in class. (It was these same faculty members who did not stand behind the Nisei when war broke out.) But even though I did not attend classes regularly that graduate year, it was the most satisfying educational experience I ever had. It was the first and only time that I immersed myself in the lifestyle of the college Nisei. I did meet some Nisei who were active in the larger campus activities, but they seemed to be set apart from the rest of the Nisei student body. A few set themselves apart from the entire college because of fear that someone would find out about their outcaste background from Japan. I learned that there was no such thing as a "typical" Nisei.

I made many non–Nisei friends that year, but the two groups never seemed to interact. It seemed that almost five hundred Nisei undergraduates were a separate student body. I did not understand until much later some of the social pressures in our society which created this situation. The barrier was not language, but a self–imposed reserve which the Nisei brought with them from the pre–war communities. I did not have this kind of experience, so it was difficult to comprehend at that time. Naively, I believed that the Japanese–American student clubs were segregating themselves without any awareness of external forces which left them with limited options. I also did not understand why many Nisei women seemed to be on campus mainly to find husbands who belonged to their same social class and economic levels. Only a few openly rebelled to prepare for non–existent careers.

The other thing I learned that year was that the Nisei brought all of the pre–war community social and class distinctions to the campus. I could not comprehend, for example, why it was so important for them to know the prefecture (*ken*) from which my parents had emigrated in Japan. This puzzled me to the point where I would respond that I was an outcaste and this even mortified my liberal Nisei friends. I did not feel that it was necessary to explain that my grandfather was exiled from a Tokyo samurai tradition to the small island of Hachijo, where political exiles were sent, or that my father had run away from this island at age 15 to come to America. There were also campus divisions based upon urban or rural background, Buddhist or Christian affiliation, and parents' occupational status. I misunderstood their ethnic pride as symptomatic of political identification with military Japan. I did not understand that the expression "Jap," used frequently by summer workers, was never to be used outside the group. Being a Japanese–American was the common bond which held all of the divergent campus Nisei together.

On December 7, 1941, the Nisei confusion about the future became a reality. Our world was shattered. Many students went into shock as no one knew how to cope with the situation. The students worried about their families, as the FBI quickly rounded up many Issei heads of households. Banks were closed. There was no real leadership left in the Japanese–American community. On the campus there were no Nisei leaders, and many of the students left in droves to be with their families at the first hint of internment. Others left to join the military. In this crisis, the UC Berkeley faculty and the San Francisco media were not very encouraging, and most of the liberal, civil liberties organizations were immobilized. Even the churches were lukewarm; they only passively protested, although they did play an active role in assisting the Japanese–Americans to prepare for mass evacuation.

Few Japanese–Americans protested the military decision to evacuate, and most Issei businesses lost their life work and savings. Some left–of–center Nisei individuals and organizations, like the Young Democrats Club of Oakland, tried to openly protest the violation of constitutional rights by petition, but they did not get the support of the campus Nisei, the Japanese–American community, or even their own national offices. Even my non–Nisei friends, who planned an underground route to keep me out of the camps, had to give up the idea when they realized that they would all soon be dispersing. They could only offer in the end the comfort of playing the record "The Cradle Will Rock" on the last evening before evacuation.

A Time of Crisis and Confusion

This hysteria built from January 1942 until the end of spring. The campus mood among Nisei was one of growing confusion. The military and the government made uncertainty and indecision the rule of the day. It was in this crisis that some Nisei students emerged as leaders. Among them were Tom Shibutani and James Sakoda, who were seniors studying social science. They organized study groups for discussing how to cope with the many rumors sweeping the campus each day. A curfew kept the Nisei away from the local Japanese–American communities.

At the same time, Dr. Dorothy S. Thomas, who taught rural sociology, decided that it was vital to record objectively what was happening to the Japanese–American communities. She had anticipated an exclusion policy as soon as the war erupted. She got initial funding from the university for an immediate survey which traced the rapidly changing situation: the dramatic deterioration of the pre–war Japanese–American community, the developing antagonisms of the military, the racist appeals of the powerful agricultural lobby in Sacramento, and the shifting of the media and politicians from lukewarm sympathy to Japanese–Americans to openly racist antagonism. Dr. Thomas began to recruit a few Nisei undergraduates and non–Nisei graduate students, and they became the nucleus for the JERS staff.

In the early months of 1942, when mass internment became more than a rumor, both Shibutani and Sakoda urged the Nisei members of the dwindling discussion group to record exactly what was happening to the Nisei students, their families, and the Japanese–American communities nearby. In the meantime, Thomas had obtained Giannini and other foundation grants to expand the scope of her project to cover the entire Japanese–American population on the West Coast. Dr. Frank Miyamoto of the University of Washington and other qualified researchers were added to the staff. For Shibutani and Sakoda, the immediate assignment was to locate other Nisei on campus who might have some research orientation.

With the announcement of evacuation, the Japanese–American community floundered, due to the removal of the Issei leaders plus the ineffectiveness of Nisei organizations, such as the JACL and churches, in providing direction. JERS immediately gave priority to this aspect of community disorganization. Since Shibutani was aware that I had some contacts in the San Francisco Japanese–American community among the fringe groups, he nominated me for the JERS staff even though I did not have any background in sociological methodology. I was very hesitant about my role as a researcher since I had no formal training in this discipline. I was persuaded by the possibility of a small, weekly honorarium from the university. And I did have the advantage of free run of the Bay Area without regard to the military curfew as my friend, Harry Lee, gave me a Chinese student ID card.

Keeping a Wartime Diary

In early spring, 1942, I met with Thomas and her husband to discuss what role I could fill in JERS. I had kept a diary from Pearl Harbor, as Sakoda had insisted that daily records should be recorded. I showed some of my entries to the Thomases, and they emphasized that if I continued with my efforts that it would be valuable to JERS. I was hired for a $12.50 weekly honorarium just before evacuation to Tanforan Assembly Center. In the confusion of this mass internment, I lost most of my pre–war records and the diary from Pearl Harbor to Tanforan. But I did keep a daily diary throughout my stay in Tanforan and later in Gila, and still later during the Chicago resettlement and post–war periods. These materials are now in the archives with my Chicago life histories, my main contribution to JERS.

My diary assisted me in dealing with much of my confusion about being a Nisei and with pressures created by stress. Its main value during the 1940s was to help me sort out problems in research methods, in recording life histories, and in evaluating interview techniques. It was of crucial value to resolve the issue of confidentiality, as the Nisei were most sensitive about any written records. They were aware that FBI files could damage their resettlement aspirations. They were more at ease when they accepted that these records could be of value to JERS research and that this information would not be released to any government agency. The fact that I was a resettler myself was an asset in establishing a positive interview relationship. This gave JERS an advantage over the WRA Community Analysis Section, which represented the camp administration and was mistrusted by evacuees.

While in the camps, I refined my ability to take brief notes with my own kind of shorthand, as the camp administration was suspicious of JERS. While at Tanforan, we were never allowed to have a staff meeting with Dorothy S. Thomas. I also worked for the camp newspaper, and this exposure allowed me to make many contacts among the population as well as give me additional experience in interview techniques. The University of California had sent my social welfare degree to Horse Stable #10, but I was unable to use it while at Tanforan.

Without direct supervision from the Berkeley JERS office, the staff in Tanforan was forced to work independently and select study projects on a random basis. We were all in our early twenties and inexperienced in formal research. We came from diverse backgrounds and held different opinions, but somehow we became increasingly productive in our own areas of research. We never wavered in our belief that JERS was an important project.

As a single Nisei interested in social interaction, there were occasions when I had conflicts over whether I should record some of my own unorthodox social activities. I was concerned from the beginning about issues of confidentiality and research needs. Over a period of time, the research focus became primary and this was reflected in the growing objectivity of my diary reports. This understanding of my research role was later to be most helpful when I began to write life histories. Complete detachment and objectivity was the ideal goal, but not always completely possible. Since I was also a participant in the evacuation and resettlement, I was always very much aware of how my own personal orientation could influence the research process. For this reason, I later often expressed my personal orientation about the role of the Nisei in my diary in order to consciously prevent these sentiments from entering the framework of the life history interviews I did in Chicago.

From the beginning, Dorothy S. Thomas did not have any formal guidelines to offer the JERS staff, other than to gather as much data as possible and worry about the interpretation later. Because of this permissive direction, the staff gradually produced a general outline of what to observe during evacuation and resettlement. We formulated a wide range of topics for individual study. As a result, there never was a uniform assignment for all of the staff in the various camps. Since I was given such a loose assignment initially, it was possible for me to work in the employment office, the newspaper in Tanforan, and in the welfare office in Gila to gather data and develop interviewing techniques on my own. In time, my own orientation did not stand in the way of interviewing individuals with sharply different views.

At Gila, I was asked by the administration to organize the social welfare department (because I was the only Nisei among the thousands who held a graduate degree in this field). I immediately discovered Issei resistance to the Nisei college women I was training as social workers. This attitude prevailed among many of the male block managers and other professionals, but it was strongest among the many single farm workers who had followed the migratory crops for many years and were now destitute. They had a cultural bias of male domination, so many insisted that I, not the women I had trained, interview them, despite my lack of Japanese language skills.

Conversely, it was this experience which made me aware of why so many college–educated Nisei women had placed such a heavy pre–war emphasis on campus social activities, despite their considerable academic achievements. It was at Gila that many of these women got their first experience in a professional role, and some of their repressed resentment about their pre–war status spilled over. They found they could compete equally with men and, in time, their dedication as social workers won over the resistant Issei applicants. They worked long hours for their $21 per month professional status. Their efforts influenced my later decision to include many Nisei women in the life history sample in Chicago, even though the male resettlers outnumbered females ten to one initially.

The other significant influence in my learning to accept Japanese cultural patterns involved one of my co–workers in Gila, Robert Spencer. He arrived in the desert camp shortly before I did. He had interrupted his Ph.D. dissertation in the anthropology department at the University of California to do work for JERS. He related exceptionally well to all evacuees because of his genuine interest in Japanese culture, which he deeply felt should not be rejected by the Nisei. Evacuees did not view Spencer with suspicion because they knew that he did not work in the WRA Community Analysis Section. He led me to participate in Japanese cultural activities, from which I had previously kept my distance. As a result, I learned about sumo, *go*, *mochi* pounding at New Year's, Zen ceremonies, Japanese kinship, and many other aspects of culture in the seven months that we worked together. My view of Japanese culture moved from negative to tentative. We redefined our own JERS roles to enable us to work more closely together, and we wrote up a joint report on the Gila community structure under a research framework, which he mostly devised and I followed. Spencer also made a significant contribution to my life history interview techniques, as his approach was less goal–oriented than my social work interview approach.

The Emerging Role of Life Histories in JERS

By early 1943, W. I. Thomas had persuaded his wife that the writing of life histories should play a larger role in JERS. A staff meeting was held in Salt Lake City to formulate a specific outline for life histories during the resettlement phase. We went on to the Poston camp for further discussion with another staff worker, and the outline was completed. Possible collaboration with the Alexander Leighton research group in Poston was cancelled because of a riot erupting at that time over the "loyalty" registration, which had led to disturbances in most camps. The WRA then began its policy of leave clearance for the Midwest, with the intent of closing the camps, a policy which appealed mostly to single Nisei as an alternative to military service.

Since I was philosophically opposed to a segregated Nisei military unit, I did not volunteer, and I was not qualified for the military language schools. I requested an assignment in my educational specialty, which gave me clearance for resettlement, and it took the Army two years to decide in my favor. In March 1943, I left Gila armed with many copies of the life history questionnaire, two teenage dependents, and a JERS stipend of $175 per month. I went through all the resettler problems of adjustment which confronted the thousands who came later. I began a 30–month project to collect life histories. It became my sole responsibility to select the sample and make connections.

The JERS staff was located at the University of Chicago, and daily meetings were held initially to decide how the resettler population could be studied. I was able to gain valuable sociological insights from Dr. Frank Miyamoto and others on the staff. I also went out to Berkeley to review life history concepts with the Thomases. They emphasized that the life histories were my official priority in Chicago before going into the Army (where I became the only Nisei in a team doing psychological profiles of military prisoners and court–martialed GIs). From then on, I spent an average of 18 to 20 hours a day on this project. My practice of sleeping only four hours a night had started during college.

To remember methodological process in detail after so many years and without any available JERS references at my disposal is most difficult. I can only generalize on how I made initial contacts with the resettlers. I do remember that one of the important conditions for life history selections was the Chicago climate. In the winter when it was windy, I only selected resettlers who were within easy streetcar range. I did get some guidelines in statistical procedures from other JERS staff, but these guidelines were followed loosely at best. I had wanted to do 100 life histories when the resettler population was less than 500, but I had to give up this goal when the resettler population exceeded 20,000. Thousands more passed through Chicago on their way back to colleges in the Midwest and East.

Many resettlers were initially contacted through relatives and friends, by word of mouth, through social agency connections, the field office, employment offices, churches and hostels, dances and bars on Clark Avenue, and through private social gatherings. I met hundreds of resettlers over this period. At one time Togo Tanaka, who worked in an employment agency when not doing JERS research, referred to me resettlers identified by pre–war residence and occupational and educational groupings. I was able to follow up on perhaps one out of 20 of these referrals. In this trial–and–error method, I did manage to cover most of the career lines known to the Nisei before the war.

Since most of the interviews had to be arranged for the evening hours or on weekends, it was an extremely time–consuming process. On occasion, the interview had to be broken up over a full day. I also spent much time in writing up my notes late at night, and I usually dictated to Louise Suski, the office secretary for JERS, the following morning. She could type as fast as I could dictate. I did not change the content of any interview, but I did rearrange some of the sections to generally follow the life history questionnaire form. I usually gave this outline to the resettler, but it was never followed point–by–point since it was more important to keep the person talking on whatever was on their mind at the moment. In my dictation, I tried to capture the tone of expression as closely as possible. I was able to dictate entire verbatim comments, a skill I no longer possess.

It probably would have been easier had I done the life histories of only those who were articulate, cooperative, and interesting, but this was not my goal. In order to avoid some of the biases of sampling, I tried to include resettlers who were angry, hostile, or unresponsive. Many were resentful that the WRA had sent them to a strange city when they really wanted to return to the West Coast. They believed it was further evidence of racism. Others made no attempt to adjust to Chicago as they were waiting to be inducted into the Army, and they did not plan to return to the Midwest. In some instances I did follow–up interviews over a two–year period, but some of this data was not included in the finished life history collection. Another problem was in finding a suitable place for conducting interviews, as it was too incovenient to hold them in the JERS office, which was located on the south side of the city. In time, most of the interviews took place in the cramped apartments of the resettlers, usually before and after dinner. There was no such thing as a tape recorder in those days, so that the interviews proceeded in a conversational way over a wide range of topics. Since I was trying to define my own attitudes about the role of the Nisei in American life, I had to be on constant guard not to project my own cultural and political biases on the resettler being interviewed. This was not always an easy task. My social work training held some of my potential biases in check. In most instances, I found that all of the resettlers were very open in expressing views.

My Changing Frame of Reference

There were shifts in my own frame of reference by the time I got to Chicago. I modified some of my attitudes about resettlement and the future of Japanese–Americans. I believed the Nisei would be best served by rapidly integrating into American society. In time, I realized that the path to this goal was an individual choice; there was no mass solution to a "melting pot." I concluded that this process of integration could best be achieved by a move to the East Coast. I was careful not to express this attitude through the tone of my voice in the life history interviews. I discovered that many Nisei were even more vocal than I that assimilation was the only path for Japanese–Americans. But others had equally strong beliefs that their future was back on the West Coast, and they were bitter that the government policy had forced them to move to the Midwest. Despite this anger, most of the single Nisei did not oppose military service. From their viewpoint, they had no choice but to become assimilated as their cultural heritage had been destroyed along with the pre–war Japanese–American community. The dilemma at that time was that there were no guidelines as to how Japanese–Americans were supposed to find their proper role in American life. This issue still confronts Asian–Americans today.

Surprisingly in the face of a wide range of attitudes among resettlers, I never had a problem gaining their confidence and cooperation. I discussed the issue of confidentiality immediately, and this assurance of privacy resulted in free expression after the first meeting. Because of my earlier commitment (while in the internment camp) to protect the identity of a subject—when, on those occasions the issue of confidentiality clashed with research goals—I discarded a few of the life histories prior to completion of the interviews. These individuals feared that the material would damage their post–war status. I was aware that a change of name and geographical location was insufficient for total protection of these individuals. At the same time, the line between my social life and my research work was often blurred, and these activities were sometimes intertwined. In the 1940s, promiscuity for Nisei women was taboo, so I did not continue with life histories where there was personal involvement, especially with young Nisei wives who had resettled from the camps while their husbands had joined the military.

My connection with JERS ended after I had written 64 life histories by the time I entered military service, but it resumed in the early 1950s when Dorothy S. Thomas, James Sakoda, and some graduate students at the University of Pennsylvania began to prepare the resettlement data for publication. I was invited down on weekends to review the life histories. I did some of the preliminary selection of life histories for publication, and I prepared the brief introduction to each selection. Thomas made the final selection of the 15 life histories included in *The Salvage*. She chose those which were most representative of the evacuation and resettlement process and which had been statistically discussed in the first section of the book. The life histories used were not abridged, as far as I can recall.

All the life histories had in common the experience of leaving the internment camps and starting new careers in an unknown part of the country. The Nisei left behind their families in most instances until they could get economically settled. This resettlement broke the period of isolation of life behind barbed wire in the camps. It started the long process of individual economic and social adjustment in society. JERS was able to capture the essence of this process. When *The Salvage* was published (the life histories constituted three-fourths of the volume), all of the JERS files were returned to the Bancroft Library in Berkeley. In the early 1970s, John Modell edited my Tanforan diary for publication, and this was to be my last connection to JERS for many years.

Opening the Floodgate of Memories

It was the University of California conference on JERS in September 1987 which opened a floodgate of personal memories. It brought me full circle to my past. I am even now sorting out the real meaning of how the decade of the 1940s, through the JERS connection, shaped my lifelong adjustments. I learned that JERS was not forgotten history. Many of the documents were being researched by a new generation of scholars. On this occasion, I had a reunion with many of the JERS staff. Most had gone on to prestigious careers, and those in the academic environment were responsible for many publications on Japanese–Americans. They were the pioneers of the present–day Asian–American sociologists. I was left with a positive feeling that even as young and inexperienced as we were in the 1940s, the contributions we made to JERS remain a vital source of data for current researchers on the Japanese–American experience.

Out of JERS came the later development of Asian–American Studies in several universities, oral history programs, and research collections. JERS was there to record much of the complex Japanese–American world of the 1940s, from the day of mass evacuation to resettlement and the closing of the WRA camps. It was a unique situation, as most of the JERS staff had the dual role of being Japanese–Americans and being researchers during this confusing chapter in American history. The staff had the difficult chore of sorting out different values, resentments, and aspirations among evacuees. There were also deep group divisions, and some of these resentments still appear to exist. Contemporary scholars will find untapped information in the JERS files, which now seem to be taking on a second life after many dormant years. The JERS files are part of our Nisei legacy to the next generation. On a personal view from within, the JERS experience did influence my own development, both in the skills I learned and even more in my emotional growth of becoming a Nisei. Even in my newest career, devoted to traveling all over the world since 1973, I feel that I am a part of a cross–cultural experience. In addition, my wife, who is Kibei, has had notable success as a modern dancer and theater director in New York City, London, and Tokyo. She has choreographed arrangements for many dance companies all over the world, and more recently served as artistic director in the Martha Graham organization. This fortunate combination of travel and work has enabled us to meet hundreds of young people, and they view us as representatives of American society. I continue to use my interviewing skills learned in JERS to informally assist young people from many lands in their acculturation to this country. Over the years, we have also sponsored in our home many individuals from Japan, China, Poland, Germany, Costa Rica, Sweden, France, Italy, Korea, Brazil, Norway, and other countries. Their patterns of adjustment are not so different from the Nisei resettlers, except they do so by choice.

Finally, like most Japanese–Americans, I have realized that the pre–war "Nisei Problem" has disappeared in the post–war decades. JERS has played an important part in this process by bringing into balance the tensions underlying the growth from youthful ethnic confusion to an integrated, mature self–image.

When I went to the Berkeley campus after forty years for the JERS conference, I saw an astonishing number of Asian–American students, and I thought that nothing had changed. But I was wrong. A closer look revealed the faces of relaxed Asian–Americans, who freely mixed with the non–Asian students. I then concluded that the 1942 Nisei generation had left a proud heritage to the next generation. JERS was there to record this heritage. And through reflection of this past, I gained a respect for all of those thousands of resettlers who went on to make a significant contribution to the Japanese–American image.

Life History Analysis and JERS:

Re–evaluating the Work of Charles Kikuchi

DANA Y. TAKAGI

> We are safe in saying that personal life records, as complete as possible, constitute the *perfect* sociological material . . .
>
> W. I. Thomas and Florian Znaniecki[1]

> Looked at from one vantage point, the project of discovering and making available the lives and works of women is one of mythmaking—the creation of a tradition that can sustain women personally and give them a rich and lively social world.
>
> Carole Ascher[2]

Between 1943 and 1947, Charles Kikuchi devoted his life to interviewing Nisei resettlers in Chicago, taking down the details of their family history, work experiences, and perceptions of community. Kikuchi's 64 life histories constitute a unique set of historical documents in the JERS collection. In *The Salvage,* Dorothy S. Thomas used lengthy excerpts from the life histories to present the Nisei's "individual train of experience." The Kikuchi life histories stand alone as the only in–depth interviews of Nisei during relocation and resettlement.[3]

By the time that Kikuchi conducted his interviews, American sociologists were beginning to abandon the life history method, turning to survey data analysis on the one hand and grand theory on the other. The life history was originally associated with W. I. Thomas and Florian Znaniecki and other early Chicago school sociologists, including Nels Anderson, Clifford Shaw, and E. Franklin Frazier. With the decline in influence of the Chicago school came a decline in the use of life history materials. But a virtual renaissance has occurred in the last two decades. The revival embraced not only life history data, but also oral history, depth–interviews, and a renewed interest in the "subjective" aspects of individual social experience. Several outstanding works exemplify this drift toward the use of qualitative data analysis in the social sciences including, for example, Paul Willis, *Learning to Labour*, Lillian Rubin, *Worlds of Pain*, and E. P. Thompson, *The Making of the English Working Class*.[4]

The fascination with life history has reached all corners of the academy and is especially strong among feminist researchers[5] and historians.[6] And a cursory glance at the spate of new publications in Asian-American history shows that life histories are the current academic rage.[7] Amidst this current boom, it seems only fitting to assess the historical and contemporary significance of the Kikuchi life histories for research on the Asian-American experience.[8]

To start, an assessment of the Kikuchi life histories ought to be grounded in the intellectual milieu of the period in which they were gathered. The critical link between life histories in the Chicago school and life histories in JERS is sociologist W. I. Thomas. Therefore, I begin with a discussion of the important book he co–authored with Florian Znaniecki, *The Polish Peasant in Europe and America*, based extensively on life history materials. Next, I discuss the ways that the Kikuchi life histories reflect the organization of and theoretical assumptions found in Thomas and Znaniecki's work. I then move on to look at more recent approaches to life history analysis, pointing out two major differences between their methods and those of the Chicago school. My final comments concern the overall usefulness of Kikuchi's life histories.

From Polish Peasants to Nisei Resettlers

The five–volume epic by W. I. Thomas and Florian Znaniecki, *The Polish Peasant in Europe and America*, was first published between 1918 and 1920. The book influenced a wide circle of sociologists and set the intellectual groundwork for a sociology that stressed the importance of studying experience from the subject's point of view. The Chicago school sociologists of the 1920s and 1930s were in general agreement with Thomas and Znaniecki on this point. Studies such as *The Hobo* by Nels Anderson and *The Jackroller* by Clifford Shaw sought, as did Thomas and Znaniecki, to offer a faithful portrayal of the subject. And to get an accurate portrayal of the subject's experience meant conducting depth interviews, gathering personal documents, collecting life histories, and, in some instances, engaging in participant observation.

The Chicago school sociologists did not make the distinctions between oral history, life history, biography, and autobiography that social scientists are likely to make today. For example, Clifford Shaw referred to his subject's (Stanley's) account of delinquency as "own story" and as life history. Similarly, Thomas and Znaniecki referred to Mr. Wladek's 350–page written account of his past (written at their request) as "personal record," "life–history," "life–record," and "autobiography." In addition to "life histories," the bulk of Thomas and Znaniecki's work relied on "personal documents" in the form of letters written by Polish peasants.

In keeping with the tradition of the Chicago school writers, today's social scientists refer to "life history" as a subject's own account of his/her individual history. The account can be written or oral.[9] Burgess differentiates between oral and life histories in terms of the validity of each form.[10] According to him, oral histories, unlike life histories, were first used to provide evidence of social experience where there was little written, documentary evidence. But a disadvantage is that with little corroborating evidence to cross–check the oral history as a document, its use raises some questions of validity and reliability. Like autobiography, a life history offers the reader the perspective of an individual. But what distinguishes life history from autobiography or fiction, according to Becker, is the "perspective from which the work is undertaken and the methods used."[11]

What was unusual about Thomas and Znaniecki's research was 1) their use of life history data and personal documents from Polish peasants and, 2) the outline of a distinctive method or approach for analyzing qualitative data. Life history materials were not always considered useful in sociology. Thomas and Znaniecki made the first, and possibly one of the strongest, case for incorporating life histories into sociological research. It was their contention that social theory arises from two kinds of data, the objective cultural elements of social life on the one hand, and subjective characteristics of the members of the social group on the other. Objective cultural elements are, in Thomas and Znaniecki's work, denoted by social values. Social values are any data "having an empirical content accessible to the members of some social group."[12] The content of social values is sensual or imaginary, or both, and the meanings attached to them become "explicit when we take them in connection with human actions."[13] For example, food, music, and even a complex institution like the welfare system constitute social values which evoke both content and meaning.

In contrast to the objective cultural elements of a society, subjective characteristics of social groups are denoted by attitudes. Thomas and Znaniecki suggest that an attitude is the "individual counterpart to social values."[14] While social values define cultural objects, attitudes are the psychological processes of the individual that define his or her relationship to a social value. Thus, attitudes such as hunger and perceptions on the origins of poverty respectively define relationships to food and the welfare system.

The primacy of the life history as historical data can be seen in the organization of *The Polish Peasant*. In the second edition, composed of two volumes, most of the first volume of 1100 pages is devoted to peasant letters. Thomas and Znaniecki provide only their methodological introduction as preface to the work and a short introduction on the peasant letter. Analyses of the dissolution of peasant society and the reorganization of peasant communities in Poland as well as organization and disorganization of immigrant Poles in America follow in the second volume. But the crucial question, for which Thomas and Znaniecki offer only elliptical answers, is how do they analyze the peasant letter? Where do concepts such as social disorganization and reorganization come from? In a more general vein, how is life history as evidence used to conceptualize and/or theorize about social relations and social structure?

Thomas and Znaniecki's contention of the superiority of life history data over other kinds of data is embedded in their notion of what to study and how to study it. In the methodological introduction to the original edition, Znaniecki writes:

> We use in this work the inductive method in a form which gives the least possible place for any arbitrary statements. The basis of the work is concrete materials, and only in the selection of these materials some necessary discrimination has been used.
>
> The analysis of the attitudes and characters given in notes to particular letters and in introductions to particular series contains nothing not essentially contained in the materials themselves; its task is only to isolate single attitudes, to show their analogies and dependences, and to interpret them in relation to the social background upon which they appear.[15]

This inductive process was later given a more formal name, analytic induction, by Znaniecki in 1934.[16] As a methodology for analyzing life history as well as other qualitative data, analytic induction presumes that concepts like disorganization flow from the empirical data, in this case peasant letters and life histories. According to Znaniecki, analytic induction is the social science equivalent of the scientific method in the biological and physical sciences.

As a research procedure, analytic induction begins with a definition of the problem under study and a hypothetical explanation—what sociologists currently refer to as a working hypothesis—of what is being studied. The hypothesis is examined and reexamined on a case–by–case basis. Cases which do not conform to the hypothetical explanation (in sociological jargon, negative cases) can be dealt with in one of two ways. Either the researcher must reformulate the working hypothesis or, alternatively, the researcher redefines the problem under study. According to Znaniecki, this method of reformulating the hypothesis for every case, or life history, leads to the establishment of universals, or causal laws, in the social sciences.

Following the lead of Thomas and Znaniecki, several important works in the field of criminology adopted analytic induction as a research method.[17] But the claim that analytic induction uncovers causal laws in the social sciences has met serious criticism and doubt.[18] A larger issue which survives as a topic for contemporary discussion is how do researchers know that their categories, concepts and abstractions are justifiably derived from the life history? This is a topic that is subsumed under a general discussion of what constitutes method in the social sciences.

Znaniecki's analytic induction assumed that concepts (social theory) are derived from the life experiences (data). Much of contemporary sociology shares this assumption. But Znaniecki did not specify how conceptual categories are created, or in his methodological jargon, inductively generated from the data. While it is beyond the scope of this paper to review the philosophical and epistemological discussions of method in the social sciences, it is important to at least note that the subject of inferential knowledge, the inductive process of abstracting concepts from data, has been challenged.[19]

The influence of *The Polish Peasant* went beyond the introduction of a new methodology, the depth interview, direct observation, and fieldwork, so characteristic of the early Chicago school sociology. The book is also often cited in the field of family organization, immigration, community organization, and ethnicity. Thomas and Znaniecki are perhaps best known for their concept of "social disorganization." According to Thomas and Znaniecki, social disorganization of Poles, manifested in rebelliousness, juvenile delinquency, and dissolution of family, was the result of incongruence between individual attitudes and group values.[20] This dissonance model analyzed individuals and groups as caught between traditional communities and new communities, or new social worlds. The model took hold in American sociology. Eli Zaretsky, in his introduction to an abridged and edited version of *The Polish Peasant*, suggests that social policy and sociological research on minority groups have borrowed Thomas and Znaniecki's model of immigrants exiting a traditional world and entering a new social world.[21]

This model is at the heart of the Kikuchi life histories of the Nisei. In an outline of the Kikuchi interview schedule, Dorothy Thomas said that the life history portion of the JERS study is focused on

> the institutional reorganization and individual readjustments following their [Nisei] release and dispersal.
>
> The interview and document will be directed towards records of the changes in status, behavior and attitudes concomitant with the process of settling in and adjusting to a new environment.[22]

The actual format of the life history interview schedule by Thomas clearly outlines the central problem under study by JERS as the transition from one community (relocation centers) to another (Chicago).[23] And in the life histories, Kikuchi routinely comments on the adjustment process of the resettlers. For example, he notes that Shigeo, a single, 28–year–old Nisei man employed as a commercial artist, has had a "satisfactory adjustment process except for some loneliness due to the lack of social contacts," while Margaret, a 29–year–old Nisei woman employed as a secretary, is "well adjusted to the resettlement process and shows no personality problems."[24] The resettlement process refers to the transition from the camps, an all–Japanese–American environment to Chicago, a city of mixed races and new work experiences. In nearly all of the cases, Kikuchi introduces the life history with his own short summary of the individual's adaptability to dramatically different social situations.

The Kikuchi Life Histories

Each life history is divided into two distinct sections. In the first section, a preamble to the actual text of the life story, Kikuchi provides a synopsis of the individual's family and life history. Often, Kikuchi begins with a summary statement on how the individual is coping with the transition to resettlement. The second and more lengthy part of the life history is the individual's own story as told to Kikuchi.

There are two major ways that Kikuchi's life histories bear the intellectual stamp of the work of Thomas and Znaniecki. First, Kikuchi earnestly believed in the importance of an accurate account of the Nisei experience. As he explains, "no one really knew what the Nisei were thinking or feeling."[25] Kikuchi worked extremely hard at establishing rapport with Nisei in an effort to get their life stories. Also, in the interest of adding more information to an individual's life history, several of the files also include "personal documents," such as the respondent's letters to family and friends. And in some cases, additional analyses and comments are added by other members of JERS.

The general organization of Kikuchi's interview schedule is roughly similar to Thomas and Znaniecki's life record of Polish immigrants. This is not surprising since elsewhere in this anthology, Kikuchi has indicated that W. I. Thomas took an active role in developing the life history component of JERS. According to Kikuchi, both W. I. and Dorothy S. Thomas continually stressed the importance of recording the life histories of Japanese–Americans. It is quite likely that W. I. Thomas worked with his wife to draw up the outline of topics to be covered in the interviews with Nisei in Chicago. The topics, including family history, childhood experiences, work and community experiences, reflect those areas also highlighted in *The Polish Peasant*.

A second way that Kikuchi is clearly influenced by the work of Thomas and Znaniecki is his use of the concept of disorganization. Occasionally, Kikuchi refers to some of the Nisei as "personally disorganized." His use of the term "disorganized" is worth noting since the same concept figures so importantly in *The Polish Peasant*. For example, in the case of Kisako, a young, 19–year–old Nisei woman, Kikuchi writes, "she is a rather quiet girl and apparently disorganized."[26] Reading Kisako's life history, we discover that she is ashamed of the poverty of her family, that her fiance had died in the war in Italy, and that since coming to Chicago, she has not been able to find a satisfactory job. Here, Kikuchi is probably using the term "disorganized" to describe the crises and uncertainties facing Kisako. In another example, the case of Chie, a 25–year–old secretary, he says, "there is no serious personality disorganization apparent on the surface."[27] Though Chie, like Kisako, feels that the future is quite uncertain, Chie is "not unlike most of the resettled Nisei who feel that they cannot cope with all of the unforeseen environmental problems which they feel will arise."[28]

To be fair, Kikuchi is not engaged in the sociological enterprise of creating theory or hypothesis testing. Thus, while Znaniecki and Thomas were building a model of social organization and disorganization, Kikuchi is probably borrowing terms like "disorganization" for the purpose of describing an individual in crisis.

Having explained how the Kikuchi life histories are related to Thomas and Znaniecki, let me briefly comment on one outstanding difference. Thomas and Znaniecki are explicit that the object of their study is theoretical and analytical. Kikuchi's project focused on the collection of data and not on analysis. Even the publication of lengthy excerpts from 15 of the Kikuchi life histories in *The Salvage* did not occasion any analytic or theoretical discussion on the Nisei. As Thomas said, the life histories, or the train of individual experience, serve the function of complementing the demographic and statistical information profile of the Nisei presented in the first half of the book.[29]

Hiatus in Life History: 1930–1960

By the end of the 1940s, the life history method in sociology receded into the methodological background, while the use of large–scale surveys moved to centerstage. Thus, when Kikuchi had finished gathering the life histories of the Nisei, the actual use of the life history had almost vanished, at least in sociology. Life histories provided a range of experiences, but the methodology of interpreting those experiences was still problematic.

It seems to me that the analysis of life histories since that period has gone in two, somewhat overlapping directions. One direction, as I have noted earlier in this paper, has been to focus on issues of method in the social sciences. Method here should not be confused with the term technique, as in research technique. While techniques are strategies for analyzing data, method refers to assumptions about the relationship between theory and data. Many different voices contribute to the discussion of method, including, for example, Marxists, philosophers, feminists, phenomenologists, and symbolic interactionists. A central issue is whether there is a distinction between methods of analysis in the natural sciences and methods of analysis in the social sciences.

A second direction of life history analysis stems from a critique of the assumptions that characterized the analytic statements made by Thomas and Znaniecki in *The Polish Peasant*. As Zaretsky has pointed out, the influence of the book can be seen in much of the subsequent race relations research in sociology.[30] Indeed, many from the generation of social scientists after Thomas and Znaniecki focused on the ways in which the transition from traditional peasant societies to early capitalist America affected immigrants, workers, and racial minorities. This research emphasized how capitalism structured and shaped the life experiences of racial minorities, ethnic groups, and classes. In the field of race relations, for example, adaptation and assimilation became key concepts.[31] Successful groups in society were thought to "adapt" to their new environs, while the unsuccessful had failed to adapt.

Starting in the 1960s, a new generation of social scientists emerged to challenge the assimilationist bias of race relations theory, labor history, and research on immigrants. These new writers rejected the conception that individual experience can be analyzed as an "effect" of social structure. For example, William Ryan argued that the culture of poverty thesis "blamed the victim" for his or her own poverty.[32] Other critics, some of whom were part of the "new social history,"[33] charged that not enough attention was given to how the activities of working people affected the development and nature of capitalist life in America. Accordingly, social history from "the ground up" examined capitalism through the life experiences of individuals, rather than viewing individual lives as the by–product of capitalism. For example, Herbert Gutman says:

> Much remains to be learned about the past history of the American working class, much of which will enlarge our understanding of the larger social and economic processes that have shaped the development of the late twentieth–century American society. And there is much to be learned about the individual men and women who made up that changing class.[34]

The new social history calls for an unearthing of life experiences of working class individuals in biographies, diaries, letters, family documents, and even poetry and song.

The call for excavating the life experiences of those individuals and groups who have so often stood on the margins of history has resonated well in feminist and ethnic studies circles. Long ignored as subjects worthy of study, the experiences of women and racial minorities now have a place in social science research. In the field of Asian American history, for example, life histories are now standard text. In the basic introductory Asian American history courses, books such as Carlos Bulosan's *America Is in the Heart*, Akemi Kikumura's *Through Harsh Winters*, and Victor and Brett deBary Nee's *Longtime Californ'* have become typical assigned reading. These books and others like them are used to introduce students to a history through individual experience which is often ignored in college U.S. history courses and in California history courses at the high school level.

The Politics of Experience

Feminist scholarship, like the new social history and ethnic studies, takes as it subject the marginalized and excluded. Feminist researchers have charged traditional disciplines of history, sociology, and anthropology with the intellectual neglect of half of the human race. Thus, a major contribution of feminist research to social science has been the inclusion of women's experiences, both past and present.

The call for inclusion is a central part of a feminist research project.[35] This project will stop nothing short of writing a new history by redefining what is historically important and outlining a feminist research agenda, feminist theory and feminist methodology.[36] Women's experiences are crucial for rewriting history and for conceptualizing feminist theory and feminist method. And life histories as well as oral histories are a major source of documenting women's experiences.

Like the early Chicago school sociologists, some feminist researchers stress the sociology of the individual in an interpretation of the larger social world in which the individual lives. In this view, life histories are a form of factual data upon which concepts, hypotheses and theories are formulated and tested. This is a methodological perspective roughly similar to that found in *The Polish Peasant*. For example, Mary Sheridan in her book *Lives: Chinese Working Women* says:

> Life histories can illustrate the operation of the social order because through them we are able to observe how people adapt to the goals of society. They give us access to the "subjective" springs of action. The relationship between the individual and society is brought out by her life history.[37]

In a similar vein, Jane M. Atkinson bids feminist anthropologists to "replace the current split between analyses of women's personal lives, on the one hand, and male dominated social structure and ideology, on the other, with a unified picture of how the nature and experience of both sexes are socially and culturally patterned."[38] In other words, for some feminist researchers, the object of using life histories is to create a theoretical or analytic understanding of the social world.

Atkinson, Sheridan, and many others also share with their Chicago school predecessors a deep appreciation for the richness and variety of the individual experience. As C. Wright Mills has stated in the much celebrated *The Sociological Imagination*, sociologists are in the business of studying the human variety. Feminists have echoed this call with respect to the lives of women. For example, Lynn Z. Bloom, in a special issue of *Frontiers* exclusively devoted to women's oral history, says:

> Learning about the lives of women can provide an invaluable re–creation of our collective past, and provide meaningful ways to cope with our present and our future.[39]

And reiterating the call by speakers at the annual National Women's Studies Association meetings, a 1982 editorial to *Signs* urged feminists to recognize and embrace the wide variety of women's life experiences.

But the interpretation of oral and life history text by feminist researchers is significantly different from the original Chicago school sociology in two respects. First, feminist scholars view the lived experience of women as intrinsically *political*. For example, in one of the most powerful statements on this matter, Catherine McKinnon says:

> . . . women's distinctive experience as women occurs within that sphere that has been socially lived as the personal—private, emotional, interiorized, particular, individuated, intimate—so that what it is to *know* the *politics* of woman's situation is to know women's personal lives.[40]

Similarly, Mary O'Brien, issuing a challenge to feminists to critique and move beyond a male dominated theory of women's experiences, states:

> The activity that defines the Nature of Woman has been and is speculative and ideological. The activity that defines the lived conditions of women has been political and legal. Male supremacy typifies historical praxis at its most effective: a long standing but vital unity of thought and action.[41]

The assumption that women's lived experience is political means that the presentation of these experiences through oral or written life histories is also a political act. Since women's voices are frequently absent from traditional historical analyses, women's life histories break the silence of untold experiences. Thus, Sherma Gluck, borrowing from Gerda Lerner writes of the "special rhythm" of sexism governing women's lives and notes that in documenting women's lives, "we are affirming that our everyday lives *are* history."[42]

The assumption by feminist researchers that women's experience is political leads to a second important break with the Chicago school sociologists on the analysis of life histories. That is, that feminist scholars insist that the analysis of life histories constitutes a feminist *method*. For example, Susan N. G. Geiger in a review essay on the method and content of life histories says:

> The purpose of this review essay is to provide a more comprehensive examination of this body of literature considering women's life histories as primary sources for the content of women's lives and life history research as a *feminist method* for the broader and deeper understanding of women's consciousness, historically and in the present.[43] [emphasis added]

In a major departure from Znaniecki's analytic induction, feminist researchers argue that life history analysis embodies a particular relationship between researcher and subject. As Gloria T. Hull has outlined in what she calls the black feminist critical approach, the "proper scholarly stance is engaged rather than 'objective'."[44] In a more elaborate statement, McKinnon says that feminist method is based on the uniqueness of women's experience.

> Women's experience of politics, of life as sex object, gives rise to its own method of appropriating that reality: feminist method. As its own kind of social analysis, within yet outside the male paradigm just as women's lives are, it has made a distinctive theory of the *relation* between method and truth, the individual and her social surroundings, the presence and place of the natural and spiritual in culture and society, and social being and causality itself.[45]

It is the uniqueness of women's experience which gives rise to the engaged position of the feminist intellectual. Feminist method challenges the proposition that researchers act as neutral or objective observers of their subjects. Feminist researchers thus openly acknowledge the processes (and difficulties) of individuation of the self and separation from the subject that accompany the research enterprise. For example, in *Between Women* the contributing writers explain how they learned *about* their subjects as well as what they learned *from* their subjects.[46] Geiger in her review essay on feminist life history method blasts social science idealization of objectivity saying, "feminist scholars have revealed that notions of objectivity themselves are androcentric, and that higher levels of abstraction assumed to present a 'true' picture of 'reality' often represent neither truth nor reality for women."[47]

One major implication of the engaged stance of the researcher to his/her subject is that the very act of data collection, the interview, is a potentially consciousness raising interaction. The consciousness raising involves a heightened awareness of the self for both the researcher and the researched. The subject may, through the telling of her life experiences, gain new insights or perspectives on her own social experiences. And similarly, the researcher, in listening to the subject's experiences, widens his/her knowledge of the variety of women's experiences and in recording the subject's experiences validates those experiences.

In stressing the politics of experience in women's lives, feminist scholarship has called attention to the interactive nature of the relation between subject and writer in the gathering of life histories. But while feminist researchers have, I think, launched an effective critique of the notion of objectivity in social science, they have not yet succeeded in moving beyond that critique to a specification of the actual method of analyzing or interpreting life history data. While much has been written about how feminist method is different from the canons of social science methodology, there is little information about the actual content of feminist method. Instead, feminist researchers have tended to emphasize women's lived experience over questions of method and theory. This has been perhaps a necessary step since in the feminist intellectual enterprise the politics of experience is at the center of delineating feminist method and feminist theory. Thus, while Thomas and Znaniecki have an outline for a case–by–case inductive analysis of life histories, feminist methodology has not yet fully embraced or critiqued such nitty–gritty questions of negative cases, comparisons, hypothesis testing, nor the more difficult questions on the relationship between theoretical concepts and data.[48]

Analytic Induction, JERS, and the Politics of Experience

The Kikuchi life histories predate an avowedly feminist research agenda by several decades. But I think his work in one way anticipates the spirit in which feminist researchers claim life history analysis as feminist method. To be more specific, the Kikuchi life histories are often an explicitly interactive process akin to what feminist researchers characterize as consciousness raising. Kikuchi remembers that the ideal goal of the interview project was complete objectivity, but that this goal was not always possible within the actual research setting. He recalls that he often expressed critical sentiments toward Nisei in his diaries so that he would be less likely to taint his interviews with personal opinions. But he also has noted that, through his interviews with the Nisei, he acquired a more appreciative understanding of the Nisei experience.[49] In other words, the process of interviewing the Nisei was a learning experience for Charles Kikuchi. Or, in the language of feminist method, Kikuchi had his consciousness raised by the interviews.

Given the feminist emphasis on a politics of experience, how do the Kikuchi life histories stand up under feminist scrutiny? Recall that the feminist critique of social science opens with the charge that women's experience is excluded from history, while a feminist research agenda specifies the political nature of that experience. Let me discuss each of these points with respect to Kikuchi's work.

By feminist standards, Kikuchi's life histories make an important contribution to American history by documenting the social experiences of 29 Nisei women. The simple addition of women's family histories and work and resettlement experiences to the historical record should warrant feminist adulation for Kikuchi. As there are no other accounts of the Nisei female experience as told from their own perspective during the tumultuous war years, the Kikuchi life histories stand alone.

Although feminists are likely to applaud Kikuchi for documenting Nisei women's experiences, the feminist research agenda parts company with Kikuchi and JERS over the *politics* of that experience. Recall that one of the principal assumptions of the feminist approach to life history is that women's experiences are intrinsically political. Kikuchi never sought an understanding of life histories as political experience. Instead, Kikuchi wrote his preliminary summaries of each life history with concepts borrowed piecemeal from W. I. Thomas. Feminist writers would take Kikuchi to task for these brief summaries. In a feminist research agenda, labels such as "disorganization," which appear in the summaries, reflect a normative judgment made by Kikuchi about the interviewee's experiences. From the perspective of feminist writers, the value of life histories comes from what women tell us about their own experiences and how these experiences illuminate the power asymmetries of the world in which we live, and not from evaluative statements about those experiences.

Kikuchi's evaluative statements about Nisei adjustment, disorganization, and adaptation, however, are limited to the short summaries that precede the actual life histories. The bulk of each file is devoted to the verbatim record of each Nisei's life history as told to Kikuchi. And it is the actual life histories as told by Nisei women, not the short summaries that precede them, that will delight feminist writers. By feminist standards, then, the 29 life histories of Nisei women compiled by Kikuchi offer rich descriptions of work, family, and community life from which feminist writers might interpret and analyze the political nature of women's experience.

Conclusion: The Enduring Value of the Kikuchi Life Histories

A proper assessment of the Kikuchi life histories, as I noted earlier, begins with consideration of the intellectual milieu in which they were generated. Thus, although Kikuchi was not trained as a sociologist, his work for JERS bears the imprint of the early Chicago school sociologists. In particular, his work was directly influenced and, indeed, directly supervised by one of the chief figureheads in the use of life history in sociology, W. I. Thomas. The completeness and depth of the Nisei interviews certainly owe as much to the tireless efforts of Kikuchi as to the rigor of life history method under the tutelage of Thomas.

Since the heyday of life history analysis under the Chicago school sociologists, there has been an important shift in how researchers think about the use of life history and the method of collecting life histories. The impulse for that shift, which has come most consistently from feminist scholars, has dramatically shifted discussion on life histories from the interpretive and analytical questions posed by analytic induction to an emphasis on the politics of experience. The move toward uncovering and presenting women's life experiences is a crucial part of a feminist method. But presenting individual social experience is only a first step in the analysis of social structure. Among feminist scholars this emphasis on social experience in the last twenty years appears to have come at the cost of the important and necessary discussion of interpretation and analysis, the method of relating theoretical ideas to concrete, lived experiences.

From the current standpoint of feminist scholarship on life history analysis, the Kikuchi life histories are spectacular representations of the Nisei lived experience. The Nisei experience has been largely untold, and the breaking of Nisei silence through life histories is Charles Kikuchi's remarkable contribution to race relations, ethnic history, and social psychological analyses of life histories. The enduring strength of the Kikuchi life histories, in spite of shifts in life history analysis between 1920 and 1980, stems from the length, detail, and candor of each Nisei's "own story." Further analytic and interpretative work on the Nisei will no doubt emerge as life history analysis, whether it be grounded in the politics of experience or a revision of analytic induction that develops into an explicit form of data collection and data analysis.

For those in Asian-American Studies and related disciplines, our study of the Kikuchi life histories is a useful guide toward the collection and analysis of more meaningful life histories. Life histories are important for their method as well as their content. In terms of content, life histories reveal to us the events of an individual's life as well as her/his sentiments about those events. Both the Chicago school sociologists and writers from the feminist perspective will agree that one essential contribution of life histories has centered on content; life histories are valuable for what they tell us about what we have not known before.

With respect to method, the process of relating theoretical concepts to data, life histories represent a source for verifying assumptions, or creating new understandings of the Asian-American experience. Consider for the moment the question of why some Asian-American groups do well in school, earning the reputation of "model minority." A popular explanation is that Asian families emphasize the value of education in childhood socialization. Thus far, much of the support for this explanation has been anecdotal. To check out the validity of the explanation, we need a good deal of comparative information about what goes on in Asian-American families. At the moment, there is very little of this kind of information available about Asian-Americans and the newer immigrants from Southeast Asia. A comparative analysis of life histories would be one way to examine the "model minority" issue.

Notes

This research is supported by a Faculty Research Grant from the University of California, Santa Cruz. The following people patiently heard out my ideas and made helpful reading suggestions: Rebecca Klatch, Cheryl Barkey, Pamela Roby, and Paul Takagi. I would also like to thank Yuji Ichioka and Glenn Omatsu for their helpful comments on an earlier draft of this paper.

1. W. I. Thomas and Florian Znaniecki, *The Polish Peasant in Europe and America*, edited and abridged by Eli Zaretsky (Urbana: University of Illinois Press, 1984), 294.

2. Carole Ascher et al., eds., *Between Women: Biographers, Novelists, Critics, Teachers and Artists Write About Their Work on Women* (Boston: Beacon Press, 1984), xviii.

3. There are many other accounts of the relocation experience that can be found in literature and autobiographical material, but all of these accounts are retrospective. The main problem with retrospective accounts is that they are colored by subsequent historical events and individual experiences.

4. Paul Willis, *Learning to Labour* (Westmead: Saxon House, 1977); Lillian Rubin, *Worlds of Pain* (New York: Basic Books, 1976); and E. P. Thompson, *The Making of the English Working Class* (New York: Random House, 1963).

5. See, for example, Lynn Z. Bloom, "Listen! Women Speaking." *Frontiers* 2 (1979), 1–2; Jane Monnig Atkinson, "Review Essay: Anthropology," *Signs* 8 (1982), 236–58; and Susan N. G. Geiger, "Women's Life Histories: Method and Content," *Signs* 11 (Winter 1986), 334–51.

6. See, for example, Herbert Gutman, *Work, Culture and Society in Industrializing America* (New York: Vintage Books, 1966); Thompson, *The Making of the English Working Class*; and Eric Hobsbawm, *Primitive Rebels* (New York: W. W. Norton and Company, 1959).

7. Some recent examples include Yoshiko Uchida, *Desert Exile: The Uprooting of a Japanese–American Family* (Seattle: University of Washington Press, 1982); Akemi Kikumura, *Through Harsh Winters* (Novato, California: Chandler and Sharp, Inc., 1981); Eileen Sunada Sarasohn, *The Issei: Portrait of a Pioneer* (Palo Alto: Pacific Books, 1983).

8. The Kikuchi life histories have attracted recent attention. Isami Waugh and Jere Takahashi have used some of the materials in their doctoral dissertations. See Isami Arifuku Waugh, "Hidden Crime and Deviance in the Japanese American Community, 1920–1946," Ph.D. dissertation, University of California, Berkeley, 1978, and Jerrold H. Takahashi, "Changing Responses to Racial Subordination: An Exploratory Study of Japanese American Political Style," Ph.D. dissertation, University of California, Berkeley, 1980. See also Jere Takahashi, "Japanese American Responses to Race Relations: The Formation of Nisei Perspectives," *Amerasia* 9:1 (1982), 29–57. In addition, my own work has made extensive use of the Kikuchi life histories. See Dana Takagi,

"Personality and History: Hostile Nisei Women," in Gary Y. Okihiro, Shirley Hune, Arthur A. Hansen, and John M. Liu, eds., *Reflections on Shattered Windows: Promises and Prospects for Asian American Studies* (Pullman: Washington State University Press, 1988), 182–92.

9. Howard Becker, "The Relevance of Life Histories," in Norman K. Denzin, ed., *Sociological Methods: A Sourcebook* (Chicago: Aldine, 1970), 419–28.

10. Robert G. Burgess, "Personal Documents, Oral Sources and Life Histories," in Robert G. Burgess, ed., *Field Research: A Sourcebook and Field Manual* (London: George Allen and Unwin, 1982), 131–35.

11. Becker, "The Relevance of Life Histories."

12. W. I. Thomas and Florian Znaniecki, *The Polish Peasant in Europe and America*, (New York: Dover Publications, 1958), I, 21.

13. *Ibid.*

14. *Ibid.*, 22.

15. *Ibid.*, 76

16. Florian Znaniecki, *The Method of Sociology* (New York: Farrar and Rinehart, 1934).

17. See, for example, Edwin H. Sutherland, *Principles of Criminology* (Chicago: J. P. Lippincott Co., 1939); Alfred R. Lindesmith, *Opiate Addiction* (Bloomington: Principia Press, 1947); and Donald Cressey, "Criminal Violation of Financial Trust," *American Sociological Review* 15 (December 1950), 738–43.

18. See, for example, W. S. Robinson, "The Logical Structure of Analytic Induction," *American Sociological Review* 16 (December 1951), 812–818; and Ralph Turner, "The Quest for Universals in Sociological Research," *American Sociological Review* 18 (December 1953), 604–11.

19. See Jurgen Habermas, *Knowledge and Human Interests* (Boston: Beacon Press, 1971). Following Charles Peirce, Habermas outlines three forms of inference: induction, deduction, and abduction. According to Habermas, abduction is the only form of inference that can actually introduce new hypotheses.

20. Thomas and Znaniecki, *The Polish Peasant* (1984).

21. *Ibid.*, 5.

22. Dorothy S. Thomas, "Evacuation and Resettlement Study: Resettlement Phase," 1943, JERS W 1.20.

23. *Ibid.*

24. Shigeo Kawasaki (case history #11) and Margaret Suzuki (case history #8) are pseudonyms, JERS R**.

25. Interview with Charles Kikuchi, February 1988, New York City.

26. Kisako Yamada (case history #51), JERS, S**.

27. Chie Yamasaki (case history #16), 5, *ibid.*

28. Preface by Kikuchi on Chie Yamasaki, 5.

29. Thomas, *The Salvage.*

30. See the introduction to Thomas and Znaniecki, *The Polish Peasant* (1984), 5.

31. See, for example, William Caudill, "Japanese American Personality and Acculturation," *Genetic Psychology Monographs* 45 (1952), 3-102; and Robert E. Park, *Race and Culture* (London: Free Press of Glencoe, 1950).

32. William Ryan, *Blaming the Victim* (New York: Vintage, 1971).

33. See Gutman, *Work, Culture and Society*; Thompson, *The Making of the English Working Class*; Hobsbawm, *Primitive Rebels.*

34. Gutman, *Work, Culture and Society*, xiii.

35. The singularity of the term feminist is unfortunate as there is no one feminist research agenda. I use the term to refer to those writers whose major research interest emphasizes the inequalities of gender in society.

36. Sherma Gluck, "What's So Special About Women? Women's Oral History," Frontier 2 (1979), 3–11, and Catherine McKinnon, "Feminism, Marxism, Method and the State: An Agenda for Theory," in Nannerl O. Keohane, Michelle Z. Rosaldo, and Barbara C. Gelpi, eds., *Feminist Theory: A Critique of Ideology (Chicago: University of Chicago Press, 1982), 1–30.*

37. Mary Sheridan, "The Life History Method," in Mary Sheridan and Janet Salaff, eds., Lives: Chinese Working Women (Bloomington: Indiana University Press, 1984), 12.

38. Janet Monnig Atkinson, "Review Essay: Anthropology," Signs 8 (1982), 236–58.

39. Bloom, "Listen! Women Speaking," 1.

40. McKinnon, "Feminism, Marxism, Method and the State," 21.

41. Mary O'Brien, "Feminist Theory and Dialectical Logic," in Feminist Theory: A Critique of Ideology, 101.

42. Gluck, "What's So Special About Women? Women's Oral History," Frontiers, 3; and Gerda Lerner, The Female Experience: An American Documentary (Indianapolis: Bobbs–Merrill, 1977).

43. Susan N.G. Geiger, "Women's Life Histories: Method and Content," Signs 11 (Winter 1986), 335.

44. Gloria T. Hull, "Alice Dunbar–Nelson: A Personal and Literary Perspective," in Between Women, 104–11.

45. McKinnon, "Feminism, Marxism, Method and the State," 22.

46. Ascher et al., eds., Between Women.

47. Geiger, "Women's Life Histories," 338.

48. As far as I am aware, there is no methodology text from a feminist perspective comparable to Thomas and Znaniecki, The Polish Peasant (1958), or Barney G. Glaser and Anselm L. Strauss, The Discovery of Grounded Theory (Chicago: Aldine, 1967).

49. See "Through the JERS Looking Glass: A Personal View from Within" by Charles Kikuchi in this volume.

PART IV

Reminiscences of a Participant Observer

JAMES M. SAKODA

The evacuation and resettlement of the entire Japanese–American population of the West Coast was an event of historic proportion as well as great sociological significance. The evacuation was of questionable military value as well as illegal, as later events have shown. From a sociological point of view, it provided an opportunity for researchers to observe the effects of a new way of life on a population divided between those who were citizens and Americanized in their behavior and their alien parents, who adhered to the Japanese way of thinking.

Dorothy S. Thomas was a specialist in demography and most at home with statistical data. Her retired husband, W. I. Thomas, would have been the more likely person to study the evacuation and resettlement, since the situation had many similarities to his well–known classic in sociology, *The Polish Peasant in Europe and America*. While his wife was clearly in charge of JERS, W. I. Thomas' influence was extensive. Frank Miyamoto, Tamotsu Shibutani and I were greatly influenced by his theoretical orientation. Thus, the use of the personal document, best exemplified by life histories collected by Charles Kikuchi, and use of participant observation as a primary method of investigation show the general approach favored by W. I. Thomas.

A distinction needs to be made between Dorothy Thomas' collection of information, both statistical and verbal, and her publication of findings. She worked closely with fieldworkers, encouraging us in the collection of data. However, when it came to publishing the material, she was quite selective, ignoring for the most part vast quantities of data we gathered. She was opposed vehemently to use of sociological theory and did not encourage her workers, who were mostly doctoral candidates, to publish beyond using data for doctoral dissertations.

In this reminiscence, I will describe how I went about collecting and analyzing data in two relocation centers—first in Tule Lake and later in Minidoka. My background, I believe, is relevant to the evaluation of the data that was collected. My "Japanesy" background and life in Japan provided a bilingual ability which enabled me to speak to Issei and Kibei as well as to a variety of Nisei. My "Americanization" in Japan and return to this country to seek a college education provided association with "marginal" Nisei and consequent contacts leading to my work with JERS and advancement into an academic career. My theoretical background was in social psychology, and my method of gathering data relied heavily on participant observation, which was suitable for studying attitudes of people. Both Dorothy S. Thomas and I were keenly interested in statistical analysis of data and took advantage of the opportunity to gather valuable information.

My "Japanesy" Upbringing

My upbringing was that of a "Japanesy" Nisei with strict moral values, Japanese language school after regular school, attendance at Buddhist church, and judo lessons. The "Japanesy" Nisei might be described as withdrawn within the family and community, with considerable indoctrination in the ways of their Issei parents.

My father came to this country with two brothers around 1902 or 1903, and they worked as laborers, then collected junk, shifted to a poultry farm and hog farm, and ended up farming alfalfa in Lancaster, California, on the edge of the Mojave Desert. He went back to Japan to get my mother around 1912. Four children were born between 1913 and 1918—I was the third child. The family moved to Los Angeles where my father ran a credit union and money lending business. We lived within the Japanese community, first near Daiichi Gakuen and later in Boyle Heights.

Our family was affected directly by the Depression. My father lost his business and ended up with a hog farm in Artesia, where I attended high school. I think we were barely getting by when the hogs in the neighborhood were killed off by the government for suspected hoof and mouth disease. At this point, my father decided to take the family back to Japan with the lump sum payment he received from the government. It was 1933. It was clear that the attitude of being a sojourner in an inhospitable country was a strong one. My mother objected to leaving before I finished my high school education, but she was overruled, and we went along without protest.

While living in Japan for six years, I became more Americanized than I had ever been. I attended the Matsumoto Commercial School, but my social life was with other Nisei. I joined the Hiroshima Nikkei Club, which had just been formed under the auspices of a Christian Church. This was the beginning of a social life, which I had previously missed. The three years in Hiroshima were probably the happiest time of my life.

We four children also learned to be more independent of our parents. Each, in turn, returned to the United States, not being able to see a future in Japan, where we would feel out of place socially. In 1939, after spending three years at Toyo University, I returned to the United States to continue my college education. My stay in Japan provided me with confidence in my identity as a Japanese–American, unlike many Nisei who could not shake the feeling of inferiority when faced with Caucasians. I could accept both the fact that I was an American citizen and a Japanese.

Back in America, I was on my own and had to fend for myself without family support. I was determined to continue my college education and attended Pasadena Junior College and then the University of California in Berkeley. I worked as a "school boy" during the school year. During vacations, I did odd jobs, including farm work while living in a Japanese labor camp and clerking at a fruit stand. I was a little vague about what I wanted to become—I thought of teaching Japanese, of becoming a writer, or taking psychology. The "Nisei Problem"—that of finding suitable jobs—had not disappeared. My brother who had finished an agricultural course at the University of California at Davis could only find jobs as a farm worker or in a nursery. Eventually he went into contract gardening, as did so many Nisei. Nisei generally looked for white collar work but were frustrated in this effort.

At Berkeley, I became active in the Buddhist church but was also able to meet the more "marginal" Nisei through Kenny Murase, with whom I "batched." He was active in the Young Democrats on campus and seemed to collect those outside of organized Nisei groups. Through Kenny, I met Charlie Kikuchi, Warren Tsuneishi, Kazumi Sonoda, Lillian Ota, Bob Kinoshita, and Tom Shibutani. As I saw it, marginality had its advantages and disadvantages. It deprived them of the security of association with an in–group but left them freer to pursue associations with Caucasians and upwardly mobile careers. The crux of marginality was the predicament of not being accepted fully by either the Japanese or Caucasian group.

At the university, I was taking a course in social psychology taught by Ralph

Gundlach, a liberal professor, when Japan attacked Pearl Harbor and war was declared. I realized the importance of studying the reactions of Japanese–Americans to the event. For the course, I wrote a paper titled "As They Await Evacuation," outlining types of Japanese–Americans and their initial reactions to the outbreak of war. The types were placed on a two–dimensional map with Nisei belonging to two different cultural spheres of influence, Issei on the one side and Caucasians on the other. The vertical dimension represented social class—upper, middle, and lower. The types selected for description were conservative Nisei, maladjusted Kibei, extremely conservative Nisei ("Japanesy" Nisei), rowdy Nisei, elite socialite ("Americanized" Nisei), progressive ("marginal" Nisei), and radical liberal.

Tom Shibutani was also enrolled in Psychology 145 and also did a paper on Japanese–American reaction to the war situation. He introduced me to Dorothy S. Thomas, who was seeking funds for a study of the relocation process. Clearly, my association with the "marginal" Nisei at the University of California provided entry into the Caucasian academic world as a paid participant observer. I went to the Los Angeles area to join my married sister, May Takasugi, and my younger sister, Ruby, and my brother, George, to wait for evacuation orders. For the first time since coming back from Japan, we were together. We were evacuated to the Tulare Assembly Center, and from there went to Tule Lake, which along with Gila and Poston, had been picked by JERS as centers to be studied.

Research Problems in JERS: Defining the Focus of Investigation

From the beginning of JERS at Tule Lake, there was a nagging question of defining the problem under investigation. In an early memorandum, Dorothy S. Thomas explained tentatively what was to be observed:

> Your immediate problem, broadly speaking, is to determine as fully as possible the spontaneous social and personal adjustments to the situation of enforced migration. In order to get this record as accurately as possible, observations should be, in the main, in terms of overt acts of behavior, including, of course, things that are said and things that are written as well as things that are done. Get records both of individuals and of situations.[1]

Life in Tule Lake began to settle down, and it appeared that a conventional study of community life might be possible. Late in August 1942, fieldworkers were requested to complete a comprehensive report based on this outline. At the same time, we were requested to follow events as they cropped up and, in some cases, to write a report. The attempt to define the problem under investigation was finally given up in favor of a "point to point" approach.

> In a memorandum dated May 12, 1942, I outlined some general questions bearing on our research and promised to plan more detailed procedures "as soon as the status of the investigation is actually settled." It is now apparent that it is unlikely that the "status" of an investigation of this sort will ever be actually "settled" (even from the administrative standpoint), and that the situation which you are observing will continue to be one of rapid and unpredictable change, with new and important problems emerging for the duration of the study, and that the application of accepted techniques of recording will continue to present great, but by no means insurmountable, difficulties.[2]

This reluctance to define the problem under investigation coincided with Thomas' distaste for sociological theory as well as with the likelihood that WRA policy would be shifting. It also coincided with a point of view expressed by W. I. Thomas:

> It is my experience that formal methodological studies are relatively unprofitable. They have tended to represent the standpoint developed in philosophy and the history of philosophy. It is my impression that progress in method is made from point to point by setting up objectives, employing certain techniques, then resetting the problems with the introduction of still other objectives and the modification of techniques.[3]

What was meant by "point to point" definition of the problem is partly clarified by the following memorandum:

> Now we come to questions of future procedure. My survey of your journal shows that at least 20 categories have emerged in the course of a month. Follow–up of all would be impossible for any observer. A periodic summary of this sort will, however, be valuable both for you and for the study. . . . Furthermore, and most important, you will begin to concentrate on certain categories for special detailed, continuous attention. . . . At the same time that you are selecting a few categories for intensive analysis, you should, by all means, continue your informal journal. In a study of this sort, we cannot determine a priori, what the significant developments will be.[4] [underline included]

In the camps, it was the occurrence of disturbing political events which commanded researchers' attention. In Tule Lake, between August and October 1942, there occurred in rapid succession the farm strike, the construction strike, the coal strike, the mess slowdown strike, the overseas broadcast issue, and the theater project issue. These were followed by the Poston strike in November and the Manzanar incident. The most compelling event was the "loyalty" registration crisis, which resulted in the segregation of the "disloyal" in Tule Lake.

Fieldworkers wrote reports on various aspects of camp life, such as religion, which was of special interest to Robert Spencer in Gila; on the Co–op, with which I was closely related; and on the Kibei in the warden's office, which I put together from an interview. I recorded many journal entries on my conversations with friends and taking girls on dates to dances. Each fieldworker had a special interest, particularly involving a dissertation topic. My interest was following the attitudes of various types of Issei, Nisei, and Kibei toward ongoing events. But the bulk of attention of JERS was on major political events which affected both the administration and the evacuees. This fascination was in some respects unfortunate in that some of the less dramatic events were not fully covered.

Participant Observation: Necessity for Subterfuge

The relocation center atmosphere of suspicion toward possible *inu* made it impossible to use conventional methods of gathering data. Carrying a notebook and taking notes were bound to cause alarm among some camp residents. I did take notes sometimes at meetings, when note–taking by other participants was usual. Circulating a questionnaire, the most popular method of sociological research, was out of the question. I did circulate one among my psychology students but gave it up as not too promising. It was also not possible to announce openly that I was a JERS research assistant; I only informed those I could trust. Finally, close association with Caucasians was risky, and I kept that to a minimum. I even kept my distance from my associates, Tom Shibutani and Frank Miyamoto.

The primary method of data collection was participant observation. For this, it was necessary to find a role as a participant and then gather data inconspicuously during the course of the daily routine. In Tule Lake, I had a number of jobs—interviewer for WRA Form 26, adult education teacher of psychology, and Co–op block representative and member of the board of directors. I was going to work for Dr. Harold Jacoby, a college professor who headed the Internal Security Section, but quit after a day because it did not appear to be a safe job. I joined the Creative Writer's group and attended some Buddhist church services. I attended many dances and other social events and could freely observe the social scene.

My brother, younger sister, and I were assigned an "apartment" in Block 25, among mostly people from rural areas around Sacramento. The block manager was from Oakland and was friendly toward me. We developed a friendly relationship with our immediate neighbor, Mr. Kaya, an Issei who was chef for the block, and his wife. With the rest of the block, we were not on intimate terms. It would have been much easier to get information if we had resided with a group with whom we were familiar.

But there were a number of ways that I developed connections. My brother became the head of the hog farm, and I became acquainted with some of his co–workers. My sister taught English to Issei women in the adult education program, and when some of the women came to visit her, I was able to talk with them. One was Mrs. Kakimoto, who came from a farm in Placer County and whose family at first opposed "loyalty" registration. I talked to her on a number of occasions and continued to visit the family when they moved to Minidoka.

Another important method of gathering information was the interview with informants, i.e., people who were willing to talk about their experiences. Often friends and acquaintances became unwitting informants. At other times I asked them about their personal background or their knowledge of a given event. They were most likely to be Nisei leaders or "marginal" Nisei, who were antagonistic toward the pro–Japan elements in the camp. For example, Fumi Sakamoto was a "marginal" Nisei girl whom I met in the Co–op office. She had been befriended by Kibei wardens, and she was willing to tell me what she knew about them, as well as about her own background. I also talked with Koso Takemoto, an educated Kibei, who was willing to help me write my report on the Co–op. Most of the interviews were more casual conversations, during the course of which I could pursue some issue of interest.

The following diary entry gives some idea of a day in the life of a participant observer.

Sunday, January 3, 1943

1. Diary

I had expected to sleep till late, but my eyes were wide awake at 8 a.m. when the mess hall gong sounded, and so got up. The lights went out a little after 9, and so I took the opportunity to go see Kazuko [my typist].

Kazuko was home, and as usual talked to her. She said that she had heard from a fellow that Mrs. Murayama was partial to members of the Little Theater and she was wondering whether she should join it or not. Then she mentioned a girl with whom she said she got along well. I asked her what sort of person she would like to associate with, and she said she wouldn't like to associate with just anybody. This got me a little disgusted, and I told her why it was good idea to get along with different kinds of people. When I left her I was feeling that I was being unduly critical of her and that I should stop discussing her problems with her. I wondered how she really took my being so fatherly in giving her these advices that I did, because they didn't seem to be doing too much good.

When I came back Ruby was having a conference with her Adult English teachers. Among the others James Otsuka, Hattie, Janey and Yoshiko Kiyono were present. There were so many persons present that I wasn't particularly sociable, partly because I came home in a not too agreeable mood. James did not say very much to me and looked as though he held some resentment against me. Kiyono mentioned that she might want to come to my class, but I did not encourage her particularly. Kiyono and James stayed longer than the others and we sat around talking, and I couldn't do any writing.

In the afternoon May and Kingo dropped in and then Hattie. We all discussed James' recent attempt to find a date. I tried to nap after everybody left, but Mrs. Ishizuka came in to taste our honey to see what it was like because she wanted to buy it, too. Then Kazuko knocked at the door. I was surprised to see her. She had brought me the rest of the mess hall section, which ran into 89 pages. She told me that the construction division people had come after her to ask her to the social they were having at the factory from which she had been omitted. It was probably that thing that weighed on her mind which made her rather restless in the morning. She said she had refused to go after the way they treated her, and she seemed to feel all right when she came to see me. She brought back Richardson's book that she had borrowed from Ruby, and borrowed two more. She also asked me to read my "As They Await Evacuation." She mentioned that the Marysville JACL was willing to sell their typewriter and asked me if I wanted to buy one for about $90. After a little consideration I said that I would like to buy it and asked her to make the arrangements for me. I figured that my portable would not last too long and that a typewriter would be a good investment anyway. We kept talking about things, and we were both in a more pleasant mood than we were in the morning.

In the afternoon I also decided that I should go to Dr. Jacoby and Elberson's places to get my reports to use on my personal adjustment section. I stopped in at Mabel's place to return her two books and also give her 2 calendars, one for her and one for Tony. She seemed to be scared to see me. Tsuyako was sewing something. I talked for a while because there was no one else in the room, although I had thought that I would just leave the books and leave right away. Tsuyako soon closed up the sewing machine and said she was going home. I said that I would go home, too, and since Mabel didn't say anything else except thank you, I left. Jacoby was out and Don was out, too. Mrs. Elberson was cleaning a living room full of soot which covered the room—it was caused by a faulty oil burner. She was very nice and found the co–op report for me.

In the evening Fumi Sakamoto dropped in to discuss [Co–op] office matters with me, and she was here till 10. She came to ask me what I thought was wrong with the squabble that was going on in the co–op office, especially between Koso and herself and Koso and Noboru Honda. She asked me whether it was her fault that relations were not very smooth. Then she also asked me about the formation of the employer relation committee, which I discussed with her. I took the opportunity to ask her background. She did not agree with her father on his relation with her mother and told him outright. This made her father take it out on her mother. Relations being like this she left home at the age of 12, and ever since lived mostly among Caucasians, and only came home to see her folks occasionally. She never associated very much with Nisei. She's going on 29 right now. She admitted she was aggressive and blunt. She said that she never felt that she was superior to the Japanese people or that Caucasians were necessarily superior to the Japanese. In fact she felt insecure among Japanese because she could not speak the language very well, and always had to keep wondering how they accepted her. She said her sick leave resulted from the fact that she had had disputes with Koso about that time. I asked her why she wanted to go out, and she said that her habits were becoming sloppy in here. Her English, for one thing, was becoming poor. Her head, she also

> thought, was not receiving much stimulation, except for her coop work. I put her jacket on for her when she left and handed her her mittens, which she admitted she had not made herself. Then I saw her to the door and suddenly realized that I should see her home. I told her to wait a minute and I would see her home. I said that I got used to thinking that she wasn't a girl. We talked as we walked home, and she put her arm through mine. She asked me when I was going to take her to a show, which I had promised at the end of the year, and I said that it would have to wait till after the reports were finished. I am pretty sure that she feels lonesome and desires some attention from men. She asked me in at her place, but I said that I would have to get back to my report.
>
> But it was getting late by the time I got back, that I decided to start writing my journal. It's 11:15 now and I still have more entries to make, but I am getting sleepy and I'll have to leave the rest till tomorrow.

Research Problems During the "Loyalty" Registration Crisis

The difficulty of carrying on research was greatly magnified during the "loyalty" registration crisis, when the threat of boys being drafted or picked up as draft dodgers was thought to be dependent on one's answers to the questions. It was not possible to wander around the camps to observe what was happening in different blocks. The field notes that we kept became possible incriminating evidence against those who opposed registration. I began to use initials for names, transposing letters to make identification more difficult. Frank Miyamoto contemplated burning some field notes, while Dorothy S. Thomas reported that she and W. I. feared being called to testify and thought about digging a hole to bury field notes.

The closest I came to being beaten up was when some Nisei boys from Block 25 grabbed at the notes I had taken at a meeting and demanded to know what I was going to do with them. I explained that I was doing a study of evacuation for my doctoral dissertation, that it was something which could not be left to Caucasians. It was cold, and they finally let me go.

The crisis exaggerated the conflict between the fieldworker's role as neutral observer and active participant. At a crucial Block 25 meeting on February 11, 1943, a Kibei stated that Kibei and Nisei should be loyal to Japan and answer "No–No" to the registration questions. I was then asked for my opinion, and I explained that Nisei were U.S. citizens and should be loyal to the United States. I thought that those from Japan would understand this argument. Also, I said that most Nisei would not be able to get along in Japan. My opinion was clearly unpopular and was opposed by many Kibei and Issei. Later, when a block vote was taken on registration, I sent in a blank sheet. I later went out and registered "Yes–Yes" and for a few weeks was ostracized by the block. The atmosphere at the height of the crisis is described by my following diary entry:

> For my own protection I can not reveal anything to anybody, and must write up my diary in a manner I do not give away too much information about things, especially the identity of people. But I must continue to gather materials for my thesis. When this war is over this whole incident is going to make very sad reading—it is going to read like a real tragedy—and the writing of such a chapter should not be left up to the WRA or any Caucasians who do not understand what the Japanese people are really feeling. The whole incident is going to make the Japanese people look very foolish if all of the factors going into disturbing the minds of the people are not brought out. The fact that I have such a task to perform makes my load easier to carry.[5]

My Work as a Participant Observer in Minidoka

Following the registration crisis, Tule Lake was declared a segregation center for so–called "disloyal" families. Tuleans who had been classified as "loyal," such as myself, had to leave. Dorothy S. Thomas wanted me to go to Gila to replace Charlie Kikuchi and Robert Spencer, but I chose to go to Minidoka to be with Hattie Kurose, whom I had met in Tule Lake. In Minidoka, Hattie and I were married, and I carried on my field research from September 1943, to March 1945. I also observed the closing of the center in the fall.

In Minidoka, Hattie and I lived in an "apartment" in Block 12. Her parents lived in the same block, and the block manager and some residents were friends of her family. Thus, unlike my stay at Tule Lake, I had some friends within the block. We were also Tuleans and considered intruders who were critical of the way in which Minidokans had knuckled under to administrative demands. For that reason we were welcomed by some Minidokans, who were dissatisfied with conditions in the camp. I took the job of labor relations advisor and chose to be located in the Community Council office. This provided close contact with labor problems and negotiations involving the council.

I became a close associate of Rev. Joseph Kitagawa (Father Joe), the Episcopalian minister who liked to meddle in politics, and Tom Ogawa, the capable

Community Council clerk. Closely associated with us were Elmer Smith, the community analyst who was an anthropologist sympathetic to evacuees, and Helen Amerman, a high school teacher. Father Joe had some high school students join us in discussions, as well as some members of the administration. Our group was able to keep close tabs on most of the important developments in Minidoka.

I also had some contacts among former Tuleans: Kintaro Takeda from Sacramento, who had led the slowdown mess hall strike in Tule Lake; and Minnie Nakano, who was Don Elberson's secretary in Tule Lake and now worked as the Minidokan project director's secretary and did my typing. The Kakimoto family came to Minidoka, rather than stay in Tule Lake as "disloyalists," and I visited them occasionally. I also had contacts with the *Irrigator* staff and the WRA statistical section.

Overall, I was able to collect a much more complete set of data in Minidoka than in Tule Lake. Thus, when I later returned to the University of California to work on my dissertation, I decided to focus my study on the situation in Minidoka.

Resources for Researchers in the JERS Archives

As a JERS field worker, I collected a vast amount of data. My data, along with that of others, are now in the JERS archives. The collection includes daily journals, reports, letters between field workers and Dorothy S. Thomas, and statistical information. The JERS collection is a largely unexploited research resource. Only a small portion has been published.

The records of field observers generally took three forms: the diary, the journal, and the report. All three forms relied on daily note–taking. When it was not feasible to take down notes, Thomas urged us to jot down topics as soon as possible and then to expand them into journal entries in the evening:

> As to detailed procedure, I cannot emphasize strongly enough the necessity of writing up your field notes daily. The unique opportunity which this situation offers is the obtaining of a socio–historical record on the spot and at the time the events are occurring. I realize that the situation makes it impossible for you to do more than jot down key words and "clues" during the course of the day. These key words must, however, be expanded into narrative form before they get "cold." You are not automatons. You are, yourselves, being modified daily by the experiences you are going through. The chances of distortion of your records are greatly enhanced if much time

> elapses between recording and writing up. So—the first point in procedure must be a daily write–up of field notes.[6] [underline included]

The daily write–up was not always possible and sometimes more than a day or two went by before the notes were written up. It was generally not difficult to reconstruct conversations and events. I often took notes at formal meetings of the Co–op or at meetings with WRA officials. Typing at night was a problem because it aroused suspicion that some nefarious activity was going on. I also had the problem of finding a secretary to retype the journal. I relied on girls who grew up outside the Japanese–American community and did not look on my work with suspicion.

Diary Notations

In my diary I wrote what I did, regardless of whether I thought it was pertinent to JERS or not. It included sometimes what was served at lunch, when I took a nap or went to bed. In it also were details of my personal life, such as encounters with girls. When the registration crisis arose, I kept the diary section separate from journal entries in order to keep material secret. The diary entries are difficult for researchers to use because entries were usually made chronologically and people I met were often referred to simply by their first names.

Journal Entries

The journal entries were given headings of their own and pertained to particular topics or persons. They included detailed minutes of meetings that I had attended. Sometimes the entries were short, but often they ran to several pages and constituted a mini–report. The following is an example of a write–up on a person:

> 1. Matsuda
>
> Norman Koyama's successor came around today to see Ruby about the locks. JS [James Sakoda] was typing a letter and was not paying particular attention to him. Somehow a conversation was started, however, and Matsuda mentioned that he was no longer popular in his block. JS said that he was in the same fix in his block. Matsuda went on to recount his position in his block.
>
> M had been in Japan for 8 years and returned to America in 1930. While his basic education was received in Japan, he has attended University of

Calif. He speaks fairly good English. He mentioned Koso Takemoto and Albert Koga as two of his associates, showing that his close friends are Kibei who are educated and Americanized. He had a group who used to get together and play the mandolin, and all 4 of the others were Kibei. He is probably about 26 or 27 years old.

Up to the time of the registration he was the leader in the block, attending meetings, making suggestions. He was in a position where most of the block people looked up to him, and treated him with respect. When the registration came up, people looked to him for leadership. He maintained a calm attitude toward the issue, and thought that it would be best if people went and registered. This incurred the anger of the few who strongly opposed registration. He found himself alienated from most of the block people. He insisted that he himself thought it was best to register. About 10 others followed him and registered, too. Thus he made himself a marked man, a leader of the opposition. At present, he says that hardly any one in the block speaks to him. The fact that he lives in Block 40, which is in the ward that has had the most trouble makes him more liable to such treatment. He says that he goes to the mess hall, eats silently, without talking to any one. Formerly he had many friends in the block—now he has practically none. One good family friend even told him not to come to see them.

He was working in the Adult Education Department, teaching mathematics. Evidently he enjoyed his work and working for the people, but now he wants to get out of here as fast as he can. His attitude toward the other Japanese here is typical of those who stood up for registration. He says that the people are ignorant. Both Albert Koga and Koso Takemoto seem to be in the same sort of fix. He saw a mandolin in the room, and asked if it would be all right if he came over to play with us.[7]

Reports

The reports were more formally written accounts, collating material from different sources to present a more coherent picture than was possible in the diary or journal. Some of the reports were devoted to clarifying the structure of the community, while others concerned a particular event, which had dominated the attention of field workers. In all I wrote 25 reports, totalling over 1,800 pages.

Letters

The letters between Dorothy S. Thomas and me are preserved in the files and make fascinating reading today. They include mundane matters, such as ordering supplies, but also problems of following events in the center. Thomas almost always responded with encouragement to the journals and reports that I sent to her. In my letters, I often summarized current happenings.

The low point for me occurred right after the "loyalty" registration, when Frank Miyamoto and Tom Shibutani were forced to leave Tule Lake. This left me alone, and Thomas sent Morton Grodzins to persuade me to go to Gila to take up where Bob Spencer and Charlie Kikuchi had left off.

2519–C, Newell
Tule Lake, California
May 24, 1943

Dear Dr. Thomas,

I was surprised, to say the least, to receive a visit from your personal emissary, all of the way from Berkeley. I knew that the news couldn't be good for him to come personally. I thought that perhaps the trip to Gila had been called off, or that I was going to be fired or something. Then when Morton started to list the advantages of my going to Gila in Bob's place, I just sank into an easy chair and looked glum. I really felt that way. I let Morton give his complete message before I said anything. He did a good job, I assure you, and even gave the same thing to me in writing, too.

Here I'm the only one left behind, since Bob [Billigmeier] is leaving now. All of my friends are leaving one by one, although I do know a great many people here yet. But I was starting to think that I wouldn't be able to stand staying here very much longer if this sort of thing kept up. I just couldn't think of leaving what few friends I had here to go to another project, although I would have been willing to go out. Life is so uncertain that I just don't count on anything continuing for any length of time. We may be drafted soon, in which case I would like to get a chance to teach Japanese, something which I am qualified for and was thinking of going into before evacuation. While I realize that my staying here means so much to me if I want an academic career, at time even I get fed up with it all. The registration has hit a great many people rather badly. I and a great many other young leaders in the community no longer feel that we belong to the people anymore. We go on our own way, and they go along theirs—why should we bother about them anymore. From now on my position is less that of a participant, and more that of a ruthless observer. And there's Hattie, too. The first thing that I asked Morton was whether it was your desire that I go to Gila. Evidently it was, but Morton said that you wanted me to make up my own mind. At that time I was just about ready to give everything up! . . .

Let me say this much. I feel grateful for the position I have on staff. Also, I feel honored to have you consider me worthy of taking over Bob's job in Gila. I shall forget all thoughts of leaving the Project in the near future, unless draft becomes imminent. Sounds rather silly, doesn't it, but I mean it.

Spent all day yesterday with Hattie up on a slope, watching the co–op picnic down below. The sun was warm, but we had a breeze, and it was a perfect day.

I hope you'll be able to find someone to take Bob's place. In the meantime I'll be looking forward to seeing you in Phoenix.

'Bye,

James Sakoda

In Minidoka I was in much better control of the situation as can be seen from the following letters:

May 1, 1944

Dear Jimmy:

I received your letter and also your documents. I am greatly impressed with your report and am immediately having it copied. The analysis I agree has some controversial points, but that is all right for it gives us something that we can discuss, and perhaps reach some conclusions about later. I shall also have that typed and will send you copies, as well as send a copy to Chicago, one to "X" and one to Hankey. You may rest assured that the materials will not fall into the hands of those who are not connected with the Study.

I am enclosing the first chart on the Tule Lake situation. Other analysis will follow very shortly. We are going to be able to check through those unknown cards so that we can get the data more accurate, as Mr. Stauber is very cooperative. He was, incidentally, most anxious for us to carry through a similar analysis on another Project and he suggested Minidoka. I feel, however, that unless we are to get a great deal of free help from WRA, the project is too big for us to undertake at this time. That is another matter that we will discuss at Salt Lake City.

I am enclosing a formal letter to you which you can submit in connection with your short–term leave.

Sincerely yours,

Dorothy Swaine Thomas

12–12–C
Hunt, Idaho
May 2, 1944

Dear Dorothy,

I was certainly very glad to receive definite news of the conference in Salt Lake City. There is nothing in your plans that will interfere, or rather I don't see anything here that would interfere in my fitting into your plans. I shall plan to be in Salt Lake City some time on the 7th. Conference—8, 9, 10, 11. After the conference I would like to visit Topaz. I was considering this anyway, and may stay there a couple of days. I shall make arrangements at this end for my train ticket to Salt Lake City and for my short–term leave, which I think I can get without any trouble.

Concerning the reports that I am to make, I have already sent in my report on the draft situation. As far as I can see, the observations that I made on the spot still holds, although I am getting some material that should be added later. As for the labor relation situation I have no manuscript thus far, except for the write–up of the boilermen walkout. I have just started on the Pickling Plant Conflict, and think that I can finish that, at least. I shall be in a position too of giving a sketch of the present warehouse conflict. Throughout these reports on conflicts within the center, I would like to point out characteristics peculiar to Minidoka compared with Tule Lake. There has been a gradual change here from the most "loyal" center to one close to pre–segregation Tule Lake. There has been a definite change, not only in the general social structure of the project, but also in the attitudes now dominant in the community. In a way this change can be considered the triumph of Tule Lake ways over Minidoka ways, although most people do not realize the close connection between the change and the attitude of the people from Tule Lake. In regards to the Tulean adjustment here, I can point out some of the things that I have observed here. This again I can best do in terms of the major conflicts that have developed on the project and the position taken by Tuleans in them. I would like to pattern my report somewhat after the method I am employing now of concentrating on the description of major incidents, rather than attempting to follow a particular item, such as Tulean adjustment. Then I can point out some of the analyses that I have made of these incidents in terms of social structure, Tulean adjustment, etc. For your benefit I am listing the major incidents within the project (mostly of a political nature) from which I can draw material:

Tulean Arrival
Housing Conflict
Meeting with Myer
Meeting with Spanish Consul
Boilerman Walkout
Creation of the Community Council
Draft
Pickling Plant Conflict
Kimball's Visit
Warehouse Conflict
Kuroki's Visit

The warehouse conflict has taken an interesting turn, with Stafford cooperating with the Council to keep the warehouses going, suspending the power of several recalcitrant Caucasian workers. It is said that Miller is behind it all, but the evidence is not strong enough to hurt him much, I think. Washington is informed of what has been going on, and it is expected that a few changes in the Caucasian staff will be made direct from Washington. Stafford is headed for trouble from the public if those who are shifted around can't take it. The whole situation may break any day now. The social structure of the Caucasian staff is now beginning to take on meaning. Here we have three assistant project directors who line up something like this: Miller highly unsympathetic and dictatorial in his ways. Pomeroy steering a middle course. Davidson supposedly sympathetic to evacuees, not too bold. Miller and Davidson are always tearing each other apart. The last time Stafford left the project he left Davidson in charge. Result: boilermen trouble. This time when he went to Washington he left Miller in charge: result pickle plant trouble which Miller managed to solve by closing the plant down. In the warehouse conflict Stafford discovered that Miller was endangering his [Stafford's] position, and he begins to cooperate with the Council against Miller and his men who were causing the trouble. One cannot help but notice certain parties collaborating to maintain their own status or to attack that of a rival. The Washington office and Council, Stafford and the staff or Stafford and the Council, Stafford and Davidson against Miller or Stafford and Miller against Davidson, the public and unsympathetic staff members, sympathetic staff members and residents. I am going to try to get as much material as possible on the attitude of staff members on this warehouse conflict.

One other item that is current is Ben Kuroki's visit. Thus far it has been highly pathetic because of the lack of response on the part of the people. The Isseis are highly incensed by his statement that he is going to bomb Tokyo, while the Niseis don't dare show too much enthusiasm. I was very much depressed the first day to notice the lack of appreciation of Ben's stand, even though I felt that there were things that he had yet to understand which the people felt deeply.

I shall do what I can before the conference. I hope I have covered everything that I was supposed to do.

'bye,

Jimmy

P.S. Hattie is not going with me.

Statistical Information: The Significance of Form 26

From a researchers' point of view, an important by–product of the evacuation was the census information collected on an entire ethnic group on the West Coast. I was a supervisor in the interviewing unit set up to collect the census information on Form 26. As a demographer, Thomas was keenly interested in the data and obtained official permission to use it. One of her former students, Evelyn Rose, who later married Rev. Joseph Kitagawa, headed the WRA statistical unit, and we were able to gain access to the Form 26 information. It was still a job to take down on cards selected information from the interviews and combine them with block addresses, information on leave clearance, and "loyalty" status. In Tule Lake I gathered together a group of Nisei to work evenings on this information.

The background information included region and town of origin on the West Coast, religion (i.e., Buddhist, Christian, None), as well as generation, education, occupation, age, sex, marital status, etc. The statistical data provided concrete evidence of behavior differences along regional and generational lines, providing a firm basis on which to support the less reliable field data. The data could also be used to compare the behavior of groups, such as segregants and non–segregants or resettlers and non–resettlers.

The WRA, in its quantitative report,[8] provided detailed statistics on camp entries and departures of evacuees and some demographic information. But it did not bother with correlation of background factors with segregation and resettler status. Thus, the data contained in Form 26 has yet to be fully exploited. A comprehensive study of Japanese–American communities based on this data is still possible.

Due to my own interest in attitude development among different subgroups of Japanese–Americans, I found the statistical data in Form 26 very useful. The bit of data presented here on factors associated with segregant status shows the extent to which it can be utilized.[9]

Responses on Form 26 enable researchers to relate background responses to behavioral responses. For example, religious identification of evacuees was particularly important because it provided an indication of degree of assimilation to American values. Generally, those who were Christians and those who specified no religion were more Americanized than Buddhists.

Responses on Form 26 also show the impact of regional differences among evacuees. In Tule Lake, the presence of both Californians and Northwesterns allowed for comparison of the two groups. The former came mostly from Sacramento and the surrounding region, including the delta and Placer County, areas with many farming communities. The latter came from the western half of Washington (except Seattle, but including Tacoma) and the western half of Oregon (except Portland and vicinity). Japanese–Americans in the Northwest were more widely scattered in small communities than California.

Data from Form 26 can also be used to study the effect of size of pre–evacuation Japanese–American communities on acculturation to American values. For example, pre–war communities for evacuees at Tule Lake were divided into three categories: those with less than 35 Japanese–American residents, 17-years and older; those with 35 to 100 residents; and those with more than 100 residents. Evacuees from Sacramento and Tacoma were placed in a separate category called "urban centers."

The Form 26 data is summarized in table 1 (see table 1 on opposite page).

Chart 1 shows the relationship between percentage of Buddhists (a measure of resistance to American acculturation) across the three categories of rural populations as well as the category of "urban centers." The chart also compares communities from California and those of the Northwest.

Table 1. Number of Segregants 17-years and older in Tule Lake by Religion, Generation and Size of Japanese Community

SIZE OF COMMUNITY OF ORIGIN

	Less than 35			35 to 100			More than 100			Total		
	Segregants	**Total**	**Percent**	**Segregants**	**Total**	**Percent**	**Segregants**	**Total**	**Percent**	**Segregants**	**Total**	**Percent**
CALIFORNIA	**130**	**261**	**49.8%**	**165**	**248**	**66.5%**	**1090**	**1780**	**61.2%**	**1385**	**2289**	**60.5%**
Buddhists	**119**	**200**	**59.5%**	**153**	**209**	**73.2%**	**955**	**1385**	**69.0%**	**1227**	**1794**	**68.4%**
Kibei	13	19	68.4%	48	53	90.6%	160	207	77.3%	221	279	79.2%
Issei	73	108	67.6%	61	91	67.0%	469	643	72.9%	603	842	71.6%
Nisei	33	73	45.2%	44	65	67.7%	326	535	60.9%	403	673	59.9%
Others	**11**	**61**	**18.0%**	**12**	**39**	**30.8%**	**135**	**395**	**34.2%**	**158**	**495**	**31.9%**
Kibei	2	2	100.0%	2	5	40.0%	12	25	48.0%	16	32	50.0%
Issei	2	11	18.2%	1	11	9.1%	57	119	47.9%	60	141	42.6%
Nisei	7	48	14.6%	9	23	39.1%	66	251	26.3%	82	322	25.5%
NORTHWEST	**140**	**559**	**25.0%**	**187**	**534**	**35.0%**	**287**	**1245**	**23.1%**	**614**	**2338**	**26.3%**
Buddhists	**95**	**262**	**36.3%**	**155**	**357**	**43.4%**	**242**	**848**	**28.5**	**492**	**1467**	**33.5%**
Kibei	19	26	73.1%	30	53	56.6%	25	64	39.1%	74	143	51.7%
Issei	64	188	34.0%	103	232	44.4%	152	462	32.9%	319	882	36.2%
Nisei	12	48	25.0%	22	72	30.6%	65	322	20.2%	99	442	22.4%
Others	**45**	**297**	**15.2%**	**32**	**177**	**18.1%**	**45**	**397**	**11.3%**	**122**	**871**	**14.0%**
Kibei	10	26	38.5%	9	27	33.3%	5	14	35.7%	24	67	35.8%
Issei	19	81	23.5%	10	62	16.1%	14	110	12.7%	43	253	17.0%
Nisei	16	190	8.4%	13	88	14.8%	26	273	9.5%	55	551	10.0%

For California, the degree of population concentration was associated with lower percentages of Buddhists at both ends of the scale. For the Northwest, the picture was somewhat different. In contrast to California, Japanese–Americans were more widely scattered in the Northwest and this was accompanied by lower adherence to Japanese cultural values as indicated by the lower percentage of Buddhists. The regional diffferences were smaller for larger communities, although the Northwest consistently had smaller percentages of Buddhists than in California.

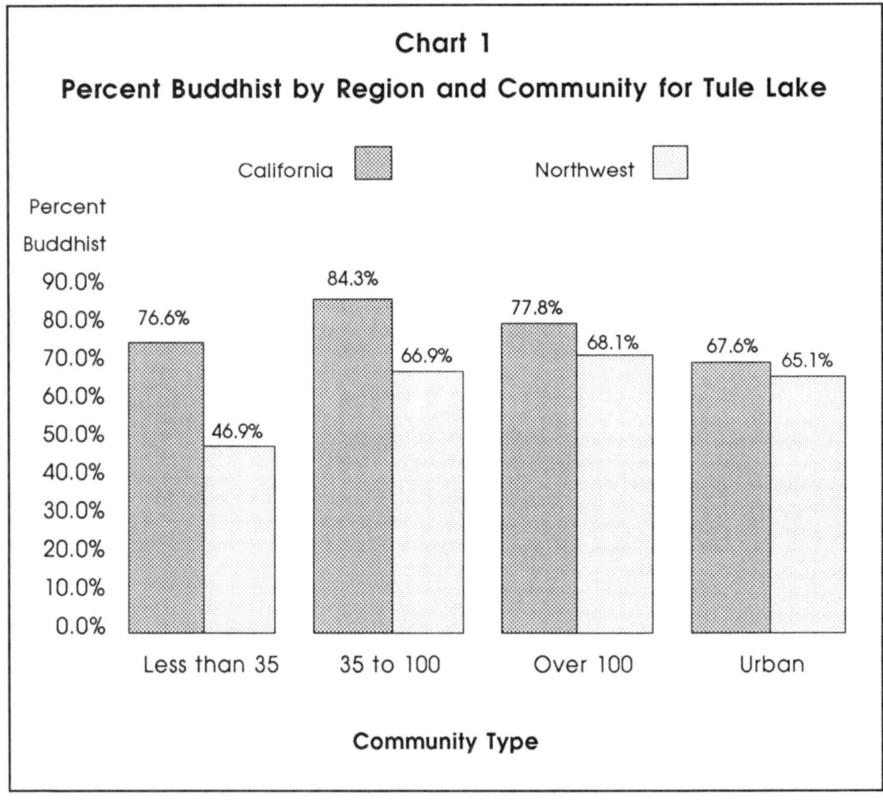

It would appear that there was greater acceptance of American cultural values at both ends of the community size continuum. The Northwest exceeded California in this respect, particularly in areas with fewer Japanese–American residents. The curvilinearity of cultural trends appears to reflect both the effects of scattering of the Japanese–American population, which reduced Japanese cultural practices, and urban living, which promoted Americanized values. This finding deserves further study.

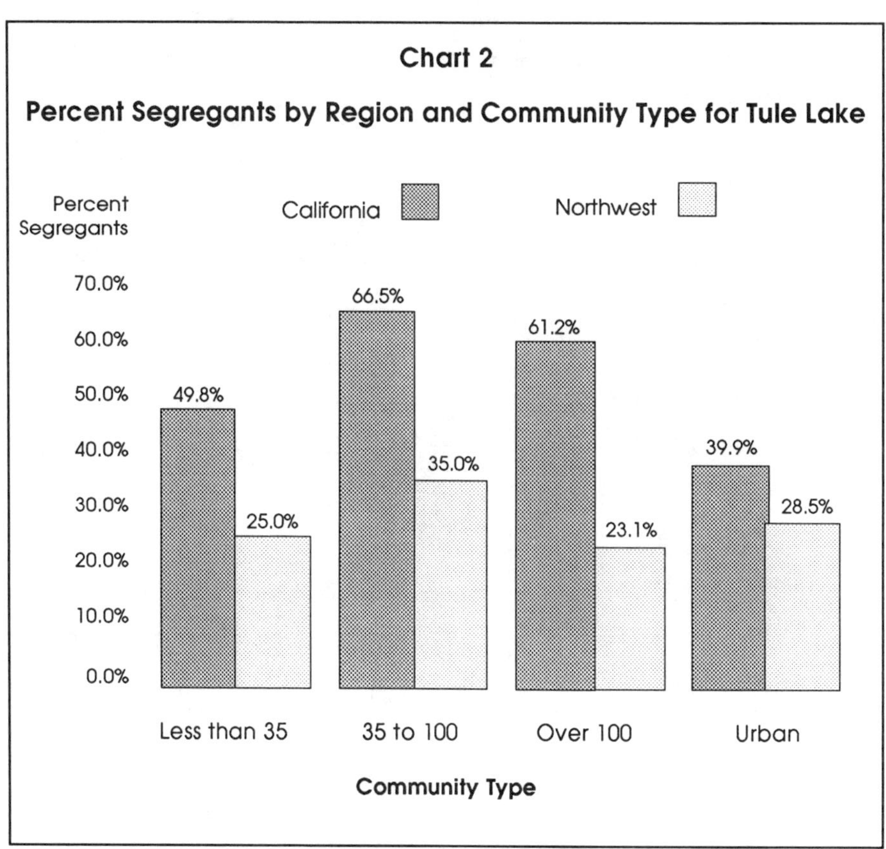

Chart 2 shows the percentage of segregants in Tule Lake by community size. The charts shows both a California–Northwest difference and a curvilinear relationship across community types. The exception is the rise in percentage for Tacoma, which may not have been typical of Japanese–Americans in a large, urban center.

Chart 3 shows the percentage of segregants by religion and generation. In my own research, I have referred freely to differences in attitude and behavior of Kibei, Issei, and Nisei and also to "Japanesy" Nisei and "Americanized" Nisei. Statistical evidence presented here shows definitely that these are not simply stereotypes but real distinctions. Among Buddhists, the percentage of Kibei who became segregants was about twice as large as for Nisei, and for Christians and agnostics the difference was greater than twice as much. The percentage of segregants for Buddhist Kibei was more than four times that of Nisei who were not Buddhists.

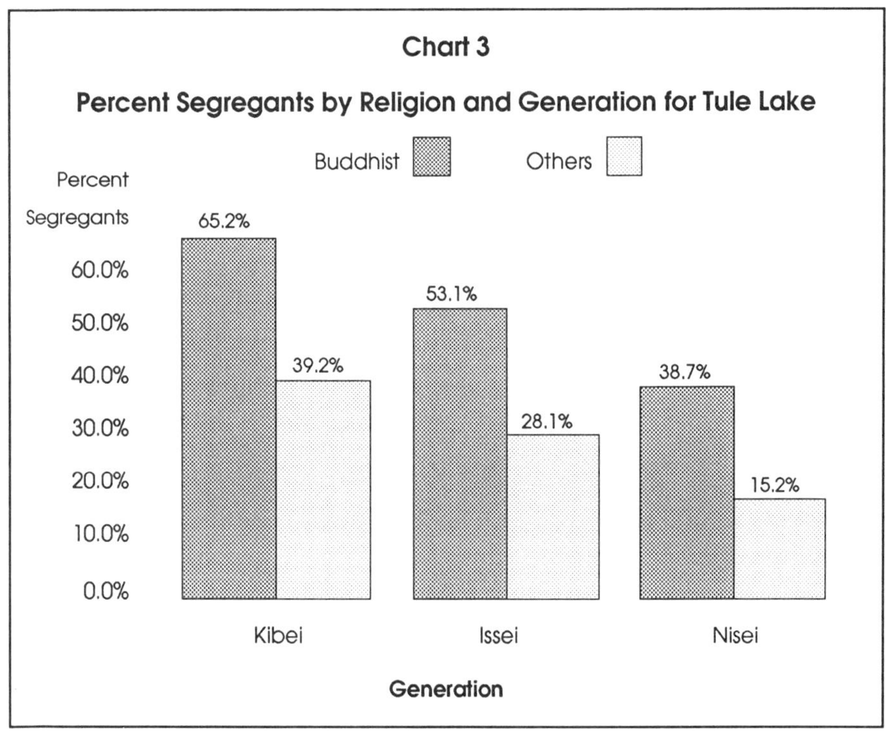

Evaluating the JERS Publication Record

In view of the large quantity of field data gathered in relocation centers, particularly in Tule Lake and Minidoka, the JERS publication record was meager. Dorothy S. Thomas originally planned three books based on the field data. Her plan could be interpreted as a demographer's view of a population under investigation.

In *The Spoilage*, events leading to the registration crisis were covered succinctly. In the chapter on segregation, direct quotation of verbatim record hearings by Robert Billigmeier and other field notes were used extensively, providing excellent insight into the desire for security which motivated many evacuees to opt to be declared "disloyal" and remain in Tule Lake rather than risk being forced to resettle had they been moved to another center. The remainder of the book was devoted to a study of militant, pro–Japan segregants and factions within the camp population. Here, there was great reliance on field notes of Rosalie Hankey, which documented attitudes leading many to renounce their U.S. citizenship. The account was historical, and no effort was made to make a theoretical analysis. Nonetheless, it was to the authors' credit that they made considerable use of field notes. Unfortunately, reliance on one fieldworker resulted in the charge of lack of objectivity.[10] One participant, in spite of being referred to in the book by a pseudonym, claimed harm to her reputation.[11]

In *The Salvage*, secondary material was used to recount the adjustment of Japanese immigrants in this country. There was a section on evacuation titled "Forced Mass Migration." This was followed by statistical analysis using "migration differentials," such as region (California–Northwest), generation, occupation (agricultural and non–agricultural), sex, and religion (Christian–Secular–Buddhist). Here, Thomas was on familiar ground and able to deal adequately with the problem of explaining how migrants differed from non–migrants, without resorting to sociological theory. The remaining two–thirds of the book were taken up with life histories gathered by Charlie Kikuchi. The case histories were presented without theoretical explanations or classification into types.

"The Residue," the third book, was not published. Dorothy S. Thomas and Richard Nishimoto explained in the introduction to *The Spoilage* that the "residue" could not be studied until their adjustment on the West Coast was determined. They apparently conceived the study as one involving migration from relocation centers rather than a study of those remaining in the centers. Thomas tried unsuccessfully to hire Tom Ogawa when Minidoka was about to be closed, and perhaps she wanted to use him as co–author, as she had with Nishimoto. She once offered to publish my dissertation if I would take out the theoretical section, but I was unwilling to do that and she did not bring up the matter again. Why she did not write a book about those who remained in the relocation centers is still a mystery to me, since they constituted the largest portion of the evacuated population and the subject of the largest amount of field research.

I was not consulted on the writing of either *The Spoilage* or *The Salvage,* even though I was mentioned on the title page as a contributor on both volumes. The statistical data I had been responsible for gathering in Tule Lake and Minidoka was turned over for analysis to George M. Kuznets, a statistician and colleague of Thomas. When I wrote my own paper using the data to study the effect of size of Japanese–American communities on acculturation as measured by answers to the "loyalty" questions, Thomas did not show much interest and I stopped efforts to publish it.

It would appear that if Thomas had been a social psychologist interested in theory, the JERS publications would have been quite different. She was most at home conceiving of JERS in demographic terms—in particular, as a study in migration from the relocation center, using statistical data. She was comfortable with presenting field data in historical terms, as she did in *The Spoilage,* or offering case histories without commentary, as in *The Salvage.* She chose not to use terms, such as "definition of the situation," "cultural conflict," "organization" and "disorganization," as W. I. Thomas had in *The Polish Peasant in Europe and America.*

It is difficult not to reach the conclusion that a great deal of valuable data was collected by JERS fieldworkers, but much more could have been published. Those of us who were closest to the data must share part of the blame for not doing more than writing a doctoral dissertation and turning to the pursuit of our own careers. But this hardly justifies Peter T. Suzuki's conclusion that "JERS was a failure,"[12] particularly when he looked at only the published material and did not examine the materials deposited at the Bancroft Library in Berkeley.

As I look back on the data, I can see that much more can be done. Many Sansei seek identification with their past, but do not have the language skills and familiarity with Japanese culture to do so easily. The JERS field data are written in English, and the Form 26 data are coded for statistical analysis. Perhaps some younger scholars can be persuaded to take up the task that an earlier generation failed to complete.

Notes

1. Dorothy S. Thomas, "Memorandum" (May 12, 1942).
2. Dorothy S. Thomas, "Memorandum to Field Collaborators" (August 27, 1942).
3. Letter, W. I. Thomas to Robert E. Park, quoted in Herbert Blumer, *Critiques of Research in the Social Sciences* (New York: Social Science Research Council, 1939), 166.
4. Dorothy S. Thomas, "Memorandum to James M. Sakoda" (July 15, 1942).
5. James M. Sakoda, "Diary" (February 22, 1943).
6. Dorothy S. Thomas, "Memorandum" (August 27, 1942).
7. James M. Sakoda, "Journal" (March 17, 1943).
8. War Relocation Authority, *The Evacuated People. A Quantitative Description* (Washington, D.C.: GPO, 1946).
9. Data analysis in this section is based on James M. Sakoda, "Tule Lake Community Study of Acculturation," unpublished manuscript, 1947, 1–19.
10. Marvin K. Opler, "Review of *The Spoilage*," *American Anthropologist* 50 (1948), 307.
11. Violet Kazue (Matsuda) de Cristoforo, "A Victim of the Japanese Evacuation and Resettlement Study," unpublished manuscript, 1987.
12. Peter T. Suzuki, "The University of California Japanese Evacuation and Resettlement Study: A Prolegomenon," *Dialectical Anthropology* 10 (1986), 189–213.

The "Residue":

The Unresettled Minidokans, 1943–1945

JAMES M. SAKODA

Besides *The Spoilage* and *The Salvage*, Dorothy Thomas had planned a third volume entitled "The Residue," which however was never published. This book, possibly based on my fieldwork at the Minidoka Relocation Center in Idaho, was supposed to deal with those evacuees who declared themselves "loyal" to the United States, but stubbornly resisted War Relocation Authority pressure to leave the relocation centers. When the WRA announced camp closures at the end of 1944, many wanted to remain "like Indians" in the security of the camps. Under the threat of expulsion, some had fantasies of being rescued by a victorious Japan. The vast majority of the Issei, along with their dependents and some Nisei and Kibei, comprised this unresettled group of evacuees about whom hardly anything has been written.

This article concentrates on the "residue" at Minidoka. Their story begins at Tule Lake, where I started working as a JERS participant observer. This center was populated by Japanese–Americans from both California and the Pacific Northwest. However, after the "loyalty" registration, which sorted out "loyals" from "disloyals," many "loyal" Northwesterners went to Minidoka, which was already occupied by Japanese–Americans from the Pacific Northwest. I joined this group and stayed at Minidoka almost until it was closed in late 1945. Based upon my extensive observations, I later devoted my doctoral dissertation to a study of Minidoka.[1]

Theoretical Framework: Social Interaction and Development of Attitudes

For my analysis of the "residue" and other relocation camp data, I used the viewpoints of W. I. Thomas and Kurt Lewin. The central concept was the interaction of participants with varying attitudes or definitions of the situation. Attitudes were organized around predominant values, such as the Issei's need for security. Attitudes were directed toward specific situations and were redefined with variations in the situation. Redefinition of attitudes was toward tension reduction. The study of social interactions was based on Kurt Lewin's notion of approach and withdrawal, i.e., an individual approached those for whom he held a positive evaluation but withdrew from those he viewed negatively. This approach–withdrawal theorem provided the basis of a social structure, which developed according to the movement of people with varying attitudes. In the course of writing my dissertation, I developed a checkerboard model of social interaction. The model showed how two groups of checker—assigned with varying combinations of positive, neutral, and negative attitudes toward members of their own group and those of an opposing group—developed over time different arrangements representing the social structure. The model, which is described in more detail in the appendix to this article, showed that individual attitudes and the social structure were different aspects of the same phenomenon. This model was later computerized.[2]

In applying this model to Japanese–Americans, I realized that the social situation included not only the family and the Japanese and American communities but also the cultural environment and the relationship between Japan and the United States. The participants included Issei, Nisei, and Kibei, as well as various subgroups with distinct attitudes and values. Thus, to understand the predicament of those who became the "residue," it is important to study each group, both prior to evacuation and during confinement, first at Tule Lake and later at Minidoka.

Pre–evacuation Attitudes and Values

The Issei with Families

For most Issei, life prior to evacuation was not easy, particularly after the depression. Livelihood was based on small farms or small retail stores within the Japanese community, and earning a living required hard work and the help of family members. A long–term goal of most was to earn enough money to return to Japan to live in comfort. In the meantime, they generally withdrew into the protection of the community. One important value of the Issei was education for their children, including college education even when prospects for professional employment were not favorable.

The Issei identified with Japan. Japan was their country, and most expected to return to the homeland. But because of the connection with their Nisei children, the Issei often suppressed expressions of overt identification with Japan.

The Issei Bachelors

The migrant workers were a sorry lot. The Immigration Act of 1924 cut off any chance of obtaining wives from Japan. Without the help of wives, they faced great difficulties in becoming independent farmers or store owners. The Issei Bachelors, along with the Kibei, were the disgruntled, dissident group within the relocation centers. They did not have ties with children to provide integration with the American community. They did not have the financial means to enjoy life.

Their identification with Japan was expressed more openly than by Issei generally. Without a family and without an economic stake in America, they expressed hope that Japan after winning the war would reward them by providing a haven in places like Java, which Japan had occupied. This notion of reward for loyalty was voiced often in the relocation centers but also prior to evacuation.

The Kibei

The Kibei were victims of the Issei's sojourner attitude. In order for an Issei couple to work freely and to provide their children with a Japanese education, the children were sent to Japan for upbringing by grandparents. When the depression came and it became increasingly clear that the family would be unable to unite in Japan, the Issei recalled the children. Some were in their teens by this time and spoke little or no English. Returning to America, they became a maladjusted group. Their ambition was to get a good education and learn English, and some succeeded. For most, however, job prospects were poor and association with Nisei limited.

After Pearl Harbor, the Kibei were like the Issei Bachelors in their expression of support for Japan. Although there were no attempts at sabotage, the Kibei's frustration with their lot in the United States led to expressions of hope in Japan's victory.

The "Japanesy" Nisei

These Nisei were most likely to be Buddhist, to have taken Japanese language schoolwork seriously, and to have been greatly influenced by their parents' interest in Japanese things, such as judo and movies. They could speak Japanese sufficiently to communicate with their parents and sometimes spoke it fluently. They were most likely to be passive in social situations. They believed in the need for *gaman*—to grin and bear it in times of adversity, to forego pursuing pleasure when duty called for work. They were generally not comfortable with *hakujin* and generally avoided contact with them.

Nisei, in general, were not concerned about loyalty to Japan or America, since their main interests were in social matters. However, the "Japanesy" Nisei were sometimes influenced by attitudes of their parents toward Japan. They did not really understand the importance of loyalty to America. However, they were American citizens, and not many planned to go to Japan. Thus, they were prepared to be drafted but not to volunteer to prove their loyalty to America.

The "Americanized" Nisei

These Nisei were largely Americanized in their external behavior. They generally spoke English exclusively. They were more likely to think of America as their country, not Japan. Many were members of Christian churches, which helped them to become socialized in American ways. Before evacuation, I became acquainted with some of these Nisei at Pasadena Junior College and noted the following:

> Was talking to Setsuko and George today during a study period. George started the whole thing by demanding why he didn't chuck his school work. "Why don't you?" I said. "But what can I do?" he asked and then added, "Work in a fruit stand?" "Why not work in a fruit stand?" I insisted. Setsuko said that George wasn't ambitious enough. Why didn't he go on with his studies. Why didn't he go to China, where he could get a job without the knowledge of Japanese. But I interposed and told Setsuko that she couldn't blame the boys because there wasn't so very much that they could do. How about the boy that won all honors and couldn't find a job. But I turned around and insisted to George that he ought to take a chance on it and at least do his best. We thought that there might be some chance in civil service. Setsuko knew of a Nisei at the head of the mail department. She also knew a nurse receiving good pay. She thought also that Tajima had a good job as a secretary in Japan. She also knew a mechanic who fixed boats. There was another Nisei in an airplane factory.[3]

The pre–war job prospects for Nisei on the West Coast were dismal. Working in a fruit stand or as a gardener was not appealing but was the common fate of many Nisei.

"Rowdies"

There was a rowdy element among Nisei. Some were Hawaiian Nisei or

Kibei. They were essentially groups of boys who played together without much adult supervision. They were reputed to cause trouble, such as breaking up dances. Their favorite activity was sports. They were not the type to take studies seriously or to attend church. Hence, when it came to finding jobs, only manual labor was available to them. Their problem, as with other Nisei, was the poor prospects for suitable jobs, which prevented them from meeting girls and settling down.

The "Marginal" Nisei

Everett V. Stonequist wrote a book called *The Marginal Man*,[4] which described the dilemma of a person belong to two cultures but not accepted by either one. The Marginal Nisei disliked Japanese as a group and usually avoided belonging to Japanese students clubs or Japanese churches. They were most likely to adopt American ways and show few Japanese traits. Their marginal status was likely to leave them psychologically disturbed. They wanted to associate with Caucasians but often were not fully accepted by them. Unlike other Nisei, they often acted like Caucasians—more outspoken and forward in their behavior. Since they lived only on the fringe of the Japanese–American community, they were quite ready to leave if the opportunity arose. This willingness to leave and seek the help of Caucasian associates often helped them to pursue successful professional careers. The loyalty of Marginal Nisei to the United States was generally unquestioned. They saw other Japanese–Americans as being too clannish, and some believed that the community had brought the evacuation on itself.

Adjustment to Center Life at Tule Lake

The Tule Lake Relocation Center was designed to hold 16,000 "residents." It became the home for Japanese–Americans from the Northwest and Sacramento and surrounding rural areas. The initial WRA policy was benign with emphasis on making evacuees as comfortable as possible within the limitations of criticism from the outside that they were being pandered. Life in the relocation center was not unlike roughing it at a summer camp. There was enough to grumble about, but many families soon settled down. Most Issei, who had struggled for a living, for the first time found time for leisure activity. If they worked on the farm or the construction crew, they did not have to work hard. Some chose not to work and spent time with hobbies.

For Issei Bachelors, camp life was in some ways ideal. Living in a bachelor's quarters was not much different from living in a pre–war laborer's bunkhouse. Meals were served three times a day. The men could get together in the boiler room and talk about how Japan was faring in the war or play games, such as *shogi*.

Initially, Nisei were selected for key positions in the center. They ran the project newspaper, farm, and hospital and taught in the schools. These opportunities contrasted to the situation on the outside where white collar jobs were hard to get.

Socially the situation was attractive to many. Weekly dances were organized in several recreation halls and required little money to attend. There were weekly movies, church services, ping pong contests, baseball leagues, and beauty contests.

There were complaints that the small "apartments" and eating in the common dining hall weakened family ties. However, from the viewpoint of Japanesy Nisei, who had been under strict family control, the new arrangement provided an opportunity to socialize with other Nisei.

Even for Marginal Nisei, camp life provided a chance to work with Caucasians for the benefit of other Japanese–Americans. For example, Kazuko Tanabe worked as a personal secretary to the head of the construction section. While she did not care for Japanese–Americans generally, she was in a position to do favors for her block by getting building material. Living in close contact with Japanese–Americans, however, put pressure on Marginal Nisei. During the registration crisis, Tanabe became ill and had to stay home for several weeks.

Camp conditions were not advantageous for the typical Kibei. One group from the Northwest became wardens. Another group took courses in English and organized a club. They kept its existence secret because they did not want other Kibei to become involved. The more educated Kibei obtained office jobs and were able to associate with Nisei.

Conflicts among Groups

Evacuation brought a shift in community leadership from the Issei to the Nisei. In the camps, many leadership positions went to Nisei, even though many were still in their twenties and not mature enough to handle supervisory jobs. The WRA specified that representatives to the Community Council, an advisory group to the administration, had to be citizens. This angered older Issei. Some of the early explosions in Manzanar and Poston were, in essence, generational struggles for political control.

In Tule Lake, the Nisei dominance of the Community Council was offset by a practice of referring issues back to the block for approval, where Issei sentiments prevailed. Issei also organized a Planning Board with representatives from each block. The Cooperative Enterprise was guided by Don Elberson, who was liberal in viewpoint and patiently educated people to the concept of an evacuee–owned and –run enterprise. Both an Issei and Nisei representative from each block were selected, and both English and Japanese were spoken at meetings, depending on the preference of the speaker. Issei, Nisei, and some Kibei all worked together to run the enterprise.

Food shortages began to appear in July 1942. On August 15, farm and construction workers in Block 18 refused to go to work when they were served only two little pancakes and tea because of the lack of sugar. The strike spread to other parts of the project. In negotiations with the administration, leaders pointed out the food shortage was due to the Caucasian assistant project steward, who had a policy of stocking only a two–day supply of food. The administration agreed to increase the supply and asked the workers to go back to work. That afternoon, workers held a mass meeting with speeches by protest leaders—Kibei and Issei. But more level–headed opinion prevailed, and the workers decided to return. On August 17, breakfast consisted of grapefruit and a piece of ham besides the usual mush, French toast and coffee. Several residents commented that it was good to have a strike now and then. The movement to get rid of the assistant project steward continued and finally succeeded with the aid of a slowdown strike.

Crisis at Tule Lake: "Loyalty" Registration and "Segregation"

The registration crisis, which occurred early in 1943, came as a surprise to both the administration and Japanese–American residents. Early in its program, the WRA provided for student relocation and seasonal work for laborers in sugar beet fields. It also toyed with the establishment of industries within the centers to take advantage of evacuee manpower. But by the end of 1942, the WRA decided on a program of permanent resettlement and eventual dissolution of the centers. Early in 1943, two programs were combined to register all evacuees on a "loyalty" questionnaire. The first was a plan by the

War Department to establish an all–Nisei combat team. The second related to the WRA's need to clear those who desired to relocate to the outside world. Unfortunately, the registration was poorly handled in Tule Lake. A question on the swearing of loyalty to the United States was accompanied by a question on the willingness to serve in the U.S. Armed Forces. It was not clear whether answering "yes" to both meant volunteering for military service. In Tule Lake, many refused to register. As a result, 42 percent of those 17-years and older at Tule Lake were declared "disloyal," in contrast to 10 percent at other camps.

The registration issue affected almost everyone. Kibei became protest leaders, declaring loyalty to Japan and dominating meetings to force the entire block not to register. They were also willing to take out repatriation papers in order to avoid having to register and seemed to welcome the opportunity to return to Japan. Later the administration announced that they would still have to register. The more educated Kibei and those who had learned English and got along with Nisei were more tempered in their attitude and were often willing to register.

Most Issei were concerned that their sons were being forced to volunteer for the Nisei battalion and that by filling out registration forms labeled, "applications for leave clearance," they themselves would be forced to leave the center. The more educated or socially successful Issei were more tempered in their point of view:

> Mrs. Akahoshi is an intelligent lady and a shrewd observer of people. She sees things in better perspective than probably any other person living in Block 25. She remarked to JS [James Sakoda] yesterday that people had started to make plans to leave the project and start farming and working on farms. But this registration had closed their minds entirely to the idea of going out. The people do not want to return to Japan right away and would prefer to wait till the end of the war to see how things are going to turn out before making their decision. . . . Since the young people have been required to take out repatriation papers, it has become necessary for the parents to do so, too. Most of parents are not willing to let their children return to Japan alone, and feel that they have to sacrifice their property for the sake of their children. The Government handled the registration in a poor manner. It was introduced in such a way as to make the people believe that they were going to be sent off to war to be sacrificed, through the creation of a special Japanese combat unit. The officials do not seem to realize

this state of mind of the Japanese people.[5]

Many Nisei boys said very little at block meetings and were evidently confused by the arguments. Nisei often mentioned the injustice of being asked to volunteer while still being incarcerated. They clearly did not relish answering "no" to the question of loyalty to the United States because most had little attachment to Japan. Nonetheless, many were unwilling to buck the trend in their block or to oppose the wishes of their parents. The great fear was that of being forced to volunteer by answering "yes" to both questions. The Japanesy Nisei, who were in the habit of obeying their parents, were the most willing to go along with their block.

The Marginal Nisei were more vocal in their condemnation of others for not taking this opportunity to volunteer for the Nisei battalion. They openly announced their position and were denounced as traitors. Frank Miyamoto and Tom Shibutani, my JERS co–fieldworkers, felt that they could not stay in the center for fear of violence and left soon after the registration crisis.

The crisis subsided when the administration announced in writing that those answering "no" to both questions would not be volunteering for the Nisei battalion nor likely to be drafted. At a crucial meeting, Mr. Kaya, the chef, made a stirring speech, asking the people in the block not to make a serious mistake by sticking to the resolution not to register and running the risk of being jailed. He cried and won people over to his point of view. The block manager offered to get a written statement from the project director, which would make registration safe. The block then decided to register, the protest leaders withdrew, and the block returned to a more normal state. Protest leaders were tolerated or even welcomed at the time of the crisis. However, when the crisis passed, they became a threat to peaceful existence.

But the crisis had caused a cleavage in the population. Nisei in increasing numbers left for college or work on the outside. Some changed their registration answers when they found that they needed clearance to go to work or school. The decision to segregate all the "disloyal" in Tule Lake made it necessary for others who had not registered, or had answered negatively, or who had taken out repatriation papers to change their stand. Finally, many families felt it was safer to stay in Tule Lake than to face uncertainties in another center. They became the "Old Tuleans," in contrast to the incoming "segregants" from other centers who were more anti–administration and pro–Japan.

The Nisei Leave—Sometimes Reluctantly

Although increasing numbers of Nisei began to relocate to the outside world, they did not all leave eagerly. Shuji Kimura, a Christian Nisei from the Northwest, summarized his mixed feelings:

> Now in closing, to touch briefly upon the social aspects of the life in these relocation camps. Life within these camps is not in any sense a black hole of frustration as many might think, nor on the other hand, a light–hearted round of depraved idle pleasures as some Congressmen seem to think. There is food enough to sustain life decently. If one is ambitious one can learn many skills, learn the English language if one be deficient in it; there is work enough for everyone, and to many college trained individuals, this is often the first opportunity to exercise their knowledge actively in the community's behalf.
>
> The evils lie in something more subtle than physical privations. It lies more in that something essential missing from our lives. No matter how insulated a person was psychologically, yet he walked the streets or the roads of the countryside and saw other human beings. Here the cutting off of self is complete. The barbed wire with its watch tower is a real and actual demarcation line between two real worlds. It cuts into the efforts toward real integration of life for which the nisei has been so hungry, the successful balancing of our lives of all the elements of the three worlds of which he is a part.
>
> The primary problem is that of keeping alive in the residents the sense that they are a part of the national effort. The most devastating effect upon a human soul is not hatred but being considered not human. The only true solution to the problem of the nisei lies in solving the problem, not humanely, but in a human manner, of restoring the sense of oneness with the world at large.[6]

Jobo Nakamura was from Sacramento and at the time of evacuation was a student at the University of California. He worked as an itinerant farm worker with his father and found life in Tule Lake enchanting. He was a hard–working staff member of the *Tulean Dispatch*. His urge to relocate was half–hearted:

> Now that I have made plans to leave the Project, I feel like staying here a little longer. Life here has made me soft and indolent. I'm clothed, sheltered and I don't have to worry about where my next meal is coming from. I feel as though I've become a part of the dust. I no longer gripe about the physical conditions of this camp.

> There is no economic pressure living in a socialized world such as here, and I am living day to day in purposeless drifting, planning frivolous things to do tomorrow. It's funny. . . . I want to prolong this sort of life but [if] I procrastinated I'll be here for the duration and I don't want to be here when the war ends. My better conscience tells me that the sooner I re–establish myself in a normal American community, the better I would be prepared to meeting the postwar future.
>
> I must go out and make my living the hard way again. Yet doubt and fear disturb my mind. Would I be jumping out of a frying pan into the fire? Will I be happy outside in a strange community? To go out means to depart from my life–long friends. It means to tear myself away from a life of comparative ease and security to start life all over again. It makes me feel weary. I hope this will be the last time I'll have to move again.[7]

The Sorting of "Loyals" and "Disloyals"

About half of the Tule Lake residents had to choose another center when Tule Lake became a segregation center for the "disloyals." The "loyals" from the Northwest generally chose to go to Minidoka, which was already occupied by people from Washington and Oregon. They entered Minidoka after exposure to Californians, who were more militant in dealing with WRA blunders, and became allies of Minidokans dissatisfied with the acquiescent leaders and residents.

As a declared "loyal" resident, I had to leave Tule Lake and chose to go to Minidoka, where I married a girl from the Northwest whom I had met in Tule Lake. I obtained a job as labor relations advisor and became an associate of the Community Council. From this vantage point, I was able to examine labor problems and become involved in negotiations between the Council and the administration. I also became a close associate of Rev. Joseph Kitagawa, an Episcopalian minister, and Tom Ogawa, secretary of the Community Council. The three of us kept a close watch on political developments. I stayed in Minidoka until the spring of 1945 and returned in the fall to cover the closure procedure.

The Unresettled Minidokans, 1943–1945

During the latter part of 1943 and all during 1945, the WRA encouraged voluntary, permanent relocation to the Midwest and East. In December 1944, it announced that all centers would be closed within a year, and relocation became mandatory. At the time, 73 percent of all evacuees were still in centers.

The "un–relocated" consisted of 85 percent of the total Issei population and 67 percent of the total Nisei. In terms of gender, 72 percent of Japanese–American males and 76 percent of females remained in the centers.

Minidoka had distinguished itself early not only for its high number of Nisei volunteers for military service—with less than 7 percent of the male population, it provided 25 percent of the volunteers[8]—and its small number of "segregants." Also, Minidoka had the highest relocation rate for all–centers. In 1943, the average monthly rate of leaves, both permanent and temporary, was 22 per 1,000 residents, in contrast to the rate of 14 per 1,000 for all centers. However, during 1944, following the arrival of Tuleans, the Minidoka monthly leave rate dropped to 21, while the all–center average increased to 21. Minidoka no longer led the relocation parade.

On January 1, 1943, there were 9,861 persons, including those on short term leave, in Minidoka. By September 1, 1943, the population had dropped 15.6 percent to 8,325. By December 1943, the population was up again to 9,492, following an influx of transferees, mostly from Tule Lake. On December 1, 1944, the population was 7,867, a reduction of 21.3 percent. Clearly, a majority of evacuees was still in Minidoka when forced closure was announced.[9]

The rate of departure from Minidoka was quite selective by generation, religion, and gender. Chart 1 (see Chart 1 on opposite page) shows the percentages of Minidokan males, 17- years and older, remaining in the center at the end of 1944 by religion and generation, based on the population in March 1943.[10] The most important variable was generation, since it was the older Issei who were reluctant to leave and Nisei most willing to do so. Religious differences were also important. In each generational category, Buddhists were more likely to stay behind than Christians.

For females (see Chart 2 on page 260), the rate of relocation was not only lower, but generational and religious differences played less a role than for males. About twice as many female Christian Nisei remained behind compared to their male counterparts. Issei parents were more reluctant to allow their daughters to leave the center than sons, and Buddhist Nisei were more likely to comply with this wish. It should be remembered that most of the Nisei below the age of 17 were dependents and were still in the center in December 1944.

For those contemplating relocation, there were usually two choices. One was to wait until the opening of the West Coast and to return home directly rather than going temporarily to the Midwest. The other alternative was to remain in the center at all costs. Some of those choosing the second alternative believed that Japan would win the war.

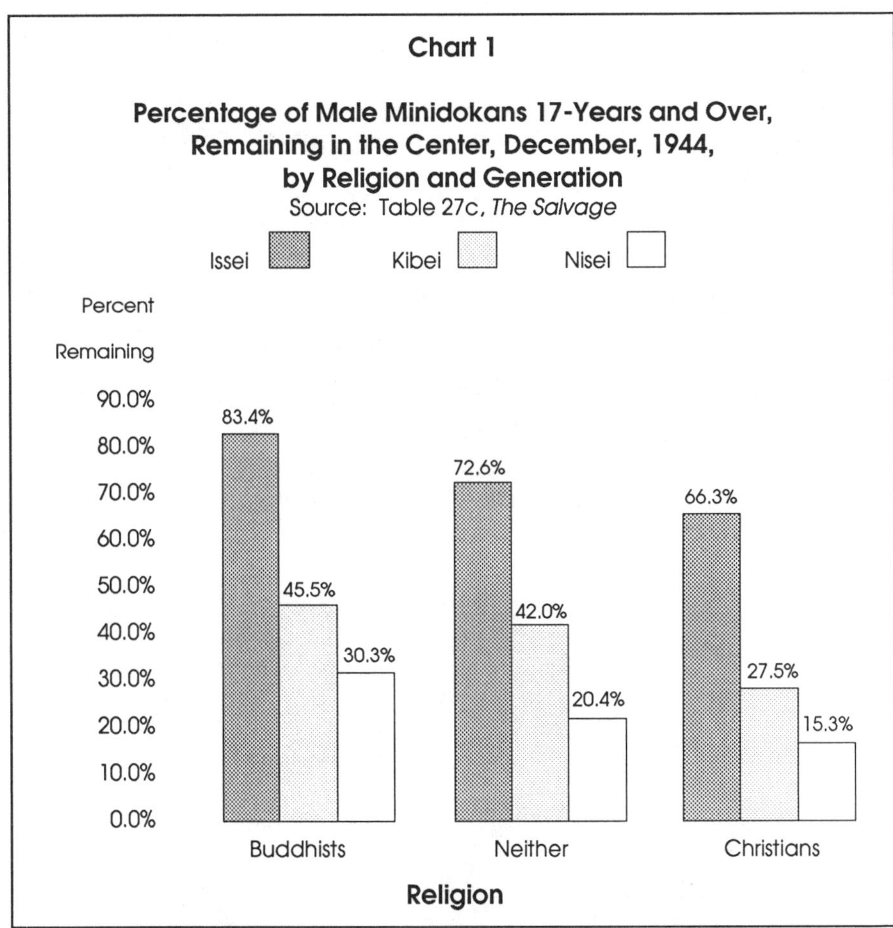

An older Issei expressed a typical viewpoint when urged by his children to join them in Chicago. His logic was sound, but his premise that Japan was winning the war was not:

> If the WRA decides to close the center, we can't do anything about it and will relocate, but I would rather wait until that time came. There's no problem about moving out of here; we can do that any time. But as things

are, I feel it's better for us to remain here for the present. We would be a burden on the children if we went out, but right now we don't need any money and we don't have to depend on anyone else. Another thing, if the West Coast is opened up and we can go back to our home in Seattle it would only require extra expense if we went to Chicago first. Fundamentally, the thing is I would go out if I thought that Japan were going to be defeated in this war, but it's evident that Japan is winning the war. I understand the American army is being pushed back in the Philippines. They'll never take the Philippines.[11]

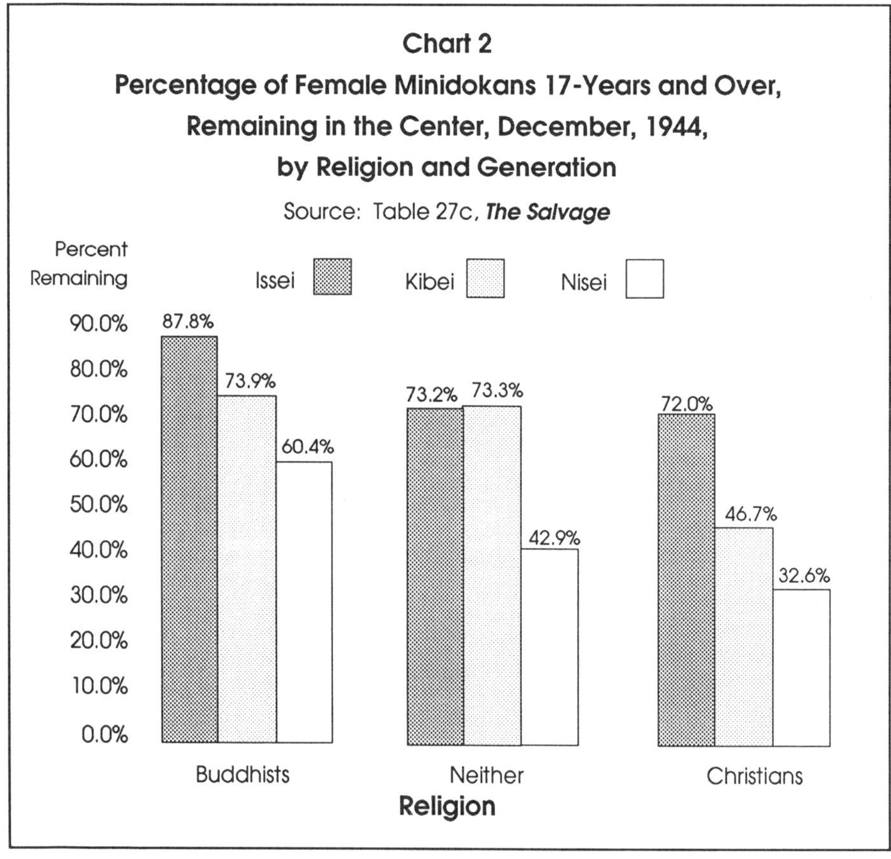

For the older Issei, there were serious risks to consider in relocation to the East. First, they would be entering hostile territory with little assurance of company from other Japanese–Americans. They wanted to relocate as a group, if possible, but arrangements were made on a family basis. Of course, one family could go first and call others, but this was no assurance enough for some. Also, they needed promises that they could return to the center if things did not work out. The administration said that they could come back, but first they should try to make other arrangements. This answer did not allay the fears of older people. Others were concerned about receiving more aid, evidently feeling that they were entitled to it since they had been deprived of their livelihood. The net result of all these factors was that older Issei and those burdened with young children chose to stay and wait out the end of the war.

The Weakening of Moral Values

A favorite theme of WRA officials advocating rapid return of Japanese–Americans to the outside world was that life in the relocation center was weakening moral fiber. Instead of working hard, evacuees were believed to not exert themselves. One example involved construction workers on the gymnasium. After arriving on the construction site, the crew would sit around a fire until the head carpenter banged on his saw. After working a couple of hours, the crew would wait for the truck to take them back to the mess hall. The procedure was repeated in the afternoon, resulting in not much more than four hours of work.

Another example involved stealing lumber. Since there was no furniture in evacuee "apartments" and lumber was not provided for this purpose, it was necessary to take lumber illegally. In Minidoka this was euphemistically referred to as "volunteering." The administration on occasion asked for volunteers to haul coal. Thus, evacuees reasoned that if the administration could ask for volunteers, they could also "volunteer" for lumber hauling.

A more subtle form of moral deterioration was the demand for aid. Before evacuation, Japanese–Americans were known for not asking for welfare from the government. When an Issei bachelor could no longer take care of himself, it was not unusual for those around him to send him home to Japan. However, now that evacuees were asked to return to the outside world, they questioned whether $25 per person, train fare, and the fund for meals provided by WRA were sufficient. Those with more than $500 in cash were not entitled to the subsidy for the trip outside, and evacuees were reluctant to reduce their own savings to venture out. Issei, particularly the elderly and those with dependents, had lost their confidence to make it on their own without government assistance. The easy life on the inside had made many willing to accept their status as wards of the government. For these Issei, the tragedy was not the guard towers or the tar–papered barracks. It was the loss of their sense of independence.

Deteriorating Relations between Evacuees and the Administration

During the first year of operation, the administration in Minidoka established a good relationship with the evacuees. Thus, the camp was able to establish a remarkable record of completing the registration process with the highest number of military volunteers among all the centers. Much credit was due to the skillful handling of the educational program by the project director's assistants.

In the middle of 1943, a number of changes occurred which fundamentally restructured the relationship between the administration and evacuees. First, the assistant project director was replaced by three heads of divisions. With the departure of the assistant, the project director became the chief definer of administrative action. His approach was to dictate orders emanating from Washington rather than to seek compromises.

The second change was the institution of a retrenchment program beginning on July 1, 1943, which reduced the labor force by one third and specified a 48–hour work week. This was coupled with vigorous efforts to encourage relocation to the outside. The apparent goal was to promote relocation by making life in the center less easy–going. This policy became a source of almost continuous conflict between the administration and evacuees.

The third change was the arrival of "loyal" transferees from Tule Lake. They arrived with experience of active protest against the administration. They criticized the Minidokans as being too docile and were welcomed by the dissatisfied residents.

Finally, newly elected leaders of the Community Council were wary of taking unpopular stands. They replaced block managers, who were considered too cooperative in dealing with the administration.

Labor Conflicts: Strikes and Walkouts

The net result was a series of labor conflicts, many of which were not settled satisfactorily and left both sides dissatisfied. When the block maintenance staff was reduced from 11 to four, work was carried on by two boiler men, one janitor and one janitress. During the summer, the work was light but as winter approached, it was necessary to keep six stoves going day and night in the laundry room and the men and women's latrines. When a fire broke out in one of the boiler rooms, the administration demanded that the three boiler men each work an eight hour shift. The boiler men were unwilling to take on additional work, and the administration responded with threat of dismissal. After a heated meeting with administration representatives, the boiler men decided to go on strike—the first for Minidoka. The Community Council took over the job of mediation from the block managers but was unable to get the project director to increase the number of workers. Instead, he decided to return workers to their old schedule. The settlement was not satisfactory to anyone. The people felt that they had lost the strike and had suffered unnecessarily, going without hot water for a week.

A similar conflict occurred when the mail carriers went on strike when their crew was reduced. They came back to work on condition that they did not have to make door–to–door deliveries; residents were required to call at the block manager's office for mail. Similar conflicts occurred with the gatekeepers, the telephone operators, the warehouse workers, the pickling plant, the community activities section, and construction crew on the high school gymnasium.

Trouble arose around the gymnasium construction when the administration objected to the four–hour work schedule of the work crew and attempted to institute an eight–hour day by assigning supervisory personnel. The construction crew quit in protest. The administration attempted to complete the gymnasium with volunteers, but no evacuees responded. The gymnasium would have remained boarded up had it not been for Rev. Kitagawa. He approached the administration for permission to have the structure opened for use as a hall to commemorate Nisei soldiers who had died. The administration agreed, and the gymnasium was opened in partially finished form. However, it stood as a reminder of administration–evacuee conflict.

Deterioration of the School System

The educational system also declined in this period. Schools had been opened under adverse conditions. Classrooms were makeshift, textbooks and supplies were not always available, and teachers were not all experienced. An innovative program, which was experimental but thought suitable for the evacuated students, was instituted at the high school. It included a core program which combined English and social studies and a work experience program. There was also a "harvest summer vacation," which allowed high school students to work in nearby fields.

However, in the summer of 1944, controversy arose over the innovative program. The project director dismissed the high school principal, and an attempt was made to change to a more traditional form of education. After the school term opened in August, there were a series of incidents between teachers and students.

In February 1945 there was a major case of vandalism of a classroom of an unpopular teacher after a class dance. Eight boys were apprehended and brought to trial before a local judge, who was pressed by local leaders not to go soft on the vandals. Rev. Kitagawa, Tom Ogawa, and the community analyst worked with the project attorney to obtain a parole for the boys.[12]

The result of these conflicts was increased hard feelings between the administration and evacuees, adversely affecting the relocation program. In September 1944, when the administration embarked on an ambitious program to recruit 500 workers for the munitions depot in Nebraska, the Community Council played a passive role in passing information to evacuees. Block meetings were poorly attended, and only 28 families were reportedly recruited. The project director suspected that some agitator was behind the resistance.

In these conflicts, the administration generally did not take the advice of camp leaders, which put the latter in an untenable position, caught between the mass of block residents and the demands of the administration. Negotiation and compromise, so necessary for settling labor conflicts, were lacking. The Issei chairman of the Community Council only made matters worse by misleading both sides by misstating their positions. He was denounced as *inu,* and his two Nisei secretaries quit in disgust. I quit my job as labor relations advisor because my position was becoming too risky with both evacuees and the administration.

The Forced Closure of Minidoka

On December 18, 1944, the WRA announced that the War Department was allowing all Japanese–Americans to return to the West Coast and that all centers were to be closed within a year. For Minidoka, the closing date was the end of

October. However, the administration decided an earlier closing, with the last train scheduled to leave on October 23. In all, there were 7,808 departures from Minidoka in 1945 before closing. From January through July, there was a gradual increase in monthly departures from 149 to 555. In the last three months, there were 1,110, 1,725, and 1,491 departures, or 4,326 total, representing 55 percent of all departures in 1945. This concentration of departures in the last few months was not peculiar to Minidoka, since it happened at other centers as well. What distinguished Minidoka was the rough manner in which the closure was carried out.

The evacuees remaining in the center were predominantly younger children and Issei, 40 years and older, and conservative Nisei. For the Issei, announcement of the closure came as a shock, and many refused to believe that the WRA could close down all of the centers. A young Issei with a family said:

> I don't want to be the first one to go back [to the West Coast] and get killed. I'm not a fool. I wonder what's going to happen to those who refuse to go out. I suppose they're going to become like Indians.[13]

A Nisei farmer with two children and a mother to support said wryly:

> I was afraid that this was going to happen. They said that we can go anyplace we like, but that's not so good. This is even worse than being evacuated.[14]

Since they were being allowed to return to the West Coast, the Issei could no longer use the excuse of not having friends to make the move together. But fear of violence remained a concern. And the most important fear was economic insecurity. Many Issei had lost farms and stores. Even those who had businesses that could be restarted had lost the will to cope with trying conditions on the outside. They had become government wards and had come to rely on this status.

Protests took the form of both seeking more financial aid and refusing to believe that the center would be closed. An all–center conference was held by delegates from each center (except Tule Lake and Manzanar) in Salt Lake City from February 16 to 23, 1945, to discuss possible group actions. The alternatives of a "hard" stand of making demands and a "soft" approach of asking for more considerations were debated. Delegates adopted a series of "soft" requests: more monetary aid, extension of time limits, and the possibility of returning to centers. But the WRA was unwilling to increase amounts of aid only to holdouts.

The delegate from Heart Mountain presented Dillon S. Myer the results of a survey indicating that 60 percent of the people were unable to relocate, that 18 percent would relocate on certain conditions, and only 9 percent planned to relocate under the WRA program. Myer replied that he was encouraged that at least 9 percent were planning to leave. When asked what would happen if some chose not to relocate, Myer replied that there was no plan to deal with such a situation. At any rate, the WRA centers were to be closed permanently.

Minidoka leaders wrote up a set of recommendations to present to Myer on his visit in the spring. These included numerous reasons for operating the center for the war's duration and requests for aid for those desiring to relocate. In a meeting with block commissioners and Community Council members and in a later address to the public, Myer skillfully replied to each recommendation, emphasizing that it would be easier for evacuees to make adjustments on the outside now than wait until the war was over.

On March 6, the Spanish Consul visited Minidoka. He bluntly stated that as a neutral representative of the Japanese government, he was not able to stop the closure of the centers. He said that there had been no word from Japan on center closure.

Among actions taken by the administration to hasten leaving was the closing of mess halls serving less than 128 people and reducing the work force. Patterned after the slowdown strike in Tule Lake, the Mess Workers Association organized a similar strike. They served meals an hour late, so that other workers could not get to jobs on time. The attempt was half–hearted, however, and on the fourth day the strike collapsed. By the end of July, seven mess halls had been closed. During August, 11 more were closed, and in September, 12 more were shut down, leaving only four mess halls open for the entire project. The quality of food also deteriorated.

Beginning October 1, laundry rooms and latrines were closed progressively, even though evacuees were still living in nearby quarters. As barracks emptied, electricity was turned off. The camp became darker and darker. In October there were still nearly 1,500 evacuees in Minidoka.

The administration also conducted a series of block meetings to explain Administrative Instruction 289, which made provisions for scheduling departures from the center. The plan included a series of 20 meetings (completed during the week of August 19–25). A second set of meetings was held for those who had not yet made relocation plans. A third set of meetings included notification of the internal security police to insure evacuee attendance. The last step involved the setting of departure dates for those who had not made their own plans:

> Step 4 represents the last activity of the educational program. If after the first three series of meetings there are still people who have no relocation plans nor dates of departure, their dates for leaving the center will be set by the Administration. They will be given a three–day advance notice of these dates and then shipped back to the places where they lived prior to evacuation.[15]

Instructions from Washington provided for scheduling departures during the last six weeks of the closing program to avoid last minute confusion. Concerning the "three–day notice," the instructions read:

> Every effort shall be made to notify residents of their established departure dates a reasonable time in advance, and no resident shall be required to leave a center with no less than three–day notice.[16]

According to an official from Washington, administrators in Minidoka were using what was meant to be a last resort procedure as a means of relocating people. The "no less than three–day notice" requirement was interpreted as "three–day notice."

As it became increasingly clear that the administration was serious about closing the center, many evacuees began to look for jobs and housing. Some accepted housing in the inconveniently located federal projects. Others made arrangements to stay at temporary hostels, which consisted of cots lined in a hall without partitions in Japanese church and language school buildings. A common predicament was that of a married Issei:

> Yes, we're leaving on the ninth [of October]. We don't have a home to go back to and will have to stay at the hostel or at a hotel until we can find something else. I want to go back to Tacoma where I lived for a long time. We will have to let our children stay in Boise for the time being until we can get a place where we can all stay together. We had a grocery store before, but my wife sold it after I was interned. She sold it very cheaply but thought it was lucky that there was any buyer. But my friends now tell me that the store is doing a thriving business . . .[17]

War Rumors and Evacuee Attitudes

Throughout their internment, some evacuees believed rumors of Japan's victory. Belief in Japan's invincibility was expressed especially by the so–called "boiler men crowd"—mostly Issei bachelors. They talked, for instance, of each evacuee receiving $10,000 to compensate for losses suffered if he remained in the center until Japan won the war. Nisei generally did not believe these rumors, and Issei were divided.

Experience on the outside helped to dispel rumors. A Kibei who had relocated to Boise realized that Japan had lost the war:

> I don't think that I'm going to stay in Boise very long. I was working in Hollywood before, but I don't want to go back there until more people return there. The weather there is good. Yes, camp is very quiet now. A lot of people are leaving for Seattle. There's no use in holding out now because they mean to close the camps. I'm resigned to staying in this country now. Japan's lost the war and there's no use in going back. I'm from Hiroshima. I have a sister and uncle there, but I suppose they're gone now. We had a house, but that's gone, too. This winter the people in Japan are going to suffer greatly. I wonder how they're going to get along. So you've been to Matsumoto Shogyo [commercial high school]. I went to Nitchu [a better school, but not the best]. It's good because you know both languages. You have a good future ahead of you.[18]

The announcement of Japan's surrender in August, 1945 came as a shock to most Issei. One woman recounted her reaction:

> John Tani [Nisei] was on the project and explained some of the broadcasts to her. When John made it clear that the war had ended, Mrs. Hirota's query was: "Japan didn't lose, did she?" John's answer was: "You talk just like my mother." At the moment, however, she was glad at least that the war was over and her son overseas had survived without being hurt. It was more important to her that her children were safe, she said, than how the war ended.[19]

Belief in the war rumors caused conflict between Issei and their children and sometimes between husband and wife. The Kakimotos moved to Minidoka from Tule Lake. They were a conservative family, and the children were generally obedient but strains were beginning to show:

> The subject of the surrender was brought up by Mrs. K. in a rather

> roundabout manner, which suggested that she was not too sure about her point of view. She was more concerned about the question than was Mr. K. She first introduced the subject by relating what Koshiyama, the *johobucho* [news chief] had told her. Koshiyama was a well–educated bachelor, who expounded theories which some people laughed at. Recently Koshiyama told Mrs. K. to stay within the center because the Japanese troops were now only five miles from the camp. The most recent news was that the head of the family would receive over $10,000 from both the Japanese and American governments. Each member of the family would also receive $7,000 each. In March a special ship would come to pick up those who desired to return to Japan, and they would be given first class passage. They would be taken on a tour through the South Sea Islands. When they arrived in Japan the government would build them a beautiful home and would pay them a pension of 85 yen a month. Mrs. K. went on to relate:
>
> "I laughed at him, and he said to me seriously: 'There's no need to laugh.' When I asked him how he knew all this, he said that he had studied the matter for three years. It's really too fantastic.
>
> "I hear that they're going to sign the peace terms in Tokyo next month. The surrender terms signed in Tokyo Bay was only for the cessation of hostilities. It can't be true that Japan gave up unconditionally. If that's true, we would really be broken up. That story of Tojo's attempted suicide is all false. The pictures in *Life* magazine were made in Hollywood. A man who has *yamato damashii* wouldn't do such a thing as shooting himself in the head if he intended to kill himself. His wife would have helped him to die if he really had to commit suicide. Nisei just don't know about *yamato damashii*. If it's true that Japan surrendered unconditionally, then it's pitiful—there couldn't be any God or Buddha."
>
> Mr. K. was more reserved in his stand. He said: "I take the middle course. I say that there's no way of telling right now which side is right. I listen to both sides. Time will tell which is true." He seemed to be less upset about the matter than his wife.[20]

But rumors of Japan's victory continued to circulate. As the closing of the center approached, rumors intensified. Japan was sending special ships to the West Coast to rescue the evacuees. Ships had reportedly landed in San Francisco, Seattle, and Portland, and Japanese troops were already in Salt Lake City. Some made plans to welcome the troops, and there were victory celebrations in scattered parts of the project:

> There was singing and shouting from the direction of Block 6, and I guessed that there was another celebration going on. . . . I asked one of the girls to go with me, and Anne [Nisei] offered to come along. As we walked along, I explained some of the rumors about the fleet coming in and all. She was surprised and kept saying: "Gee, but how could they believe such a thing." As we passed Mess 6, we could hear someone singing Japanese. There was a row of tables with white paper or tablecloth, and men and women sitting on either side. I walked on toward Block 8. Anne said: "Why don't we stand by the window and listen to what they're saying. I certainly wish I knew more Japanese." I told her that it was not a good idea to arouse suspicion.[21]

These rumors influenced some relocation plans. For some, it became important they not be considered to have left voluntarily for fear of missing out on the reward. They insisted on getting a three–day notice, but were packed and ready to go when they were picked up and taken to the train station.

The major source of rumors was eliminated when several "news analysts" were given three–day notices and evicted. But the diehards continued to believe the rumors.

The Final Push: Eviction from Minidoka

At the time of evacuation, Japanese–Americans were shocked but lined up and got on the train without protest. At closing time for the camps, some were very reluctant to leave and had to be literally dragged to the station and forced on trains.

Perhaps it is just as well that events turned out the way they did at Minidoka. When one visits the former location of the camps, there is more to remember than the drab surroundings, the muddy or dusty roads, the sagebrush, and the watch towers. We can remember the deteriorating relationships between *hakujin* caretakers and their wartime wards.

During the month of October 1944 the majority of evacuees came to accept the inevitability of leaving the center with the characteristic Japanese expression: *shiyo ga nai*. Two old men were telling each other:

> *Shiyo ga nai*. If we stay, they're going to kill us. From the 18th, we're going to have to walk to Block 24 in order to eat. It's better to go.[22]

Some waited for three–day notices. They could claim that they had not left willingly:

> According to O'Neill [community analyst], 27 three–day notices were served for today. We saw one family being brought on a WRA car. They got out without any evidence of emotional upheaval. As Mrs. Fukushima observed, some of the families claimed that it was better to receive a three–day notice because the WRA brought boxes, helped to pack, and brought the family to the station on a private car.[23]

Some even appeared to have interpreted receiving a three–day notice as placing them in a privileged class:

> The Kokawas looked disturbed when they arrived in Shoshone. They were well–dressed and had a white–collarish look about them. Mr. and Mrs. Kokawa appeared to be in their early 40s. Besides their baggage they had a dog in a box. Since the station agent was anxious to find the owner of the dog, I went around asking for a Mr. Kokawa until I found them. They had the health certificate for the dog ready, and I gathered that they were not unprepared to leave. I left Mr. Kokawa standing in line to check his baggage. About half an hour later he was out of line and approached me and asked in Japanese: "Aren't those with three–day notice served first?" I told him that I didn't think so.[24]

The impersonal and vindictive manner of some "program–minded" staff who carried out the closing procedures could be interpreted as a reaction to past frustrations in dealing with evacuees in matters such as the gymnasium construction. There was a facetious reference to an evacuee "manhunt" after October 23. As one staff member related to an official from Washington:

> There had been plans for a project–wide manhunt after the evacuees were relocated on the 23rd. But before then the A.P.s [appointed personnel] were going on a drunk which was to last about a week. Since the hunting season was opening on the 23rd, he wanted a round of shells for each A.P. with which to go on the manhunt. Evacuees remaining would probably be starved by then. If they weren't, they could be chalked up as having drowned in the canal or something.[25]

I did not find out exactly how many three–day notices were issued or how many people were actually forced on the train at Shoshone. A Japanese–American church worker, who first observed the closing program at Granada and then came to Minidoka, was surprised at what he saw:

> The contrast is interesting, to say the least. The closing procedures in Granada seemed bad enough when I was there. There had been pressures brought to bear on the bachelors to get them out of the Center some weeks previous and prior to my arrival. There had been one case of a forced removal and eviction of an elderly man, but the repercussions from the remaining residents were soon recognized by the administration and apparently the pressures had been abandoned. But when I arrived in Minidoka I was totally unprepared to find procedures operating that can only be described as "gestapo" methods. Severe pressures were being used. There was not only one but many removals and evictions. Repercussions had been quickly evident. Resentments, bitterness and further resistance to relocation were manifest. This, to the Minidoka administrators, called for further stringent methods and pressures.[26]

The Hirose Case

Hirose was an old Issei who was more stubborn than most evacuees about staying. His treatment showed the aggressive approach of the administration toward evacuees. Hirose was scheduled to leave on September 18, according to the project attorney, but his departure was held up because his old–age grant had not been approved. He refused to set a new date for departure. His wife and children left for their home in Washington, leaving him behind. Camp officials received notification of approval of Hirose's pension, and he was immediately served a three–day notice to leave on October 1. The project attorney and an internal security officer served the notice, but Hirose evidently refused to pay much attention to it.

The relocation officer in charge of the case related the administrative point of view:

> The law now states that anyone who refuses to accept a date will receive a three–day notice. The man was originally scheduled to leave in the middle of August, and again changed his date to early October. He was finally told to leave on the 16th. He threw his paper back and said that he would not go. I handed his name in for a three–day notice [because he refused to accept the date of departure]. That's why he had to leave yesterday [October 12]. You know what he was doing? He was hiding under his barrack. So they took him some time around noon. They locked his apartment; later they'll pack his things and send it to him.
>
> I told him that the man was under the impression that he was supposed

to leave on the 16th and did not know that he had to leave yesterday. The relocation officer laughed and did not seem to think that it was very important that the man knew when he was supposed to leave. Anyone who refused to accept a date was to be served a three–day notice unless they were special cases.[27]

On October 12, Hirose was escorted out to the Shoshone station, and an envelope with his ticket to Seattle and travel grant were slipped under his arm. He refused to accept it and sat down on the sidewalk. I was at the station and after persistently asking some questions was finally able to get Hirose's version of what had happened. He appeared to be confused and at times spoke indistinctly:

> This morning three men came to see me when I was making a box. They then went away. I went out to get my meal and was eating when they came again. They asked whether I was eating and waited for me. Then they brought me here. I didn't receive any sort of notice. No, I didn't receive any notice. Maybe among the papers I received there was a notice of some sort. I thought that I might have to leave on the 16th, but of course it could have been the 12th. I don't know, because I didn't read anything. I can't read.
>
> My record is clear, and they should know where I stand. When I was once questioned before, I told them that I would not go any place unless the war was over and settled. I haven't worked for a day since coming here. I told them that I didn't want any money from them because I hadn't done any work. You say that the war has ended, but I don't think so. If it has ended, there should be some news of the settlement reached between Japan and America. Until that occurs, I can't leave the project. I've made that clear to the people at the office. I wouldn't talk to them any more and came home. Once after that they asked me what I was going to do about my wife and children. I told them that I wasn't able to take care of myself and wasn't going to be responsible for my wife and children. They could do as they pleased.
>
> There should be some place where they can send me until the war is over. I'll go any place they send me until the war is ended. Even if this camp is closed, there should be a place where we could go. Anyway, I'm going home. They can send me where they like—even to jail.[28]

The community analyst, who was also at the station, went to look for the project officials who had brought Hirose to the station. He asked them to take responsibility for the man, but they refused on the grounds that their authority did not extend to forcing an evacuee to take the train. Their duty was over, they said, after having taken him out of the project. Evidently, they contacted the local sheriff. When the west–bound train pulled into the station, the sheriff forced Hirose on the train, seated him in the men's smoker room, and left the envelope with him.

Hirose stayed on the train and got off at Seattle. The Seattle WRA office evidently had not been notified of his arrival, and the officers there did not know what had become of him. After some inquiry, I learned that Hirose had wandered out to the market where he was seen by some pre–war, Italian acquaintances. His relatives heard about him and went after him. By that time the immigration official had already picked him up and sent him home.[29]

The Kawakami Case

I was able to talk to Mrs. Kawakami when I went to their shop to get a haircut. Mrs. Kawakami was a Kibei with an Issei husband and three children. Prior to evacuation, the family operated a barber shop in Seattle. Her equipment had been rented to a Filipino. The barber shop was taken over by another party, according to Mrs. Kawakami, and she was advised by the WRA to sell the equipment. She refused and stored the equipment with the WRA. Her income from the barber shop stopped coming, and she was under the impression that the WRA had "tricked" her. Evidently, she believed the rumor that Japan had won the war and refused to leave the center voluntarily. Both she and her husband complained of poor health but refused to apply for welfare aid. She received her two–week notice and calmly waited for the three–day notice. On October 12 she received a notice to leave on October 16.

The Kawakamis refused to leave, and the administration delayed action for a few days, hoping that the use of force would not be necessary. I had consulted with the Welfare Section and suggested two alternative plans. One was to do the packing for the family, and the other was to extend the departure date to the last day, October 23. The Relocation Section requested that the family be sent out the following day, while the Welfare Section was willing to be as lenient as possible. The project attorney doubted that it would do much good to talk with Mrs. Kawakami. It was decided that the family should be sent out on October 21.

A welfare interviewer called on Mrs. Kawakami and offered to help her with packing and informed her that someone would be waiting in Seattle to help them on arrival. Mrs. Kawakami then slightly changed her negative attitude and declared that she did not want to go back to Seattle. She would go any place she pleased. She offered to do her own packing and go quietly provided she was able to get a statement from the project attorney and Acting Project Director Phillips. From the former, she wanted a statement referring her to the immigration office, asking to be sent to an internment camp. From the project director, she wanted a statement that because he had ordered the closing of mess halls and latrines, people were required to walk some distance to other blocks.

The Welfare Section was willing to meet these requests. The project attorney was willing to write the statement she requested, but the acting project director refused. He pointed out that she might misuse such a statement and that a copy of the information bulletin should be sufficient. Mrs. Kawakami thereupon refused to let her freight go out ahead of schedule. On October 21, when the family was supposed to leave, they locked the apartment and went into hiding.

On October 21 three mess halls were theoretically open, but the few remaining evacuees took home food to cook themselves. In the evening, Mrs. Kawakami took her family and several old people in the neighborhood to look for food. At Mess 15, they found some cake, but no one in charge. They went on to Mess 24 and found some fish. They then proceeded to the administration area to demand some food. Several of the staff members brought some and gave it to the group.

The Kawakamis did not leave on the last train. Four days later, I would learn what happened to them.[30]

The Takagi Case

Meanwhile, I left with Father Joe (Rev. Kitagawa) on the last train to Seattle, while Mrs. Pepper, his assistant, and Mrs. Ogawa, who looked after his needs, drove the church car to the city. There was a small group leaving on the train, including the Takagis, who had received a three–day notice.

> The Takagi family arrived at the station shortly before the train pulled in. According to the report by an internal security man, the family was not prepared to leave and was told to go to the hospital. According to Mr. Takagi, he wanted to stay to see that the packing was done right by the

> WRA. Later in the day they were given a 30–minute notice to leave. A truck was used to put on loose baggage around the apartment. Shopping bags, carton boxes, and suitcases were randomly packed with the belongings of the family. The family was forced into a WRA car. At the gate Mrs. Takagi was seen struggling with Roth to get out of the car. The family and the baggage arrived shortly before the west–bound train was due. Jobu, the community analyst, and I helped to segregate the baggage between those which were checkable and those which were not. Only about a dozen of the mass of baggage could be checked. All of the shopping bags—out of which things were continually falling out—cartons, violin case, etc., were placed on a handcart to be loaded on the train directly. One of the baggage men poked around and saw baloneys in two of the cartons, and they had to be placed on the handcart. [The baggage men were very pleasant and helpful, and they certainly deserve a lot of praise for their cheerful attitude.] The girls in the family seemed underdeveloped and subnormal in intelligence. The whole family stood around as if in a fog and did not know what to do. They allowed us, however, to make the necessary arrangements. Soon after the train pulled in, and the last two coaches were reserved for the evacuees. Since the number leaving was not large, there was plenty of sitting space for everyone. After everyone was on, the community analyst pulled up the cart with Takagi's baggage, and we stacked them up in one of vestibules. I did not speak with the family, except when it was necessary to move the baggage once.[31]

Upon arrival in Seattle, I learned that the WRA office had received no notification about the Takagi family. I dropped in at the Methodist hostel to see how they were faring, and Mr. Takagi seemed glad to see me. He had refused to go to the WRA office to see about getting housing. He was over 65 and entitled to welfare aid. I talked to WRA officials and arranged for housing and got an assurance that a special interviewer would be sent to the hostel about welfare aid.[32]

Conclusion to the Kawakami Case

Meanwhile, Father Joe and I went to the station to meet the Kawakamis, who were reported to be arriving.

> Only a handful of people arrived on this train, and the Kawakamis were the last ones to come up the steps from the train. The father and the children looked grave. Mrs. Kawakami was all broken up. All the fight that she had shown until now was out of her. She began to cry and tell me what

had happened. As usual she was somewhat difficult to understand. I helped her with her baggage and introduced her to Mr. Matsushita. But she insisted on telling her story. She and her husband had been put in the Jerome jail. Richmond, when she went to the warehouse after some food, had cussed her out. She had also had an argument with N., whom she now despised. He had not acted like an adult education teacher, she said. Church had tried to get her to come along. She didn't know that they were going to take her to the Jerome jail, but that's what they did. Her husband was picked up separately and placed in a different cell from her. At the jail she was accused of believing that Ickes had said that she could stay in Minidoka, she said, when she had made no such statement. She tried to get a statement showing that she had been put in jail, but she was unable to get it. She was determined not to get any aid from the WRA.

She and her family were taken to the Methodist hostel. I told her that she should not live too long at the hostel because it was not good for her children and also suggested that she have a welfare worker visit her. She said that she would not take any aid from the WRA.[33]

Aftermath: The "Residue" Return Home

The return home was not as bad as some had anticipated, but neither was it easy for those without means. Those who owned homes or businesses could start up again. There had been vandalism to greenhouses, for example. There were still some "No Jap" signs around. For those without means, housing was the most acute problem. They usually started out in one of the church hostels, where beds were lined up in a hall, and then moved to rooming houses in the city or moved in with friends. The WRA arranged for good federal housing in Renton and also on the outskirts of Seattle, but some thought they were too far away. Welfare was needed by some families, and it required some effort to arrange for it. My uncle's predicament was typical of the problems of the needy:

I heard that Uncle had been staying at the Western Hotel instead of proceeding to Renton. Since it was close, I went to see him before dinner. He and his wife had taken a very small room in Western Hotel [run by the Shimizus] and were cooking and eating with another couple in the same hotel. Their room was not large, but it had running water and sufficient space to set up a hot–plate and a table on which all four could eat. They had begun to eat when I got there, and they seemed to enjoy the *sukiyaki* and rice which they had cooked. All four seemed to be well–adjusted to the new mode of life. The other couple had already found work. The wife was working at a plant operating a power sewing machine.

Uncle's primary problem was a place to settle down in. Soon after he arrived in Seattle he had managed to get his aid from the government. One of the first statements that he made was that he did not want to go to Renton. The next was that they were getting $40 for food, $8 for clothing and incidentals, and the rent was paid for them. "I don't have to work now. But I can't sit still and want to find a suitable job if I can. This is much better than the WRA." He was walking around everyday, he said, looking for a suitable place to live. Concerning the war news, he said that I had been right. The ships had not come into Seattle. [Gradually the diehards who believed in rumors were beginning to give in].[34]

Uncle went mushroom hunting and had succeeded in finding some. He gave me some to take home. They invited me to dinner. We got to talking about the war. *Obasan* said: "Don't worry. The surrender wasn't unconditional. There's going to be a peace talk yet. Mr. Moriyama says that we shouldn't worry because the time is going to come when we are going to feel very much relieved. He says he knows ten persons who believe as he does."

I couldn't stand that sort of talk after leaving camp, and I gave them the cold facts of life. I told them that there would be no more peace terms because the terms were known when the surrender was announced. Both seem surprised to hear this. I told them what the terms were. Korea, Formosa, Manchuria, Karafuto were all going to be taken away. For the first time they seemed to believe the actual news. *Obasan* said: "That's terrible. It means that we can't go back to Japan." I told her that if she went back she would starve for lack of food. Uncle said bravely: "It must have been due to the atomic bomb that Japan surrendered. Anyway, she put up a good fight for a little country."[35]

Conclusion: The Lesson of Forced Closure

I have presented three themes in this article. The first relates to the sorting out of "the salvage," "the spoilage," and "the residue" following the registration crisis. The "residue" consisted of those Kibei, Issei, and Japanesy Nisei who chose to remain in camp. Some had property or jobs on the West Coast, or simply decided to wait until the end of the war. However, other evacuees—mostly Issei Bachelors and Issei with dependents—having lost their belongings during evacuation, felt so insecure that they believed they had no choice but to remain in camp. Many enjoyed the relatively easy life, with opportunities for leisure activities. Unknowingly, however, they came to accept their status as wards of the government.

The second theme concerns the relationship among evacuees, evacuee leaders, and the administration. The failure of Caucasian personnel to understand the attitudes and values of the evacuees repeatedly led to hard feelings. In Minidoka, the relationship with the administration started out well, but after the arrival of Tuleans it deteriorated due partly to changes in WRA policy.

The third theme concerns the tragedy of the final closure of Minidoka. It came as a shock to many Issei when the WRA announced forced closure. Many felt that they could not survive in the outside society. WRA administrators, angry at their inability to make evacuees follow orders, finally resorted to forced evictions.

If there is a lesson to be learned, it is that treating a group of hard–working people as wards of the government, however good the intention, is a serious mistake. The WRA's attempt to rectify the situation through resettlement proved largely unsuccessful, requiring it to resort to forced closure of the centers. This tragic story of "the residue" and their desperate attempt to cling to the security of the camps has been missing from most accounts of the wartime evacuation and incarceration.

Notes

1. James M. Sakoda, "Minidoka: An Analysis of Changing Patterns of Social Interaction," Ph.D. dissertation, University of California, Berkeley, 1949.

2. James M. Sakoda, "The Checkerboard Model of Social Interaction," *Journal of Mathematical Sociology* 1 (1971), 119-32.

3. James M. Sakoda, "Diary" (April 1, 1940).

4. Everett V. Stonequist, *The Marginal Man* (New York: Charles Scribner's Sons, 1937).

5. James M. Sakoda, "Journal" (February 20, 1943).

6. Shuji Kimura, "A Single Leaf," in Tulean Dispatch, *Tule Lake Interlude, May 27, 1942–1943*, 1943, 15.

7. Jobo Nakamura, "A Nisei Diary," in *ibid.*, 109.

8. Dorothy S. Thomas and Richard Nishimoto, *The Spoilage* (Berkeley: University of California Press, 1946), 6.

9. War Relocation Authority, *The Evacuated People: A Quantitative Description*, Washington, D.C.: U.S. GPO, 1946.

10. See table 27c in Dorothy Swaine Thomas, *The Salvage* (Berkeley: University of California Press, 1952), 619.

11. Letter, Fieldworker to Dorothy S. Thomas (December 15, 1944).

12. James M. Sakoda, "Journal" (March 2, 8, 1945); Helen Amerman, "Education Report" [n.d].

13. James M. Sakoda, "Journal" (December 18, 1944).

14. *Ibid.*

15. *Information Bulletin*, August 29, 1945.

16. War Relocation Authority, Administrative Notice, No. 289, August 1, 1945.

17. James M. Sakoda, "Journal" (October 14, 1945).

18. *Ibid.* (September 21, 1945).

19. *Ibid.* (October 1, 1945).

20. *Ibid.* (September 29, 1945).

21. *Ibid.* (October 7, 1945).

22. *Ibid.* (October 11, 1945).

23. *Ibid.* (October 18, 1945).

24. *Ibid.*

25. *Ibid.* (October 19, 1945).

26. Jobu Yasumura, mimeographed report on visit to Minidoka, October 13–23, 1945 (November 5, 1945), for the American Baptist Home Mission Society.

27. James M. Sakoda, "Journal" (October 13, 1945).

28. *Ibid.* (October 12, 1945).

29. *Ibid.* (October 25, 1945).
30. *Ibid.* (October 17, 19, 22, 1945).
31. *Ibid.* (October 23, 1945).
32. *Ibid.* (October 24, 25, 1945).
33. *Ibid.* (October 25, 1945).
34. *Ibid.* (October 24, 1945).
35. *Ibid.* (October 28, 1945).

APPENDIX
Checkerboard Model of Social Interaction

I developed the checkerboard model of social interaction when I was at Harvard's Department of Social Relations on a one-semester scholarship from the Social Science Research Council (with which Dorothy S. Thomas was associated) working on my dissertation under Clyde Kluckhohn's supervision.

The model was developed to cope with the problem of showing the interaction between the psychological fields of two different participants. I had portrayed evacuees, evacuee leaders, administrative leaders, and the administration as circles on a sheet of paper. Evacuee leaders and administrative leaders met in the middle. I wanted to show the effects of the approach–withdrawal theorem: positive evaluation of a substructure of a situation is characteristically accompanied by approach toward it, while negative evaluation by withdrawal, except for approach for the purpose of aggression. This was the basic notion under which Kurt Lewin had outlined the approach–approach, approach–withdrawal, and withdrawal–withdrawal conflict situations.

It occurred to me that it might be possible to use checkers on a checkerboard to represent individuals with different attitudes interacting with one another. I set up a six–by–six checkerboard area with six checkers of two different colors. Each red checker was assigned an attitude toward members of its own group and the same or another attitude toward members of the opposite group. The same was done for the black checkers (see diagram of Checkerboard Model on opposite page). Checkers were given random positions on the board (see figure 1a) and allowed to move one step in accordance with its attitude, moving to a position which was most in line with its attitude—toward friends and away from enemies. Checkers which were the closest were given the greatest weight in determining a move. Later the procedure was computerized to calculate moves based on distances from all checkers.

Initial trials with simple set of attitudes assigned to the two groups produced interesting results. In the Crossroads situation (figure 1b), each group had positive attitudes towards its own group and ignored the other group. The question was whether being "clannish," as some Nisei were accused of being, reduced contact with the other group. The model showed the two groups coming together near the center of the board, showing that positive attitudes toward one's own group under certain conditions could increase con-

Checkerboard Model of Social Interaction

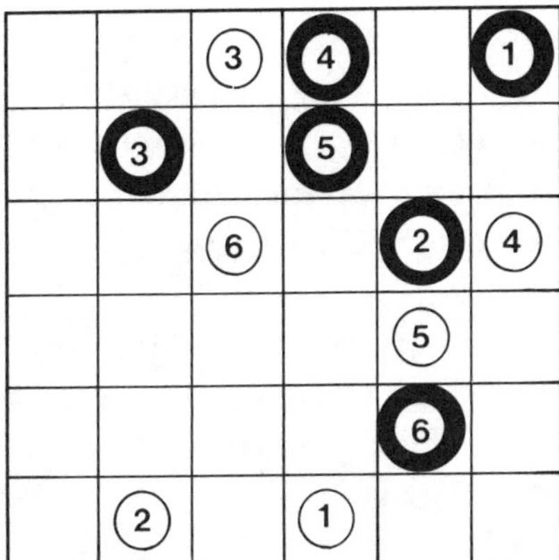

a. Random Starting Position. Each checker is moved in turn one step at a time in accordance with attitudes assigned at the outset. The moves are continued until a stable state is reached or stopped after an unstable state is determined.

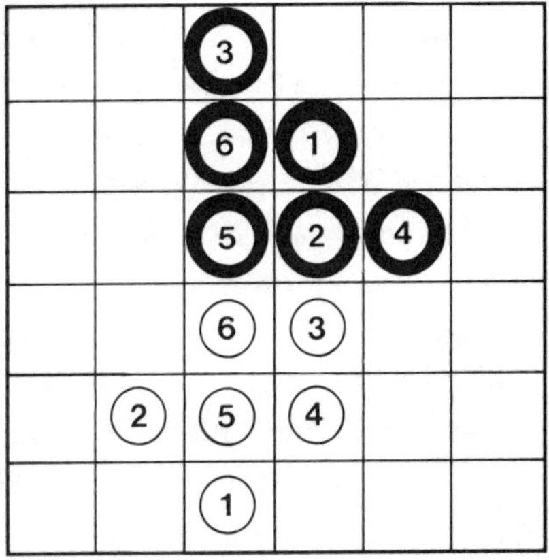

b. Crossroads. Both groups have positive attitudes toward one's own group and neutral attitudes toward the other. Both groups form in-groups near the center next to one another.

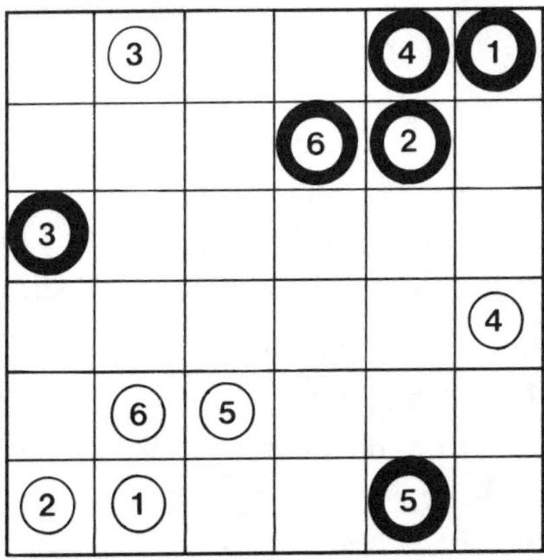

c. Mutual Withdrawal. Both groups have negative attitudes toward the other group and neutral attitudes toward one's own group. The two groups separate from one another, but form only a splintered in-group.

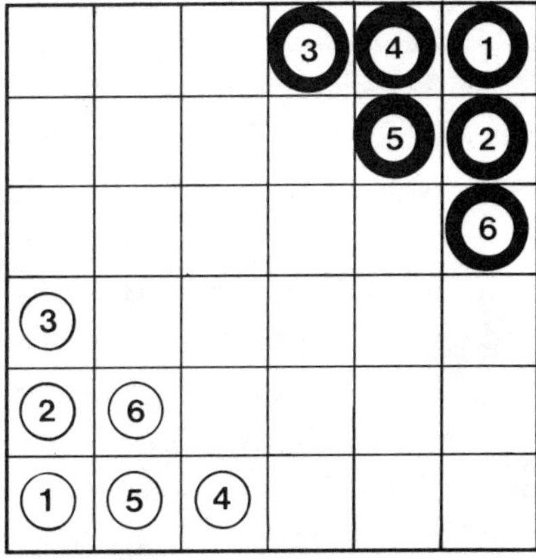

d. Segregation. Both groups are assigned positive attitudes toward one's own group and negative attitudes toward the other. Both groups form a strong in-group in opposing corners.

tact between groups. An important condition here was that the pieces were assigned initial positions randomly.

In the Mutual Withdrawal situation (figure 1c), both groups had negative attitudes toward the other group and ignored other members of their own group. The two groups separated out but did not produce a solid in–group. It took a combined negative attitude toward the other group and positive attitude toward one's own group to produce the Segregation situation (figure 1d), in which the two groups moved to opposing corners.

The checkerboard model helped to bridge the gap between subjective attitudes and the more objective group structure. The group structure could be seen as an overview of the separate pieces interacting on the board, driven by assigned social attitudes. The two were different aspects of the same phenomenon. However, to gain an understanding of the underlying dynamics of a situation, it was necessary to get at attitudes and the process of definition of a situation.

For instance, during the registration crisis in Block 25, protest leaders opposed registration, which appeared as a threat to boys of draft age. They urged those at block meetings to pass resolutions against registration. When the administration offered assurance that those answering "no–no" to the registration questions would not be subject to the draft, people became more critical of the protest leaders, and they withdrew as leaders. The rise and fall of the protest leader coincided with attitudes of welcome at the time of crisis, and criticism when the crisis passed.

In Minidoka, the administration originally had a benign attitude toward evacuees. With the emphasis on relocation and the introduction of work force reduction, positive evacuee attitude toward the administration turned negative and resulted in withdrawal. This gap between the administration and residents was aggravated by the project director's attempt to impose his will on them. This situation could be described as increased social disorganization—i.e., the decreasing influence of existing social rules.

Over the years in my teaching social psychology at the University of Connecticut (1952–1962) and Brown University (1962–1981), I used the checkerboard model to explain the relationship between attitudes and social structure. The model was later computerized by my son, William J. Sakoda.

NOTES ON CONTRIBUTORS

JAMES A. HIRABAYASHI is Professor Emeritus of Anthropology, San Francisco State University, and Curator at the Japanese American National Museum in Los Angeles. He received his Ph.D. in anthropology at Harvard University. His dissertation was on social change in a Japanese mountain community. He co-authored with Lane Ryo Hirabayashi "A Reconsideration of the United States Military's Role in the Violation of Japanese-American Citizenship Rights" in W. A. Horne, ed., *Ethnicity and War* (Madison: University of Wisconsin, 1984).

LANE RYO HIRABAYASHI teaches in the Asian American Studies Department at San Francisco State University. Trained in the field of socio-cultural anthropology, he received his Ph.D. from the University of California, Berkeley (1981). He is currently completing a book, tentatively titled *Migration, Peripheral Capitalism, and Regional Associations: Rincon Zapotec in Mexico City.*

YUJI ICHIOKA is Research Associate and Adjunct Associate Professor of History at the University of California, Los Angeles. He is the co-compiler of *A Buried Past: An Annotated Bibliography of the Japanese American Research Project Collection* (Berkeley and Los Angeles: University of California Press, 1974), and author of *The Issei: The World of the First Generation Japanese Immigrants, 1885-1924* (New York: THE FREE PRESS, 1988) and of numerous essays on Japanese-American history. His book, *The Issei,* was nominated for the 1988 Los Angeles Times Book Prize in History and received the 1989 Best Book Award of the National Association of Asian American Studies.

CHARLES KIKUCHI (1916-1988) was a JERS research assistant from 1942-1945. His major contribution to JERS was the 64 life histories of Nisei resettlers he compiled, 15 of which were incorporated into *The Salvage.* His Tanforan Assembly Center diary has been published as John Modell, ed., *The Kikuchi Diary* (Urbana: University of Illinois Press, 1973). An account of his unusual early life has been published under the title "A Young American With a Japanese Face," in Louis Adamic, *From Many Lands* (New York: Harper & Brothers, 1940). During the post-war years, Kikuchi pursued a successful career as a social worker with the Veterans Administration. His voluminous wartime and post-war diaries are deposited in the Department of Special Collections at UCLA.

S. FRANK MIYAMOTO is Professor Emeritus of Sociology, University of Washington. He was a JERS research assistant from 1942-1945. He earned his B.A. and M.A. degrees in sociology at the University of Washington before the war. His master's thesis was published as a monograph, *Social Solidarity among the Japanese in Seattle* (1939). He attended the University of Chicago for his doctorate, completed all but his dissertation, and had just begun his first faculty appointment at the University of Washington when the United States entered World War II. His observations of protests at Tule Lake were later assembled as his doctoral dissertation (1950). At the end of World War II, in 1945, he was invited to rejoin the Department of Sociology at the University of Washington, where he remained throughout his academic career.

JAMES M. SAKODA is Professor Emeritus, Brown University. He was a JERS research assistant from 1942-1945. He received his doctorate in psychology from the University of California, Berkeley. Before his appointment in the Sociology Department at Brown University, he taught at Brooklyn College. He now pursues his interest in origami, creating new forms and writing instructions for them on a Macintosh computer. He is the author of *Modern Origami* (New York: Simon and Schuster, 1969).

ROBERT F. SPENCER is Professor Emeritus of Anthropology, University of Minnesota. He was a JERS research assistant from 1942-1943 at Gila River. His doctoral dissertation, written at the University of California at Berkeley, was titled "Japanese Buddhism in the United States, 1940-1946." His major publications are: *The North Alaskan Eskimo: A Study in Ecology and Society* (Washington, D.C.: Smithsonian Institution, 1959); with J. Jennings, *The Native Americans* (New York: Harper & Row, 1977); and *Yogong: Factory Girl* (Seoul: Royal Asiatic Society, Korea Branch, 1988).

PETER T. SUZUKI is Foundation Professor, University of Nebraska at Omaha. Borned in Seattle, he was interned in Puyallup Assembly Center, Washington, and Minidoka Relocation Camp, Idaho. He left Minidoka by himself at age 15 to continue his high school education in Michigan. He earned his B.A. (1951) and M.A. (1952) degrees at Columbia University; did doctoral work at Yale (1952-1953); and earned his M.Phil. and Ph.D. degrees (1955 and 1959 respectively) in anthropology at Leiden University, Holland. He has published extensively on urban and transportation planning in the Lowlands, urbanization in Turkey, guestworkers in West Germany, and Nias, Indonesia.

DANA Y. TAKAGI is Assistant Professor of Sociology, University of California, Santa Cruz. In additon to her interest in analyzing the Kikuchi life histories, she is currently studying the alleged use of quotas by top American universities against Asian-Americans. Her other interests include social class and political organization in minority communities.

INDEX